Soul Stirring Sermons:
Evangelistic Voices
from the
Past & Present

Compiled & Edited by
Ken Lynch

Evangelist Ken Lynch
1810 Edgmont Ave.
Chester PA 19013-5306
(610) 876-1984

Printed in the USA by

𝓜ORRIS
PUBLISHING

3212 E. Hwy 30
Kearney, NE 68847
800-650-7888

Dedication

to
all the fundamental evangelists
and
their families
who, down through the years, have devoted their lives to
the propagation of the Gospel of Jesus Christ!

Introduction

With so many books of sermons already on the shelves, why another one? Basically, for three reasons. One, to bring glory and honor to the Lord Jesus Christ Whom we love and serve. It is Christ Whom this collection of sermons seeks to exalt; Christ on His Cross, Christ in His Call to salvation, surrender, and service, and Christ in His Coming. It is the desire of the compiler, as well as each evangelist represented, that the Saviour be exalted, sinners converted, and the saints edified and encouraged.

A second reason for a book like this is to present a unique collection of seventeen sermons by seventeen different evangelists; men who have devoted their lives to the ministry of evangelism. Some of these men have served in the pastorate or other ministries at one time or another. But all of them are known, first and foremost, as evangelists. Seldom, if ever before, has there been a collection of evangelistic preaching by evangelists, themselves.

The third reason for such a compilation is to help preserve the preaching and testimonials of men like these whose lives have touched so many over the years. Evangelists have not always been well received by the Church to whom they were given as a gift from God (Ephesians 4:11-13).

In his autobiography, the famous British evangelist, Gipsy Smith, relates an interesting incident from his own ministry in this regard. Since this book is extremely rare and you are unlikely to find a copy, allow me to quote him here.

"My work in New York was not at first looked upon with friendly eyes by all the ... ministers of the city. During my mission in the Harlem church I attended the usual Monday meeting of the ... ministers in company with Dr. Day. Dr. Day told his brethren something of the revival at his church, saying that it was a revival on old-fashioned Methodist lines. Whereupon a certain Dr. Hamilton rose and said: **'I do not believe in evangelists.** [emphasis mine] I have been in the ministry many years, and I have never had an evangelist in my church, and I never shall have. When the wind blows the dust blows, and when the wind settles, the dust settles. I believe in hand-picked fruit, in conversions which result from the ordinary work of the ministry. But I am glad to see Gipsy Smith present this morning, and I shall be glad to hear him.' The brethren called out loudly for 'Gipsy Smith! Gipsy Smith!' I had no desire to address the ministers, and unless called upon by the president I had no right to do so, but the cries for me were persistent, and I was invited to have my say. I began: 'Mr. Chairman, gentlemen, and brethren, - If I were at home in England, among my brethren and the ministers who know me, who have watched me, and who know my manner of work, I would venture to reply to Dr. Hamilton. But as I am a stranger in a strange land, and your guest, I prefer to be silent. If I am only a gipsy boy, I know what belongs to good breeding.' Then I sat down.

"The brethren present shouted in American fashion, 'Good, Brother Smith! Good, good, good!' and urged me to go on. 'Very well,' I said, 'very well, if you will hear me, you shall. It may be a very smart thing to say that when the wind blows the dust blows, and when the wind settles the dust settles, but it is not a Christlike thing to say of a brother and his work,' and turning to Dr. Hamilton, **'if God has given to the church evangelists, it is because you need them.** [emphasis mine] What God has called clean, do not you call common.' There was a cry of, 'Good, good, that's so, Brother Smith!' 'Well,' I added, 'you say you believe in hand-picked fruit; so do I. It fetches the highest price in the market; but what are you to do when the fruit is too high for you to reach it, and you have no ladder? Everybody knows, too, that some of the best fruit is on the top of the tree. Are you going to lose that fruit because you are not tall enough or strong enough to get it? I won't! I will ask the first godly brother who comes along to help me shake that tree, and we will get the fruit though we bruise it in the getting. I would rather not have said this. I do not believe in defending myself, or setting myself against my brother in the ministry. I have tried always to be the pastor's help, and I never allow myself in public or in private to say one disparaging word of my brethren. It hurts and grieves me when I hear a pastor speaking disdainfully of the work of the evangelist, remembering as I do that God has given to the church some apostles, some prophets, some evangelists, as well as pastors and teachers. (Gipsy Smith: An Autobiography, Fleming H. Revell, 1906; pp 200-202)'"

The months of preparing this volume have been a tremendous blessing to me, personally, as I have had to read **many** sermons in an effort to select those I wished to use, especially in the "Voices From The Past" section. I have had to listen and listen again to many other sermons on cassette tape in the course of transcribing them. If your heart is stirred only a portion of what mine was, you will be richly blessed.

A special word of thanks is due the following for their help in putting this volume together: my dear and faithful wife for her faithful support and patience during the many hours spent in preparing this volume, and help in proofreading; Dr. David Beale for his help in locating three extremely rare and hard to find books by Gipsy Smith, including a rare autographed copy of the Gipsy's autobiography; Robin Heller (commercial artist and friend) for his excellent sketch of Christmas Evans, his accurate reproductions of several signatures from old photographs, and his artistic designs framing the photographs; Unusual Films, Greenville, SC, for the photograph of Dr. Bob Jones, Sr.; Bob Jones University Press for permission to reproduce the sermon by Dr. Bob, Sr.; Mrs. Monroe Parker and Mrs. Glen Schunk for their help in providing background information and sermons of their late husbands; and an extra-special word of thanks to all of the living evangelists who have contributed to this volume. Thank you, one and all. KWL

Table of Contents

Part One

Voices From The Past

CHRISTMAS EVANS

1

The Fall & Recovery Of Man

BIOGRAPHICAL SKETCH

Christmas Evans
(1766-1838)

The name "Christmas" was given to the first child of Samuel and Joanna Evans in honor of the day on which he was born: Christmas, 1766. Due to his mother's inability to keep the family together after the death of her husband a few years later, Christmas and the other children were sent to live with various relatives. Christmas went to live with his maternal Uncle Jim on a farm in the country. Uncle Jim was a profoundly wicked man who had a negative influence on the young Evans.

In 1778, after several close calls with death on his uncle's farm, Christmas ran away and for several years traveled about working when and where he could as a farm boy.

In 1782, the seventeen year old youth found himself under the influence and preaching of the Reverend David Davies, a Presbyterian minister. It was then that he found Christ as his Saviour and peace from his sins. Shortly after his conversion, Pastor Davies taught the youth how to read and write.

At the time of his conversion, he had been running with a bad crowd who were not, in the least, sympathetic toward his new found faith in Christ. In fact, they gave him such a terrible beating one day that he was left unconscious and nearly completely blind in one eye. Years later, he would become known as the "one-eyed man from Anglesey."

In 1788, Evans became a Baptist, and, soon after his baptism, began preaching in numerous churches. He was married in 1792, but had no children. He pastored in Anglesey for more than twenty years during which time, many came to know Christ.

When the great Welsh Revival broke out, more than six hundred converts were recorded. As a preacher, Evans would hold audiences spellbound with his animated enthusiasm and dramatic gestures. One author even goes so far as to suggest that Evans may have been the first preacher to include dramatic story-telling in his sermons.

He started a number of churches and led many men to the Lord who later pastored those churches. His last message was a two hour sermon preached on July 15, 1838 in Swansea. He died on July 19, 1838 at the age of 72 and is buried in the Baptist cemetery in Swansea. KWL

THE FALL AND RECOVERY OF MAN
Christmas Evans

"FOR IF, THROUGH THE OFFENSE OF ONE, MANY BE
DEAD, MUCH MORE THE GRACE OF GOD, AND THE
GIFT OF GRACE, WHICH IS BY ONE MAN, JESUS
CHRIST, HATH ABOUNDED UNTO MANY." Romans 5:15

Man was created in the image of God. Knowledge and perfect holiness
were imprest upon the very nature and faculties of his soul. He had
constant access to his Maker, and enjoyed free communion with Him, on
the ground of his spotless moral rectitude. But, alas! the glorious diadem
is broken; the crown of righteousness is fallen. Man's purity is gone, and
his happiness is forfeited. "There is none righteous; no, not one." "All
have sinned, and come short of the glory of God." But the ruin is not
hopeless. What was lost in Adam is restored in Christ. His blood redeems
us from the bondage, and His gospel gives us back the forfeited inheritance.
"For if, through the offense of one, many be dead; much more the grace
of God, and the gift by grace, which is by one man, Jesus Christ, hath
abounded unto many." Let us consider, first, the corruption and condemnation of man; and secondly, his gracious restoration to the favor of his
offended God.

I. To find the cause of man's corruption and condemnation, we must
go back to Eden. The eating of the "forbidden tree" was "the offense of
one," in consequence of which "many are dead." This was the "sin," the
act of "disobedience," which "brought death into the world, and all our
wo." It was the greatest ingratitude to the divine bounty, and the boldest
rebellion against the divine sovereignty. The royalty of God was con-
temned; the riches of His goodness slighted; and His most desperate
enemy preferred before Him, as if he were a wiser counsellor than infinite
wisdom. Thus man joined in league with hell against heaven; with demons
of the bottomless pit against the almighty maker and benefactor; robbing
God of the obedience due to His command and the glory due to His
name; worshipping the creature instead of the creator; and opening the
door to pride, unbelief, enmity, and all the wicked and abominable passions. How is the "noble vine," which was planted "wholly a right seed,"
"turned into the degenerate plant of a strange vine."

Who can look for pure water from such a fountain? "That which is
born of the flesh is flesh." All the faculties of the soul are corrupted by
sin; the understanding dark; the will perverse; the affections carnal; the
conscience full of shame, remorse, confusion, and mortal fear. Man is a
hard-hearted and stiff-necked sinner; loving darkness rather than light,

because his deeds are evil; eating sin like bread, and drinking iniquity like water; holding fast deceit, and refusing to let it go. His heart is desperately wicked; full of pride, vanity, hypocrisy, covetousness, hatred of truth, and hostility to all that is good.

This depravity is universal. Among the natural children of Adam, there is no exemption from the original taint. "The whole world lieth in wickedness." "We are all as an unclean thing, and all our righteousness is as filthy rags." The corruption may vary in the degrees of development, in different persons; but the elements are in all, and their nature is everywhere the same; the same in the blooming youth, and the withered sire; in the haughty prince, and the humble peasant; in the strongest giant, and the feeblest invalid. The enemy has "come in like a flood." The deluge of sin has swept the world. From the highest to the lowest, there is no health or moral soundness. From the crown of the head to the soles of the feet, there is nothing but wounds, and bruises, and putrefying sores. The laws, and their violation, and the punishments everywhere invented for the suppression of vice, prove the universality of the evil. The bloody sacrifices, and various purifications, of the pagans, show the handwriting of remorse upon their consciences; proclaim their sense of guilt, and their dread of punishment. None of them are free from the fear which hath torment, whatever their efforts to overcome it, and however great their boldness in the service of sin and Satan. "Mene! Tekel!" is written on every human heart. "Wanting! wanting!" is inscribed on heathen fanes and altars; on the laws, customs, and institutions of every nation; and on the universal consciousness of mankind.

This inward corruption manifests itself in outward actions. "The tree is known by its fruit." As the smoke and sparks of the chimney show that there is fire within; so all the "filthy conversation" of men, and all "the unfruitful works of darkness" in which they delight, evidently indicate the pollution of the source whence they proceed. "Out of the abundance of the heart the mouth speaketh." The sinner's speech betrayeth him. "Evil speaking" proceeds from malice and envy. "Foolish talking and jesting" are evidence of impure and trifling thoughts. The mouth full of cursing and bitterness, the throat an open sepulcher, the poison of asps under the tongue, the feet swift to shed blood, destruction and misery in their paths, and the way of peace unknown to them, are the clearest and amplest demonstration that men "have gone out of the way," "have together become unprofitable." We see the bitter fruit of the same corruption in robbery, adultery, gluttony, drunkeness, extortion, intolerance, persecution, apostasy, and every evil work - in all false religions; the Jew, obstinately adhering to the carnal ceremonies of an abrogated law; the Mohammedan, honoring an imposter, and receiving a lie for a revelation from God; the papist, worshipping images and relics, praying to departed saints, seeking absolution from sinful men, and trusting in the most absurd mummeries for salvation; the pagan, attributing divinity to the works of his own hands, adoring idols of wood and stone, sacrificing to malignant demons, casting his children into the fire or the flood as an offering to imaginary deities, and changing the glory of the incorruptible God into the likeness of the beast and the worm.

"For these things' sake the wrath of God cometh upon the children of disobedience." They are under the sentence of the broken law; the malediction of eternal justice. "By the offense of one, judgment came upon all men unto condemnation." "He that believeth not is condemned already." "The wrath of God abideth on him." "Curst is every one that continueth not in all things written in the book of the law to do them." "Wo unto the wicked; it shall be ill with him, for the reward of his hands shall be given him." "They that plow iniquity, and sow wickedness, shall reap the same." "Upon the wicked the Lord shall rain fire, and snares, and a horrible tempest; this shall be the portion of their cup." "God is angry with the wicked every day; if he turn not he will whet his sword; he hath bent his bow, and made it ready."

Who shall describe the misery of fallen man? His days, tho few, are full of evil. Trouble and sorrow press him forward to the tomb. All the world, except Noah and his family, are drowning in the deluge. A storm of fire and brimstone is fallen from heaven upon Sodom and Gomorrah. The earth is opening her mouth to swallow up alive Korah, Dathan, and Abiram. Wrath is coming upon "the beloved city," even "wrath unto the uttermost." The tender and delicate mother is devouring her darling infant. The sword of men is executing the vengeance of God. The earth is emptying its inhabitants into the bottomless pit. On every hand are "confused noises, and garments rolled in blood." Fire and sword fill the land with consternation and dismay. Amid the universal devastation wild shrieks and despairing groans fill the air. God of mercy! is Thy ear heavy, that Thou canst not hear? or Thy arm shortened, that Thou canst not save? The heavens above are brass, and the earth beneath is iron; for Jehovah is pouring His indignation upon His adversaries, and He will not pity or spare.

Verily, "the misery of man is great upon him!" Behold the wretched fallen creature! The pestilence pursues him. The leprosy cleaves to him. Consumption is wasting him. Inflammation is devouring his vitals. Burning fever has seized upon the very springs of life. The destroying angel has overtaken the sinner in his sins. The hand of God is upon him. The fires of wrath are kindling about him, drying up every well of comfort, and scorching all his hopes to ashes. Conscience is chastizing him with scorpions. See how he writhes! Hear how he shrieks for help! Mark what agony and terror are in his soul, and on his brow! Death stares him in the face, and shakes at him his iron spear. He trembles, he turns pale, as a culprit at the bar, as a convict on the scaffold. He is condemned already. Conscience has pronounced the sentence. Anguish has taken hold upon him. Terrors gather in battle array about him. He looks back, and the storms of Sinai pursue him; forward, and hell is moved to meet him; above, and the heavens are on fire; beneath, and the world is burning. He listens, and the judgment trump is calling; again, and the brazen chariots of vengeance are thundering from afar; yet again, the sentence penetrates his soul with anguish unspeakable - "Depart! ye accurst! into everlasting fire, prepared for the devil and his angels!"

Thus, "by one man, sin entered into the world, and death by sin; and so death passed upon all men, for that all have sinned." They are "dead in trespasses and sins," spiritually dead, and legally dead; dead by the mortal power of sin, and dead by the condemnatory sentence of the law; and helpless as sheep to the slaughter, they are driven fiercely on by the ministers of wrath to the all-devouring grave and the lake of fire!

But is there no mercy? Is there no means of salvation? Hark! amid all this prelude of wrath and ruin, comes a still small voice, saying, "Much more the grace of God, and the gift by grace, which is by one man, Jesus Christ, hath abounded unto many."

II. This brings us to our second topic, man's gracious recovery to the favor of his offended God.

I know not how to present to you this glorious work, better than by the following figure. Suppose a vast graveyard, surrounded by a lofty wall, with only one entrance, which is a massive iron gate, and that it is fast bolted. Within are thousands and millions of human beings, of all ages and classes, by one epidemic disease bending to the grave. The graves yawn to swallow them, and they must all perish. There is no balm to relieve, no physician there. Such is the condition of man as a sinner. All have sinned; and it is written, "The soul that sinneth shall die." But while the unhappy race lay in that dismal prison, Mercy came and stood at the gate, and wept over the melancholy scene, exclaiming - "Oh, that I might enter! I would bind up their wounds; I would relieve their sorrows; I would save their souls!" An embassy of angels, commissioned from the court of heaven to some other world, paused at the sight, and heaven forgave their pause. Seeing Mercy standing there, they cried:- "Mercy! canst thou not enter? Canst thou look upon that scene and not pity? Canst thou pity and not relieve?" Mercy replied, "I can see!" and in her tears she added, "I can pity, but I cannot relieve!" "Why canst thou not enter?" inquired the heavenly host. "Oh!" said Mercy, "Justice has barred the gate against me, and I must not - cannot unbar it!" At this moment, Justice appeared, as if to watch the gate. The angels asked, "Why wilt thou not suffer Mercy to enter?" He sternly replied: "The law is broken, and it must be honored!

Die they, or Justice must!" Then appeared a form among the angelic band like unto the Son of God. Addressing Himself to Justice He said: "What are thy demands?" Justice replied: "My demands are rigid; I must have ignominy for their honor, sickness for their health, death for their life. Without the shedding of blood there is no remission!" "Justice," said the Son of God, "I accept thy terms! On me be this wrong! Let Mercy enter, and stay the carnival of death!" "What pledge dost thou give for the performance of these conditions?" "My word; my oath!" "When wilt thou perform them?" "Four thousand years hence, on the hill of Calvary, without the walls of Jerusalem." The bond was prepared, and signed and sealed in the presence of attendant angels. Justice was satisfied, the gate was opened, and Mercy entered, preaching salvation in the name of Jesus. The bond was committed to the patriarchs and prophets. A long series of rites and ceremonies, sacrifices and obligations, was instituted to perpet-uate the memory of that solemn deed. At the close of the four thousandth year, when Daniel's "seventy weeks" were accomplished, Justice and Mercy appeared on the hill of Calvary. "Where," said Justice, "is the Son of God?" "Behold Him," answered Mercy, "at the foot of the hill!" And there He came, bearing His own cross, and followed by His weeping church. Mercy retired, and stood aloof from the scene. Jesus ascended the hill like a lamb for the sacrifice. Justice presented the dreadful bond, saying, "This is the day on which this article must be canceled." The Redeemer took it. What did He do with it? Tear it to pieces, and scatter it to the winds? No! He nailed it to His cross, crying, "It is finished!" The victim ascended the altar. Justice called on Holy Fire to come down and consume the sacrifice. Holy Fire replied, "I come! I will consume the sacrifice, and then I will burn up the world! It fell upon the Son of God, and rapidly consumed His humanity; but when it touched His deity, it expired. Then was there darkness over the whole land, and an earthquake shook the mountain; but the heavenly host broke forth in rapturous song "Glory to God in the highest! on earth peace! good will to man!"

Thus grace has abounded, and the free gift has come upon all, and the gospel has gone forth proclaiming redemption to every creature. "By grace ye are saved, through faith; and that not of yourselves; it is the gift of God; not of works, lest any man should boast." By grace ye are loved, redeemed, and justified. By grace ye are called, converted, reconciled and sanctified. Salvation is wholly of grace. The plan, the process, the consummation are all of grace.

"Where sin abounded, grace hath much more abounded." "Through the offense of one, many were dead." And as men multiplied, the offense abounded. The waters deluged the world, but could not wash away the dreadful stain. The fire fell from heaven, but could not burn out the accurst plague. The earth opened her mouth, but could not swallow up the monster sin. The law thundered forth its threat from the thick darkness on Sinai, but could not restrain, by all its terrors, the children of disobedience. Still the offense abounded, and multiplied as the sands on the seashore. It waxed bold, and pitched its tents on Calvary, and nailed the Lawgiver to a tree. But in that conflict sin received its mortal wound. The victim was the victor. He fell, but in His fall He crusht the foe. He died unto sin, but sin and death were crucified upon His cross. Where sin abounded to condemn, grace hath much more abounded to justify. Where sin abounded to corrupt, grace hath much more abounded to purify. Where sin abounded to harden, grace hath much more abounded to soften and subdue. Where sin abounded to imprison men, grace hath much more abounded to proclaim liberty to the captives. Where sin abounded to break the law and dishonor the Lawgiver, grace hath much more abounded to repair the breach and efface the stain. Where sin abounded to consume the soul as with unquenchable fire and a gnawing worm, grace hath much more abounded to extinguish the flame and heal the wound. Grace hath abounded! It hath established its throne on the merit of the Redeemer's sufferings. It hath put on the crown, and laid hold of the golden scepter, and spoiled the dominion of the prince of darkness, and the gates of the great cemetery are thrown open and there is the beating of a new life-pluse throughout its wretched population and immortality is walking among its tombs!

This abounding grace is manifested in the gift of Jesus Christ, by whose mediation our reconciliation and salvation are effected. With Him, believers are dead unto sin, and alive unto God. Our sins were slain at His cross, and buried in His tomb. His resurrection hath open our graves, and given us an assurance of immortality. "God commendeth his love toward us, in that while we were yet sinners, Christ died for us; much more, then, being now justified by his blood, we shall be saved from the wrath through him; for if, when we were enemies, we were reconciled to God by the death of his Son, much more, being reconciled, we shall be saved by his life."

"The carnal mind is enmity against God; it is not subject to the law of God, neither indeed can be." Glory to God, for the death of His Son, by which this enmity is slain, and reconciliation is effected between the rebel and the law! This was the unspeakable gift that saved us from ruin; that wrested with the storm, and turned it away from the devoted head of the sinner. Had all the angels of God attempted to stand between these two conflicting seas, they would have been swept to the gulf of destruction. "The blood of bulls and goats, on Jewish altars slain," could not take away sin, could not pacify the conscience. But Christ, the gift of divine grace, "Paschal Lamb by God appointed," a "sacrifice of nobler name and richer blood than they," bore our sins and carried our sorrows, and obtained for us the boon of eternal redemption. He met the fury of the tempest, and the floods went over His head; but His offering was an offering of peace, calming the storms and the waves, magnifying the law, glorifying its Author, and rescuing its violator from the wrath and ruin. Justice hath laid down his sword at the foot of the cross, and amity is restored between heaven and earth.

Hither, O ye guilty! come and cast away your weapons of rebellion! Come with your bad principles and wicked actions; your unbelief, and enmity, and pride; and throw them off at the Redeemer's feet! God is here waiting to be gracious. He will receive you; He will cast all your sins behind His back, into the depths of the sea; and they shall be remembered against you no more forever. By Heaven's "unspeakable gift," by Christ's invaluable atonement, by the free, infinite grace of the Father and Son, we persuade you, we beseech you, we entreat you, "be ye reconciled to God"!

It is by the work of the Holy Spirit with us that we obtain a personal interest in the work wrought on Calvary for us. If our sins are canceled, they are also crucified. If we are reconciled in Christ, we fight against our God no more. This is the fruit of faith. "With the heart man believeth unto righteousness." May the Lord inspire in every one of us that saving principle!

But those who have been restored to the divine favor may sometimes be cast down and dejected. They have passed through the sea, and sung praises on the shore of deliverance; but there is yet between them and Canaan "a waste howling wilderness," a long and weary pilgrimage, hostile nations, fiery serpents, scarcity of food, and the river of Jordan. Fears within and fightings without, they may grow discouraged, and yield to temptation and murmur against God, and desire to return to Egypt. But fear not, thou worm Jacob! Reconciled by the death of Christ; much more, being reconciled, thou shalt be saved by His life. His death was the price of our redemption; His life insures liberty to the believer. If by His death He brought you through the Red Sea in the night, by His life He can lead you through the river Jordan in the day. If by His death He delivered you from the iron furnace in Egypt, by His life He can save you from all perils of the wilderness. If by His death He conquered Pharaoh, the chief foe, by His life He can subdue Sihon, king of the Amorites, and Og, king of Bashan. "We shall be saved by his life." Because He liveth, we shall live also. "Be of good cheer!" The work is finished; the ransom is effected; the kingdom of heaven is open to all believers. "Lift up your heads and rejoice," "ye prisoners of hope!" There is no debt unpaid, no devil unconquered, no enemy within your hearts that has not received a mortal wound! "Thanks be unto God, who giveth us the victory, through our Lord Jesus Christ!"

BOB JONES, SR.

Yours truly,
R. R. Jones

2

Why Trimmest Thou?

BIOGRAPHICAL SKETCH

Bob Jones, Sr.
(1883-1968)

Robert Reynolds Jones, affectionately known as "Dr. Bob," was born on October 30, 1883, in south eastern Alabama a few miles north of Dothan in the little town of Skipperville. The eleventh of twelve children born to Georgia (Creel) and Alex Jones, Dr. Bob was the only preacher in the family and was destined to achieve international fame, both as evangelist and educator.

He was saved at the age of eleven, the result of a five year spiritual struggle which culminated in a gospel meeting where he sat spellbound under the preaching of an eighty year old preacher. The young Jones was the first to respond when the invitation was given.

His first brush arbor meeting, out of which came a small country church of fifty-four members, was preached when he was only thirteen years old. He was ordained to the ministry before the age of fifteen. By the time he was seventeen, both of his parents had died.

On June 17, 1908, the Lord blessed him with a lovely wife, Mary Gaston, who was his faithful help meet for just under sixty years. Later, the Lord blessed their home with a preacher-son, Bob Jones, Jr.

As an evangelist, Dr. Bob, Sr. was on par with such other great evangelists as Billy Sunday, R.A. Torrey, and Gypsy Smith. The crowds that flocked to the old wooden tabernacles were equaled only by those of Billy Sunday. It is reported that he had seen over one million converts by his forty-second birthday.

Burdened by the growing apostasy in America, along with the infidelity in so many colleges and universities (even "religious"), and heartbroken by the scores of spiritually "shipwrecked" young people who "lost their faith" at some state school or some modernistic religious school, the Lord led him to found Bob Jones College in 1927. First located in Panama City, Florida, then in Cleveland, Tennessee, the college eventually moved to its current location as a full-fledged university in Greenville, South Carolina in 1948. As a bastion of fundamentalism, Bob Jones University has grown from a student body of less than one hundred to a student body exceeding six thousand from every state and numerous foreign countries. It remains unquestionably the world's leading fundamentalist Christian university, well deserving of its former nickname, "The World's Most Unusual University."

Dr. Bob, Sr., was called home to glory on January 16, 1968. His last words, just before slipping into a semi-coma state, were to his wife, "Dearie, get my shoes; I must go preach!" More than 5,000 people, including faculty, friends, and students attended his funeral. What a privilege it was for the compiler of this book to have been a student on that sad, yet joyful day! KWL

WHY TRIMMEST THOU?
Bob Jones, Sr.

The text is Jeremiah 2:33: "Why trimmest thou thy way to seek love?" The literal meaning of seeking love, as it is used here, is "to seek favor." In other words, "Why trimmest thou thy way to stand in with people, to seek the approval of men?"

Let us turn back to the beginning of this chapter. God is talking to His own people, Israel. He says to Jeremiah, the prophet, "Go and cry in the ears of Jerusalem, saying, Thus saith the LORD; I remember thee, the kindness of thy youth, the love of thine espousals, when thou wentest after me in the wilderness, in a land that was not sown. Israel was holiness unto the Lord, and the first fruits of his increase: all that devour him shall offend; evil shall come upon them, saith the Lord" (vv. 1-3). God is saying here, "I have said that I would take care of you, Israel, and I have fulfilled my promise."

"Hear ye the word of the LORD, O house of Jacob, and all the families of the house of Israel: Thus saith the LORD, what iniquity have your fathers found in me..." (vv. 4-5). There is something pathetic about these words. Sometimes a father says to a son who has turned his back on his father and his father's good training, "Son, how could you do this to me? Why are you acting this way?" Or a mother says to her wayward daughter, "Honey, I don't see how you could do this to me. You have disgraced me." That is what God is saying to Israel: "You have gone back on Me."

"Thus saith the LORD, What iniquity have your fathers found in me, that they are gone far from me, and have walked after vanity, and are become vain? Neither said they, Where is the LORD that brought us up out of the land of Egypt, that led us through the wilderness, through a land of deserts and of pits, through a land of drought, and of the shadow of death, through a land that no man passed through, and where no man dwelt? And I brought you into a plentiful country, to eat the fruit thereof and the goodness thereof; but when ye entered, ye defiled my land, and made mine heritage an abomination:" (vv. 1-7). "How could Israel go back on God?" you ask. I ask, "How can we do what we have done? How can America do what she has done to God?"

"The priests said not, Where is the LORD? and they that handle the law knew me not: the pastors also transgressed against me, and the prophets prophesied by Baal, and walked after things that do not profit" (v. 8). In other words, Israel went after things that did not pay off. They "sold God down the river," so to speak, and went after false gods.

Skip down to verse 17: "Hast thou not procured this unto thy self, in that thou hast forsaken the LORD thy God, when he led thee by the way?" Now look at verse 13: "For my people have committed two evils; they have forsaken me the fountain of living waters, and hewed them out cisterns, broken cisterns, that can hold no water." Here is a lovely, gushing fountain. It is God's fountain. All Israel has to do is to drink from it. But Israel says, "Let us get another fountain. Let us walk away from this one and fix one of our own." And they go out and hew them out cisterns which, when they are finished, will not hold water. Israel forgot that the water they had was the water of God Almighty, and they deliberately walked away from His fountain.

God goes on to say, "And now what hast thou to do in the way of Egypt...to drink the waters of the river? Thine own wickedness shall correct thee..." (vv. 18-19). You will find out Who your God is, Israel. You will find out the One upon Whom you can depend.

"But where are thy gods that thou hast made thee? Let them arise, if they can save in the time of thy trouble: for according to the number of thy cities are thy gods, O Judah. Wherefore will ye plead with me? Ye have all transgressed against me, saith the LORD" (vv. 28-29). Then on to verse 33: "Why trimmest thou thy way to seek love [or approval, or friends, or worldly things, or favor]? Therefore hast thou also taught the wicked ones thy ways." What is that? "You, by your trimming, have taught wicked ones how to trim. O Israel, What have you done?"

My friends, when I think what is going on in America, it does not concern me for myself. I am thinking about conditions ahead - about young people and all that they are going to face in this country. God has blessed America. In the early days of our history, we were not a strong nation, but we had strong character and strong faith. We had Bible-believing preachers. We won all the wars. Today the world is threatened with more and more cross-currents of interest, more danger, and more wars than it has ever faced. And at a time when we should turn back to God and thank Him for all He has done for us, we are having the greatest sellout in the realm of religion that we have ever had. What a day!

A certain congressman reported that on the Unamerican Activities list in Washington there are many thousand Protestant clergymen who are sympathetic to Communism - to atheistic Communism that persecuted Christians in Europe and has designs on devouring the world. Similar conditions have been reported in the field of education. You say, "This is terrible." I will tell you one thing about people on this list: there is not a Bible-believing man in the crowd. There has never been in this country an out-and-out, Bible-believing Christian who was ever friendly to Communism. These thousands in the ministry who are said to be sympathetic to this Godless organization represent a group of people who have walked out on God and have trampled on the Bible. That is the condition we face in so-called "Christian" America.

There are three distinct groups in Protestantism. First, there are the Fundamentalists, those who believe the Bible is the Word of God and that whatever it says is true. All in this group believe the same basic doctrines: the Bible is the Word of God; Jesus Christ is the Son of God; Jesus Christ was God incarnate; Jesus Christ died on the cross to save sinners; and He rose from the dead.

The next group is a large group and a growing group. It is the group of religious Liberals who teach that "the Bible contains or may contain the Word of God."

Then there are the compromisers who say, "What difference does it make? We'll go with 'the crowds' while America goes to Hell." This is the most dangerous group of all. I would rather be an out-and-out Liberal than to belong to this group. I have much more respect for the man who does not accept the Bible as the Word of God and who can be led astray than I have for the man who claims to believe the Bible but who sells God's orthodox people down the river. That is the situation we are facing today.

The same conditions existed in Israel. They were God's chosen people. They were getting along fine. God had signally blessed them. He had given them water, had taken them out of slavery, had set them free, had put about them His loving arms, and had said to them, "You are My people, and I want you to be true to Me." But when He brought them into the land of promise, they began to trim.

That is the way a nation starts to Hell. You might conceivably compromise a little bit on some of your methods. You may say, "This is the best method," or "That is the best method"; and as long as it is in line with Scripture, you may argue the point. But when you compromise on fundamentals, you face tragedy, you face cataclysmic judgment, and you face curses. Israel suffered for her compromise; America is going to suffer, too. All the talk we hear about revival in America does not ring true. There is less real, old-time, Holy Ghost, Bible conviction for sin, and more of the "everybody-come-along" spirit than we have ever had in this country. It reminds me of Israel. They tried to please everybody.

Under our American system of government a man has a right not to believe the Bible. He has a right to be an infidel. He has a right to go to Hell if he wants to go there. A man can be a Protestant, a Catholic, a Unitarian, or a Trinitarian. Thank God, we have religious liberty at this time. But oh, what we are facing today! God's people, by the multiplied thousands, are trimming their way to seek the favor of people who are against the God of their fathers and against the Bible their fathers believed. Preachers in the pulpit and laymen in the field--all are doing it. And so it goes up and down our land.

I feel that God has spared my life and given me a long background of evangelistic training in order that I might found Bob Jones University so that there would be in this very day of religious chaos in America a base of firm and uncompromising testimony. More and more the eyes of God's people seem to be turned this way. Good Christians know where we stand, and they respect us. Educators respect us. Men who love culture respect us. The only people who are really against us - and even they have to respect us - are the folks who are trying to trim their ways to "go along." We will not lower our standards at Bob Jones University. We will not trim our ways.

"Why trimmest thou thy way to seek favor? Hadn't you rather have Me than to have that crowd?" You cannot be on both sides. You are for Him, or you are against Him. It never has been popular to be "all out" for the Bible and for Jesus Christ, and it never will be popular until Jesus Christ sits on the throne of David, takes over the reins of government, and in righteousness reigns on this earth.

A good Christian believes the Bible and stands for something. He does not run with the crowd. Oh, he is nice to everybody. But because he feels that as a Christian he cannot do certain things, he is branded a religious fanatic. Bible-believing Christians are the ones who are being persecuted today. And they are being persecuted by the compromisers and modernists as well as by the Communists. But men cannot hurt us. "If God be for us, who can be against us? Greater is he that is within us than he that is without."

Men can put pressure on you. They will do everything in their power to get you to trim your ways. One way they do this is to put on you heavy pressure to support things in your denomination that you do not believe in. Some of you have yielded to the pressure to contribute your money to schools and colleges and universities and causes in which you do not believe. You claim to believe the Bible. You say of God, "He is my God." You say that Jesus Christ is the Son of God, "He is my God." You say that Jesus Christ is the Son of God and that He rose from the dead. But under the pressure of your leaders, you have trimmed a little and have given to modernistic causes some of the money that God has entrusted to you. "We have to get along," you say. Do you? With whom are you supposed to get along? You must face the issue.

What Is Trimming?

What is trimming? It is trying to hold the middle course between two groups in order to please both of them. It is walking down here, cutting a little bit here and a little bit there. A trimmer is a man who will not take a clear-cut stand at any time. When he hears false teachers and false teaching, he does not protest. Instead he says, "That is nice. You are lovely. It is wonderful that we are all one, that we are all children of God, and that He is the Father of us all."

I have a contempt for people like that who say, "Personally, I believe the Bible is the Word of God. But...but...but...but..."

Why Do Men Trim?

Why do men trim? They trim because they want to have standing with everybody. They want everybody to be for them. Usually, however, they wind up without the respect of anybody. And eventually they will find that there is nobody for them.

I thank God that in my long ministry over the years I have been privileged to go up and down this country preaching the Gospel. And I am thankful that I could go anywhere in America to this day and find that the old saints of God who are fighting and the old preachers who are proclaiming the Word of God would be for me. The churches that have not compromised know whose side to stand on. They are in the minority, but you can multiply it. You can take a few in one community, a few in another, a few in another, and so on; and you will find that there is a larger crowd than you thought. And Bob Jones University is not going to trim!

How Do Men Trim?

How did Israel trim? They trimmed between God and idols. They said, "It is all right to recognize these other people, these heathens, these pagans. It is a wonderful work they are doing. They are lovely, wonderful people. Everybody has a right to his own religion." And Israel went along, trying to please both sides--God AND idols.

How do men trim today? First they trim by their WORDS. I heard a preacher on television preach to a large crowd. I have been in this business so long that it is easy for me to discern certain trends. This preacher said some good words for Jesus. He quoted Scripture and implied that he believed the Bible. But at least a half dozen times I heard him say something I knew was an effort to satisfy the wrong crowd. I sat there and pitied all the people who were listening. There he was, a man who was supposed to stand with the Bible crowd, throwing kisses to those who slander the Son of God and who deny the Word of God. That preacher could have said, "A man has a right in this country to believe or not to believe. He has a right to say that he believes in the blood of Christ or that he does not believe in the blood of Christ. That is good Americanism, and I am an American. I do not believe in compulsory Christianity. I do not believe that you can make men right by pressure or law or authority." That would have been all right. But no man has a right to deceive by subtle statements; and that is what this preacher on television did. If I had been a Modernist or a trimmer sitting in that preacher's congregation, I would have gone out saying, "He surely did say nice things." If I had been one of the Bible-believing, humble Christians who was untaught in the Word, I would have said, "He is all right. Didn't you hear him say so and so?" But the other crowd would have said, "He winked at us." While he was talking to one crowd, he was winking at the other. He was trimming with words.

YOU can trim by words. The man who says that one religion is as good as another religion and that it does not matter whether you are a Mohammedan or something else, as long as you are sincere, does not have true Christianity. He is not on the side of Jesus Who emphatically said, "There is just one way, and I am that way. If you have seen Me, you have seen the Father." The Son of God always magnified the Word of God; and the folks who play down the Word of God also play down the Son of God.

Next, you can trim by your ACTS. I might have in my audience, as I preach, some men who do not abide in the doctrines of Christ. It is all right for me to preach to such men. But it is not all right for me to be sponsored by these men and have them on the platform with me and say to them, "Brother So and So, please lead us in prayer." To be sponsored by false teachers is an act. It is the act of trimming my ways to seek love.

You can trim by SUPPORTING THINGS THAT ARE NOT RIGHT. There are things which you could support without any compromise, but which are tied up in one bundle with some things you could not support. If you do not support the whole bundle, the denomination says, you do not support anything. That is bad. And it has come about by the subtle suggestion of the powerful Satan who ties us up and gets us to trim. No man goes to Hell suddenly, and no church becomes apostate suddenly. A church becomes apostate by a little trimming here and a little trimming yonder. Do not trim any longer, my friend. The first thing you know, they will have you to the place that you cannot say anything.

I could name organizations in America that ten years ago stood for the same things we stand for at Bob Jones University. I could name an organization whose creed I helped to write. Into that creed they put the same fundamentals that we have in our creed. But today there is not an organization in the country that is more completely sold out than that organization. And this selling out is sweeping America. How did that organization get started downhill? It started trimming a little bit here and there. It set somebody above the Bible. That is trimming by an act.

You can also trim by SILENCE. When an issue comes up, you can just sit there and smile and say nothing. If you do not speak out when you should speak, you have sold out. You are supposed to be a good testimony and witness for Jesus Christ. You are His ambassador (II Corinthians 5:20). As an orthodox, Bible-believing Christian it is my business to be a witness. I do not have to be ugly and go around knocking a chip off my shoulder onto somebody else's shoulder; but I am to speak out when I am supposed to speak out. And I am to stand when I am supposed to stand. It is wrong to be silent when you are supposed to speak. God help us to see this issue clearly and to pledge ourselves to stand in the tragic days we are in and the more tragic days we are facing.

WHY do men trim? They want something. Do you think that anybody can give you something that is good for you that you cannot get from God if you need it? Read Psalm 84:11. It says that "no good thing will he withhold from them that walk uprightly." Christ will settle this thing with a Christian. God Almighty promises to see that your needs are supplied. Philippians 4:19: "But my God shall supply all your need according to his riches in glory by Christ Jesus."

A mother knows what her baby should or should not have, and she acts on that knowledge. Do you not think that God knows what His child needs or does not need? As I look back over the more than 60 years I have been preaching, I realize that not one time in my life when I thought I was having a hard time did God withhold something from me without its being for my good and His glory! God takes care of us. He took care of Israel. He is still taking care of Israel. They are scattered over the face of the earth, but He is watching over them. Israel cannot be exterminated. Someday they are going to return to their land in repentance and acknowledge Him on Whom before they looked to scorn. God has never forsaken Israel, and He will never forsake us (Deuteronomy 31:6; Hebrews 13:5-6).

What a wonderful God we have! Are you going to "sell Him down the river?" Are you going to trim even a little? Are you going to give some of your money to promote something you know is contrary to God's Word? What are you going to do?

Let us consider for a moment the folly of trimming. A trimmer never wins. He always loses. You may get a position, may get recognition, may get your name in the headlines. But God Almighty will see to it that you do not win. You never have won, and you never will win, a battle for God by compromise on a fundamental principle.

The ethics of the Bible and the philosophy of the Bible are as much inspired as are the doctrines of the Bible. All of it was God-breathed. So you had better make up your mind that no matter how the tide comes in and goes out, you will stand and will keep on standing on the right side.

Results Of Trimming

What are some of the results of trimming? One result is that the wicked are influenced and encouraged. If I give Christian recognition to a man whom the Bible does not recognize as a Christian, that man is encouraged to go to Hell. It salves his conscience so that he feels that he is all right. Christian, the kindest man on earth is the preacher who preaches the full counsel of the Word and tells people the things they need to hear.

Where does trimming lead? If you trim and do not give people the warning they ought to have, you will find that sooner or later you have hurt those people. God says in this message to Israel, "In thy skirts I find the blood of the poor innocents." What an indictment! God's own people, the people He loved and called and protected, the people He fed and sheltered, the people He delivered from slavery, had in their skirts the blood of the lost. Trimmers do not take folks to Heaven by their compromise; they send folks to Hell. They damn instead of save.

"In thy skirts is found the blood of the poor innocents." I would hate to stand in the Judgment someday and see a person come forward and look at my hands and see his blood on my hands, spiritually speaking. But that is going to happen to some of you. You will not win a sinner by your compromising on principle; you will teach him your tricks as a compromiser. The sinner has enough sense to know that he is a sinner and that he is not entitled to Christian recognition. When you give him Christian recognition, you give him false hope.

Jesus Christ will see to it that all trimmers will see the consequences of what they have done. Ezekiel says, "The watchman on the wall is to warn the people." My business as a Christian is to make sinners uncomfortable in their sins. My business as a Christian is to make backslidden Christians and compromisers uncomfortable. A preacher does not have the right to make comfortable anybody who is doing wrong. The watchman on the wall in Ezekiel's day had to sound the warning or else have on his hands the blood of the people he was supposed to warn of the danger. And if you do not warn people, you will have their blood on your hands. God help you to take the right stand at all times and give the warning you are supposed to give.

SAM JONES

3

Drawing The Lines

BIOGRAPHICAL SKETCH

Sam Jones
(1847 - 1906)

Sam Jones was born on October 16, 1847 in eastern Alabama. His father, John J. Jones, held the rank of Captain during the Civil War and served the Confederacy with distinction.

At age six, young Sam gave his first public "address" which ended with the words of a little poem taught him by his mother:

> "In thunder peals, and Thorton* tones, The world shall hear from Samuel Jones."

Little did anyone realize the truth of those words until many years later.

Jones suffered from a physical condition known as dyspepsia (a digestive problem) and was advised to seek relief in the "moderate" use of alcohol. Instead of the moderate use recommended, Jones later became consumed with drink.

He married in 1869 and continued to live a life of debauchery and sin until his father, dying of consumption [tuberculosis], called him to his death-bed and pleaded with his wayward son to give his heart to God. Kneeling by his dying father's bedside, Sam Jones cried out, "God, be merciful to me a sinner!"

Though he was deeply in debt from his former life of sin and owned absolutely nothing, he at once sensed the call of God to preach. In 1872, he was accepted by the North Georgia Conference of the Methodist

---

Thorton was a well known orator of his day.

Episcopal Church, South, on a trial basis. His first appointment was to a circuit of extremely poor churches. It was during this three year period, followed by another two year circuit in a different area, that he began to develop the personality and style of preaching for which he later became famous. A contemporary of his described him as "the most unique, sensational, and effective preacher in America today." His preaching was sometimes blunt and straightforward, but often spiced with a good sense of humor. His grammar was not always correct, as will be noted in the sermon reproduced here, which is taken from a collection of sermons by Jones, published in 1886.

For several years he was forced to leave the evangelistic trail for health reasons, during which time, he gave numerous lectures against the evils of the liquor industry. He was later able to return to his evangelistic work where he remained until his death in 1906 at the age of 59. KWL.

DRAWING THE LINES
Sam Jones

"Now while Paul waited for them at Athens his spirit was stirred in him when he saw the city wholly given to idolatry." (Acts 17:16)

By "them" was meant Silas and Timothy, co-workers with Paul, who were to follow and accompany him on his missionary tour.

I believe Saul of Tarsus was the greatest man in this world's history. When I measure his head I look and admire. When I measure his heart I am at a loss to know which is the greater, his head or his heart. It takes both head and heart to make a true man. If there was a leading characteristic in the life of this great man it was his sterling integrity, his downright honesty. There was never but one trouble in the mind of this great man, and that was touching the divinity of Christ. It took the biggest guns of heaven to arouse and convince him, but when once convinced he was loyal forever. I believe I am ready to say here in my place, that St. Paul being an honest man God put him straight once, and he never gave God a moment's trouble after that, until God said: "It is enough; come up higher." St. Paul was such a man as I would imitate. I admire his character, true, noble, courageous, honest. And now this man, waiting for his companions at Athens, sees the whole city given to idolatry.

The charge that God brought against his ancient people was this: "My people will not consider." The etymological definition of that word (consider) is, "to look at a thing until you see it."

I would illustrate the words "glance" and "consider" by reference to the study of a landscape picture. A glance would take in the main features, such as the mountain scenery, the stream and the hamlet. A consideration or careful examination would show the foliage of the mountain trees, the roads leading to the mansion, the cattle grazing on the hill slopes, and so on. There is quite a difference between glancing at an object and considering it. St. Paul had considered the state of affairs in Athens, and his spirit was stirred within him when he saw how the whole city was given to idolatry.

One Of Two Things

Now, I want to say right here: One of two things is true of the city of St. Louis tonight. Either the eyes of Christian people are closed to the fact, or else the facts are false-hoods; one or the other. You can take whichever horn of the dilemma you please. I can take the daily papers of St. Louis and read your local columns and see without getting at the

Bible that St. Louis is wrong, that there is something radically wrong about this city; there are too many debauched characters, too many suicides, too many murders,--too many that are drifting daily to destruction and ruin. The fact is, a man don't need a Bible to see this world is all wrong; all you need to do is just to read your morning and afternoon papers, and then walk this street with your eyes open. If you do that it will not be one week from today until you look on with horror that is indescribable.

Now, let me ask each of you: Did you ever look at your heart until you saw it? I grant you that you have glanced at it a thousand times, but did you ever kneel down and pray for light and look and look until you saw your heart? My Bible teaches me that

"The heart is deceitful above all things, and desperately wicked."
My Bible teaches me:
"Keep thy heart with all diligence, for out of it are the issues of life."
My Bible teaches:
"Blessed are the pure in heart, for they shall see God."

Different Kinds Of Hearts

I once saw a pictorial representation of the human heart. It represented the sinner's heart; full of all kinds of wild beasts, reptiles and unclean birds--a hideous sight to look upon. Then there was the heart under conviction of sin, with the heads of all these animals turned outward as if they were getting ready to leave. Then I saw the heart converted, cleansed, and it was represented with a shining light and a cross. I saw also the backslider's heart, with the heads of all the beasts and reptiles as if they had turned backwards; and I saw the apostate's heart--a Methodist's heart--as it was fill to overflowing with all manner of horrid things, and the last state of that man was worse than the first.

Oh, the heart! the heart! This world reminds me in some of its phases of the man down in the spring branch trying to clear the water, so he could get a clear drink. He was doing all he could to filter and clear the water, when some friend called out to him: "Stranger, come up a little higher and run that hog out of that spring, and it will clear itself." No trouble then. And I declare to you tonight, the hardest job a man ever undertakes in this life is to lift up his life with an unclean heart.

There is no such thing as a clean life outside of a clean heart. I know we have what we call moral men, but I don't believe you can separate morals and Christianity. In fact, the morals of this world are the paraphernalia of Christianity. The man who is moral in the sense that he will pay his debts and tell the truth, and that sort of thing, may be a villain at heart. Our Saviour looked at the most moral men this world ever saw and said:

"You white-washed rascals, you!" That is our version. His version was: "Ye whited sepulchures!" I had rather be called the former.

To Non-Professors

And I want to say, to you men that don't profess to be Christians, I don't bring a railing charge against you. In the life of Jesus Christ not a single harsh word ever escaped His lips toward a sinner. When Jesus would talk with a sinner, He would fetch up the parable of the lost sheep, where the man left the ninety and nine safe in the fold and followed the poor, wandering sheep, and when he found it he didn't take a club and beat it back home, but picked up the poor, tired, hungry sheep and laid it on his shoulder and brought it back to the fold. But I tell you one thing. The Lord Jesus Himself never lost a chance to pour hot shot and grape and canister* into the Scribes and Pharisees, and they are the gentlemen I am after, begging your pardon. Now, if the sinners about this town want to go to the theaters, and want to dance and want to play cards, and want to curse and want to live licentious lives, I say, "Go it. Go it, boys;" but if you members of the Church want to do it, I will brand you as hypocrites, until you renounce your faith in Christ and have your name taken off the Church books. I've got a right to say a few things along there, and neither this world, nor the flesh, nor the devil, will interpose any objection. Don't anybody say I interposed an objection to any man who don't profess to be a Christian, or place an obstacle in the way of his doing just as he pleases. We will attend to your case later; but now I want to look in the faces of men who have made their vows and their promises to God, and who have sworn eternal allegiance to Jesus Christ, and their lives are a shame to the gospel and a disgrace to the character they profess. That's it.

A Story Of Moody

Now let us look at our hearts. I believe this incident, related of Mr. Moody, will illustrate the point I am on. On one occasion, when he had invited penitents to the altar, there came forward a great many, and he walked back two or three pews to where two Christian ladies were sitting,

---

*"shot": small lead pellets fired from a gun; "grape": short for grapeshot, an archaic term for a cluster of small cast-iron balls used as a charge for a cannon; "canister": the container of small lead pellets, canister shot.

and he said, "My sisters, will you walk forward and talk to those penitents?" They looked up at him and said, "No, sir; Mr. Moody, we are praying for you." "Praying for me?" he said. "Am I not trying to live right and get to heaven?" "Yes, Mr. Moody; but we are praying that you may have a clean heart." And he said conviction entered his spirit in a moment, and he dismissed the services later and went home and fell down on his knees and prayed, "Lord God, show me my heart. Let me see it as it is." And he said, "When the light of heaven poured in upon my heart I saw it was full of Moody, and full of selfishness, and full of worldly pride; and then I said, 'Lord God, help me to

> "Cast every idol out
> That dares to rival Thee.'"

"and," he said, "the Lord came and washed out all unrighteousness from my heart, and from that day until now I have never preached a sermon that didn't win souls to Christ." And I declare to you, if Jesus had in this town an army of pure blood-washed hearts, we could win St. Louis to Christ. And never, never, never will we accomplish the work and bring the world to Christ until we, who profess Christ, arouse ourselves, and wake up, and shake the devil's fleas off ourselves, and get to be decent.

Hypocrites And Humbugs

I can stand anything better than I can stand a hypocrite. I always did have a hatred for shams and humbugs and cheats, and of all the humbugs that ever cursed the universe, I reckon the religious humbug is the humbuggest. You remember how the students played a joke once on the professor—at Princeton, I believe it was. He was one of those old bugologists, and I reckon he had specimens of all the bugs in the world in his frames and boxes. And the mischievous boys got the legs of one bug and the body of another and the head and wings of others and put them together like as if nature had formed them, and then they laid it on the old Professor's table, and walked in, and asked him what kind of bug it was; and he said, "Gentlemen, that is a humbug." And I tell you that when a fellow gets a little Methodism in him, and a little of theaters, and a little card-playing, and a little of most everything, and is made up out of a hundred different sorts of things, then he is a first class humbug in every sense of the word. He is just good anywhere.

Oh, my heart! With the heart right, with the fountain clear, the stream will be clear. With a good tree the fruit will be good. And I declare to you tonight that the hardest work a man ever tried to do is to be a Christian without religion; to be a good man with a bad heart.

Why, there are just scores sitting in front of me tonight, that, if it were literally true that we had wild beasts and serpents and other venomous things in bodily form in your hearts, as they are typically there, I would hate to be close round some of you, for fear I might get bit before I could get out of the way. Oh God, give us clear hearts and clear hands.

Concerning Tongues

And then I will say, to be practical all along the line, did you ever look at your tongue until you said that? Oh, these tongues of ours! These tongues of ours! We Methodists pour the water on, and the Presbyterians sprinkle it on, and the Baptists put us clean under, but I don't care whether you sprinkle, pour, or immerse, the tongue comes out as dry as powder. Did you ever see a baptized tongue? Say, did you? Did you ever see a tongue that belonged to the Church? You will generally find the tongue among man's reserved rights. There come in some reservations, and always where there is a reservation the tongue is retained. The tongue! The tongue! Pambus, one of the middle-age saints, went to his neighbor with a Bible in his hand and told him, "I want you to read me a verse of Scripture every day. I can't read, and I want you to read to me." So the neighbor opened the Bible and read these words: "I will take heed to my ways that I sin not with my tongue."

Pambus took the book out of his hand and walked back home, and about a week after that the neighbor met him, and he said: "Pambus, I thought you were to come back and let me read you a passage of Scripture every day?" And Pambus said, "Do you recollect that verse you read to me the other day?" "No," said the neighbor. "Well," said Pambus, "I will quote it: I will take heed to my ways that I sin not with my tongue.' And, said he, "I never intend to learn another passage of Scripture until I learn to live that one." Oh, me! If every man, woman, and child in this house tonight would go away from here determined to live that passage of Scripture: "I SAID, I WILL TAKE HEED TO MY WAYS THAT I SIN NOT WITH MY TONGUE. I WILL KEEP MY TONGUE FROM EVIL AND MY LIPS FROM SPEAKING GUILE."

Oh, me! Shakespeare told a great truth when he said:

> "He that steals my purse steals trash,
> But he that filcheth from me my good name
> Takes that which not enricheth him,
> But makes me poor indeed."

Violators Of Character

These violators of character--I will venture the assertion there are many, many, many here tonight--if every word you said about people in this house was posted up there in legible words, here tonight, you would immediately leave this house and never be seen in public again. You would say, "We ain't going anywhere where they put up everything we say for folks to look at." Now, I look at my tongue until I see it. There is many a man that in other things may do well, that at last will lie down in hell forever, and say: "I am conscious I am tongue-damned. I would have gone to heaven if I hadn't got a tongue."

My tongue! And I say to you tonight the best thing we can do with our tongues is to speak well and to speak kindly of all men. I dare assert here in my place tonight, when you take me from this sacred stand that I occupy tonight, I defy you to put your finger on a word of mine against the character or reputation of anybody. But I am not talking for myself up here. Understand that. Once in Jerusalem a great crowd--it was eighteen hundred years and more ago, as the legend goes, or the allegory--a great crowd was gathered in Jerusalem, and they were gathered around a dead dog, and they stood and looked, and one of them said, "That is the ugliest dog I ever saw." Another said, "Oh, he is not only the ugliest dog I ever saw, but I don't believe his old hide is worth taking off of him." Another said, "Just look how crooked his legs are." And so they criticized the poor dog. And directly one spoke up and said, "Ain't those the prettiest, pearly white teeth you ever looked at?" And they walked off and said, "That must have been Jesus of Nazareth that could have found something good to say about a dead dog." Oh, me! I like those people that always like to say something kind of people in their ways and walks of life.

Watching One's Footsteps

And then, I ask you again, did you ever look at your feet until you saw them? There is a good deal in that.

"THY WORD IS A LAMP UNTO MY FEET AND
A LIGHT UNTO MY PATH."

Oh, Lord God! I would follow in the footsteps of him who led the way to heaven. There is no circumspect Christian who does not see to it that his feet are kept in the narrow way that leads from earth to heaven. A Methodist, a Baptist, a Presbyterian, in a ball-room! Their feet, that they have pledged should follow in the footsteps of Christ, are there cutting the pigeon-wing to music! Now what do you think of that?

And I hear this expression: They say, "Well, our Church don't object to it." Now, I would say a very strong thing here, and I hope you will take it in the very spirit in which I say it, for I never said a kinder thing or a harder thing than that, you never, you never shall hear a truer thing. Whenever a Presbyterian, or a Methodist, or a Baptist, or a Christian, or a Congregationalist says that their Church don't object to dancing and theatres, and all such things as that, they could not tell a bigger lie if they would try in a hundred years! Thank God, there is not a Church named after Christ on earth that has not thundered out after these things with all the power it has got.

"Our Church don't object!" Well, now the Episcopal Church being a Church in authority--how they did thunder against these worldly amusements. That little Church you belong to may not. That rotten thing! I would not stay in it long enough to get my hat if it didn't.

A Plucky Methodist Lady

I was sitting in a train some time ago and the train rolled up to the station, and just up on the platform, nearby, were three ladies. One of the ladies said to the other, "Are you going to the ball tonight?" The other lady said, "I ain't going." "But," she said, "I forgot; you are a Methodist, and you don't go to such places. I would not be a Methodist. I want to enjoy myself." The other said, "Yes, I am a Methodist, and thank God! I don't want to go to such places." "Oh," said the other one, "I would not be a Methodist," and the train rolled off, and I felt like jumping on the top of that train myself and hollering, "Hurrah for Methodism!" And whenever she goes into co-partnership with ballrooms and with all the worldly amusements that embarrass the Christian and paralyze his power--whenever the Methodist Church goes into co-partnership with these things, I will sever my connection with her forever.* And I love her and honor her today because she has stood like a bulwark against these things, and denounced them first to last.

One of the honored preachers of this town, a man whose good opinion I value highly, one of the noblest, truest ministers of this town, said to

---

*No doubt, Sam Jones would not be a part of the mainline Methodist Church today with its church bazaars, bake sales, worldly music, not to mention its support of the homosexual movement, its modernism, apostasy, and partnership with the National and World Councils of Churches!

me, "I declare to you, our churches are little more than a graveyard. We have been killed and almost buried by this tide of worldliness that has swept over our homes year after year." And that is the truth. And I can read a ten-page letter that I got from a citizen of St. Louis today and turn every face in this house as pale as death. That man wrote like he knew what he was talking about. There is many a mother at twelve o'clock at night in this town that can sing, with the blood trickling in her heart,

"Oh, where is my wandering boy tonight?
He was once as pure as the driven snow."

Removing The Carcasses

And oh, why, why, why would I take this carcass, and that carcass, and the other carcass, that are so offensive? Why would I bring them out before this congregation? Nothing, nothing, nothing would make me do it, but to get you to take those carcasses that are despoiling the very odors of your city, and bury them out of sight forever. That is it. You all have spent two or three nights looking at me. God help you to look at yourselves for awhile. And you will think I am a beauty before you get through. I look at myself from head to foot--my hands, my heart, my feet, my tongue. I look at my ways and walks and character in this community. Did you ever look at yourself as a member of the Church? Did you ever wake up some morning, and shut your eyes, and lie there and say, "Well, suppose every member of the Church in town was just like me, what sort of Church would we have in this town? Suppose every member of the Church in town prayed as little as I pray, what sort of Church would we have? Suppose every member of the Church paid as little as I pay, how long before the whole thing would be sold out by the Sheriff?"

Oh, my brother! it is well enough, now and then, for a fellow to get a square, honest look at himself. What sort of a Methodist are you? There is a man that has promised to renounce the world, the flesh and the devil, and the vain pomp and glory of this world, and he has promised on oath, before God and man, not to follow or be led by them. What is your life? There is that Presbyterian, consecrated to God by the most solemn ceremony that heaven ever listened to. Now, what is your character? There is the Episcopalian; with the imposing hands of the clergy laid upon his head, and with a ceremony as solemn as eternity, he was dedicated in the Church to God last night, and tonight he is in the biggest ball in town, dancing his way to hell.

Salvation During Lent

And no longer ago than this very year, in one of the cities of the South, one gentleman told me--said he, "I saw the Episcopal clergyman lay his hand on the heads of a class of twenty, one night and," he said, "the next night eighteen out of the twenty were at a magnificent ball." Now, you say, "I wouldn't have done that; I would have waited a week." Well, if a fellow is going to do it at all, better get right at it. Don't you think that's so? How long ought a fellow to wait after he joins the Church before he goes at his devilment? Now, that's it.

I wish I could get all the Methodists and Baptists and Presbyterians in this city, and all other churches, to live just like they promised to live. I wish I could get all the Episcopalians in town to be as good out of Lent as they are in Lent. That would be good, wouldn't it? And I never could see why a fellow ought not to be as good one time as another. Did you? I never could. And I am going to be just as good during the year as any Episcopalian in this town is during Lent. I reckon they all hope to die in Lent. If a heap of them die out of Lent the devil will get them, in my judgment. In a great many places they dance Lent in and they dance it out. Like the Irishman talking about holy days in America--said he, "Instead of hanging our heads and sorrowing over the crucifixion of our Saviour, we Americans fire it in and fire it out."

Fighting The Devil

Now, I don't pick out any denomination and say anything about one denomination that I would not say about another. There is no denominationalism in this. I have no purpose and no desire in my heart to say one thing about one denomination that I would not say about another. That is true. I am just talking true things, and any night you come here, if you don't like the way this is rattled off, you can rack out of here, just the minute you please. For I propose, God being my helper, to speak of the truth as I see it, and I don't care what man, or devil, or cities, or earth, or hell may say, I am going to preach, while I do preach what I believe to be the truth.

And I will tell you Christian people, if you think the devil is going to surrender any ground in this town until every inch is covered with blood, you do not know the devil as well as I do. I will tell you that. I have been fighting his Majesty several years, and I declare to you that he is always ready for a fight. He has possessed nearly two-thirds of this city for nearly forty years, and if you think he is going to make a voluntary surrender of his territory you do not know him. He is going to fight and fight, and every child he has got is going to help him; you can put that down. And I tell you there is another thing: there is a heap of members of the Church going to help him, too. They will that. Some places the devil goes to he never has anything to do himself. He puts his hands in his pockets and goes round and gets members of the Church to run his devilment for him. They do his work cheaper for him than any other class. He don't have to pay them, and they board themselves. In some towns the leading ballroom dude is a member of the Church--the fellow that gets them all up and runs the thing.

Parental Responsibility

I look at myself as a member of the Church. Oh me, brother! When you see yourself as a member of the Church, as a professor of religion, it will do you good. I will ask you again, did you ever look at yourself as a father? Oh me! how close you get to a man's heart when you talk to him of his family. Brother and Sister, did you ever have your innocent child sit on your lap, put its little arms round your neck and imprint the kiss of innocence on your cheek? Have you ever looked on your lovely children lying in their bed, and said, "Of all the children God ever gave, my children have the purest and best of fathers." You can go home tonight and wake up your little Willie. Get him quite awake, and ask him, "Who is the best man in St. Louis?" He will answer, "Why, you, papa." Ask him, "Who would you rather be most like?" and he will reply, "Why, you, papa." Ask him who is the best man in the world, and he will say, "Why, you, papa." He ain't got no sense. And that is why we curse, and damn and ruin our children. They can see no harm in us, and just as we do they will follow and imitate us. A single man may drink as a single man; he may swear; as a single man he may lead a godless life; but as a married man you had better call a halt and ask where you are leading your children to day by day. You may sit in the chairs of this hall night after night; you may simply have your curiosity excited; you may simply come here to laugh but when you gather your children in your arms and see that your bad example is leading them to death and hell there is no joke about that-- no laugh about that! God pity me and pity you in our relations toward those that lean upon us; and if there is any fact in my history that I bless God for in my heart tonight, it is the fact that not a sweet child of mine ever looked in my face when I was not a Christian, trying to serve God and set a good example.

Did you ever look at yourself as a mother? Of all beings that earth claims its blessings from, it looks as though a mother ought to be the best.

Mother, what is your life before your children? Consider yourself! Did you ever look at your children till you saw them? Wife, did you ever look at your husband till you saw him? Husband, did you ever look at your wife until you saw her? If there is anything in the world I would have get to heaven, it is my wife; yet there is a husband who never talked ten minutes to his wife on religion; and there is a wife who never opened her mouth to her husband about the way of life. Oh, me; when we think of a home that has been Christless, what a sad thing!

Seeing St. Louis

And then we ask again, did you ever look at St. Louis until you saw it? Did you ever take it by streets and blocks? Did you ever count the bar-rooms in this town? Did you ever count the beer-gardens in this town? Did you ever count the number of men that went in and out of the bar-rooms and beer-gardens? I bring this question square before you. Did you ever count the number of soiled doves that curse this city and curse themselves? Oh, my God, when we look at these pictures, we have to shut our eyes and drop down upon our knees. We say, "God deliver us and God speed us." Did you ever count the billiard tables in this town? Did you ever count the gambling halls in this town? Oh, me! No wonder this one writes and that one writes, "Jones, God bless you! turn loose your guns and do your best to wake up the Christian people and show them how this town by streets and blocks is drifting to hell every day."

Now, I am going to stick to the truth while I am here, and I say to every man and to every influence in this town, unfriendly to Christ and unfriendly to the Bible, to fight back. I do not look for anything else. I want to say right now that I like to see things moving up and if you can say anything worse of me than I can of you, lamm in, and I will beat you up to the tank in that line, maybe. Pick every flaw you can in every sermon, and if I cannot pick more flaws in your life than you do in my sermons I will yield the feather to you. I say to you now, we propose to get your eyes open so that you can see yourselves. That is the first sight you ought to look at. Then look at St. Paul. When he went to the City of Athens, so wholly given up to idolatry, it stirred his heart within him. I have heard Christian people say that they had no feeling, no enthusiasm, no religious fervor; but never since I joined Christ's church have I been devoid of religious fervor and enthusiasm. The man who goes about like a corpse, with no feeling, no enthusiasm, that man is either dead to all intents and purposes, or he has closed his eyes to what is going on about him. And he went over to Mar's Hill, pointed to the inscription "To the unknown God," and preached that grand sermon generated in his soul as he walked through the streets of the city and saw that it was wholly given up to idolatry; and I tell you tonight, when we see ourselves and our city and our surroundings as they are, there is hope for us.

Seeing The Cross

There is just one more thing I want you to do--that is, to see the cross. It is the hope of the world. It is the Balm of Gilead. It has power to save. It is the redemption of the race. Oh, my brother, it was fourteen years ago and a few days, when I, a poor, wretched, ruined, lost sinner, walked up to see my father die. Oh, how I loved that father, and how I broke his heart. I have wished a thousand times that I had my father back just one hour, that I might lean my head on his bosom and hear him speak the words of kindness and advice he has spoken to me in the past. As I stood by his dying couch he took my hand in his bony hand, and a heavenly smile rested on his face just before he passed out of this world. He did not die; he did not die. His faculties were as bright and his hope as buoyant in the very agonies of death as they ever had been. As I took his bony hand he said, "My poor, wayward, godless boy! You have almost broken my heart, and you have given me so much trouble! Won't you tell your dying father, now, that you will meet him in the good world?" I stood there for a moment convulsed from head to foot. I said, "Yes, father, I will meet you in the good world." I turned away from that dying couch, and every step I have made from that time to this has been to the good world. And I mean, with the grace of God, to keep my promise. I left that bed a wretched sinner, and looked to God. I looked up there and

I saw one hanging on the tree
  In agonies of blood.
He fixed his languid eyes on me,
  As near his cross I stood.

Sure, never to my latest breath
  Can I forget that look;
He seemed to charge me with his death,
  Though not a word he spoke.

My conscience felt and owned the guilt
  And plunged me in despair;
I saw my sins his blood had spilled
  And helped to nail him there.

A second look he gave, which said:
"I freely all forgive,
My blood is shed to ransom thee,
I die that you might live."

Blessed Christ, live forever to save dying men.

MONROE PARKER

Monroe Parker

4

Climbing To Hell

BIOGRAPHICAL SKETCH

Monroe Parker
(1909 - 1994)

Monroe Parker, affectionately known as "Monk," was born into a family of preachers on June 23, 1909. His great-grandfather was a preacher, as was his grandfather, six uncles and several cousins. His brother, Jim, was also a preacher, as were two of his brother's sons. So it was no surprise that Monroe Parker, while wanting to enter the field of medicine, should be called into the ministry. In a way, he did enter the medical field, only to minister to the broken, bleeding hearts of sinful men and women across America and around the world.

According to his own testimony, Monroe Parker joined a Baptist church when he was only eight years old - and lost. For eleven years he was an unsaved church member, like many today. During those years he would alternate attending the Baptist church and the Methodist church. While attending the Methodist church, he was asked one Sunday to teach a Sunday School class of ten-year-old boys, even though he was still not converted himself. He did try to resolve to be better, but knew he was still not saved.

One day, he went to hear Dr. Bob Shuler preach and heard him say, "Boys, your sins crucified Jesus." A week later, on July 29, 1928, he was teaching his young boys about Stephen's prayer for those who had stoned him, "Lord, lay not this sin to their charge." He quoted Dr. Shuler's words to the young class and, then, admitting that his sins also crucified Jesus, he confessed that he, himself, was not saved and asked those boys to pray for him. He bowed his own head and trusted Christ that morning.

His ministry of evangelism began while he was a student at Bob Jones College in 1928, when the college was located in Florida. His ministry went on to span more than sixty-five years and more than 1500 crusades across America and around the world.

He earned his PH.D from Bob Jones and was honored by John Brown University with the honorary degree of Doctor of Divinity, and Maranatha Baptist College with the honorary degree of Doctor of Laws.

He married the former Harriet Stollenwerk in 1933, but became a widower in 1946 when she was killed in a tragic car accident. He then married the former Marjorie Parker in 1948; a marriage that brought them both more than forty years of happy fellowship and ministry together. The Lord blessed that union with two children: a son, John Monroe, Jr., and a daughter, Penelope (Penny) Anne. Brother "Monk" became a widower again on March 14, 1981 when he was 71 years of age. In the late Fall of 1982, after a somewhat brief courtship, Brother Parker proposed to the former Ruby Phillips Whitely, whose husband, Ed, had gone to be with the Lord four years earlier. She accepted his proposal and they were married on January 4, 1983.

Although Dr. Parker served the Lord in such capacities as assistant to the president of Bob Jones University, President of Pillsbury Baptist Bible College, pastor, radio preacher, founder of Christian Dells Bible Camp, and Director of the Baptist World Mission, he was first, and foremost, an evangelist. He loved preaching and he loved preachers.

His last sermon was preached in Fairbanks, Alaska on June 30, 1994 at the Bible Baptist Church. The week prior to that he participated in a Fundamental Baptist Fellowship meeting, also in Fairbanks. On July 17, 1994, he entered the presence of his Lord at the age of 85, after a bout with pneumonia. At the time of his death, he was considered by many to be the "Dean" of evangelists in America. He will be sorely missed. KWL

CLIMBING TO HELL
Monroe Parker

Our Scripture is found in the twenty-third chapter of Matthew. I shall begin to read at verse twenty-five.

"Woe unto you, scribes and Pharisees, hypocrites! for ye make clean the outside of the cup and of the platter, but within they are full of extortion and excess. Thou blind Pharisee, cleanse first that which is within the cup and platter, that the outside of them may be clean also. Woe unto you, scribes and Pharisees, hypocrites! for ye are like unto whited sepulchers, which indeed appear beautiful outward, but are within full of dead men's bones, and of all uncleanness. Even so ye also outwardly appear righteous unto men, but within ye are full of hypocrisy and iniquity. Woe unto you, scribes and Pharisees, hypocrites! because ye build the tombs of the prophets, and garnish the sepulchers of the righteous, and say, if we had been in the days of our fathers, we would not have been partakers with them in the blood of the prophets. Wherefore ye be witnesses unto yourselves, that ye are the children of them which killed the prophets. Fill ye up then the measure of your fathers. Ye serpents, ye generation of vipers, how can ye escape the damnation of hell? Wherefore, behold, I send unto you prophets, and wise men, and scribes: and some of them ye shall kill and crucify; and some of them ye shall scourge in your synagogues, and persecute them from city to city: That upon you may come all the righteous blood shed upon the earth, from the blood of righteous Abel unto the blood of Zacharias son of Barachias, whom ye slew between the temple and the altar. Verily I say unto you, All these things shall come upon this generation. O Jerusalem, Jerusalem, thou that killest the prophets, and stonest them which are sent unto thee, how often would I have gathered thy children together, even as a hen gathereth her chickens under her wings, and ye would not ! Behold, your house is left unto you desolate. For I say unto you, Ye shall not see me henceforth, till ye shall say, Blessed is he that cometh in the name of the Lord." (Matthew 23:25-39)

One night, when I had preached on the subject of Hell, a lady came to me greatly disturbed. She said it was just terrible. I answered, "Yes, M'am, Hell is a terrible place." But she said, "The idea of you preaching a sermon like that. Why, Jesus preached beatitudes. Jesus said, 'Blessed are the poor in spirit, and blessed are they that mourn, and blessed are the meek." I answered, "Yes, M'am. Have you read all of the sermon from which you are quoting?" "Oh," she said, "I've read all the beatitudes." "Well," I asked, "have you read the entire Sermon on the Mount? Have you read the part where Jesus said, 'If thy right eye offend thee, pluck it out and cast it from thee; for it is better for thee to enter into life with one eye, than having two eyes to be cast into hell, into the fire that never shall be quenched, where their worm dieth not and the fire is not quenched. And if thy right hand offend thee, cut it off and cast it from thee; for it is better for thee to enter into life maimed, than having two hands be cast into hell, into the fire that never shall be quenched, where their worm dieth not and the fire is not quenched...'" "Oh," she said, "did Jesus say that?" I said, "He certainly did. That was His first sermon. Have you ever read His last sermon? Have you read how He stood in the temple and looked right in the faces of the hypocrites and said, 'Woe unto you scribes and Pharisees, hypocrites! You are full of dead men's bones. You whited sepulchers! How can you escape the damnation of Hell?'" Why, Jesus Christ had more to say about Hell than any other character in the Word of God! If you were to take the Bible and tear out every page that has anything about the retribution said upon it, you would not have much Bible left.

Sometimes people don't like evangelists because they tell deathbed stories. But Jesus went beyond the deathbed; He told about a man who lifted up his eyes in Hell being in torment who saw Abraham afar off and Lazarus in his bosom, and he cried out, "Father Abraham! Send Lazarus that he might dip his finger in water and cool my tongue for I am tormented in this flame!" Jesus preached it! As I stated the other night, Love Incarnate preached Hell and He did not apologize for believing in it.

Oh, I know that some people will call attention to the fact that when Jesus said, "If thy right eye offend thee, pluck it out and cast it from thee. It is better to enter into life with one eye than having two eyes to be cast into Hell," that He used the Greek word "Gehenna." It was a valley southeast of Jerusalem, the valley of "Hinnom." Back in the days before Josiah became king, the ancients worshipped the god Molech in this valley. They had a great bronze image which they heated red hot, almost white hot. They practiced the most abominable ceremonies imaginable out there. They even used to practice prostitution as a religious ceremony. Little babies born as a result of these religious orgies were sacrificed to this awful god! They kept it heated red hot; they'd pull a lever, his mouth would open and they'd cast little babies into the mouth of this burning god. They also called the valley "Toph" (from "tophet"), meaning "a drum," because the beating of drums was used to drown the cry of burning infants. When Josiah became king in Jerusalem, he destroyed this idolatry and turned the valley of Hinnom into the city dumping grounds. Here the dead bodies of malefactors were cast out, dead animals were thrown, and the city sewers emptied their filthy contents there into the valley. And, of course, they kept a fire burning out there to destroy the filth. That valley became a symbol of everything that was heinous and abominable and bad!

So it was only natural, according to the law of language, that the Valley of Hinnom should become a symbol of Hell. And during the inter-testament period, so we're told by Flavius Josephus, a historian who was a contemporary of Jesus, that during the inter-testament period between the Old and New Testaments, during those four hundred intervening years, the Jews began to speak of Hell as "Hinnom", or the "Valley of Hinnom," (Gehenna as we call it). When Jesus came, He used the well known figure when He spoke of Hell. The fact that Jesus used figurative language does not destroy the fact that Hell is a literal place. He also used figurative language when He spoke of Heaven. He called it Paradise, and Paradise was originally a garden in Persia. One must conclude that if there is no Hell, there is no Heaven, if we place the reasoning upon the idea that Jesus used the well known figure.

Jesus did not confine His remarks about Hell to the Greek word Gehenna. He also used the word "Hades," which is the place of the departed. And those who translated the Hebrew Old Testament into Greek some three hundred fifty years before Christ, known as the Septuagint, used the word "Hades" to translate the Hebrew word "Sheol," the place of the departed, and is never limited to the "grave." It has some of the characteristics of the grave, and many of these characteristics are ascribed to it. But it always goes beyond the grave; it's the place where departed spirits went in the days of the Old Testament, and where the spirits of the lost go now!

It was divided into two compartments. Lazarus was in one compartment, in Abraham's bosom, in Paradise. The rich man who cried out for a drop of water was in Tartarus, the other compartment, and there was a great gulf fixed between them. You see, the Old Testament saints were not "redeemed" until Jesus died on the Cross. Their sins were covered and atoned for by the blood of bulls and goats, but the "blood of bulls and goats could not take away sin." It was not until Jesus cried, "It's finished!" on the Cross that they were redeemed.

When Jesus left the Cross, He went into Paradise. After His resurrection, He said to the woman in the garden, "Don't touch Me. I have not yet ascended to My Father." He had been to Paradise, but He had not yet been to the Father. That evening He came back and said, "Touch Me, feel Me, and see that it is I." In the meantime He had gone up to the Father, appeared in the heavenly Holy of Holies, and when He went up, he led "captivity captive." He took ALL of the redeemed of the Old Testament on to Heaven with Him! He first descended into the lower parts of the earth, and He Who descended also ascended above all principalities. He transferred Paradise to Heaven. Now when a Christian dies, he goes straight to Heaven to dwell with God and angels! When a sinner dies he goes into Hades, into the place of the departed, and one day, at the Great White Throne, Death and Hades will deliver up their dead. They will be judged every man according to his works, for there are degrees of suffering in Hell just as there are degrees of reward in the Kingdom. They are judged every man according to his works, and all who are judged at the Great White Throne are cast into the Lake of Fire!

Hell is a real place and Jesus preached it. The Apostles preached it. John preached it. The Apostle of Love preached it! And yet, there's a sickly sentimentalism over this country where some people tell us that a God of love will not allow sinners to go to Hell. I suppose they think they know more about love than He Whose very Name is love, than He Whose heart burst with love as He hung on the Cross. I suppose they think they know more about love than Jesus Christ! Jesus preached Hell! and these sentimentalists who tell you, "God will not damn sinners," blaspheme and slander God! He's a holy God! He will do right!

But, as I stated in an earlier service, He would not let any sinner who ever lived, however vile he may have been, go to Hell without making a way for his escape. I don't know much about the nature of Hell. Many people have speculated about it. I do know that Hell is a place, and I've studied every passage in the Word of God and studied it carefully. I even wrote a PhD. dissertation on the Old Testament revelation of the future life with special attention to its consistency in all periods. And I believe I know as much as anyone living about this particular subject; the consistency of it in all periods. I'm not boasting. I had to do laborious, hard work in this field because it was a field in which I wrote a dissertation.

Hell Is A Place

I believe that Hell is a place. I don't know much about the nature of it. It's God's penitentiary. It's a place of fire. It's a place of darkness. It's a bottomless pit. It's a place of dust. It's a place of punishment. It's a literal place.

A great Methodist preacher said, "The very idea of the correspondence between the character of the place and the inhabitants of the place suggest that Hell is a place of horror. It is called 'outer darkness.' It may be a dark and frightful sphere isolated from all worlds, cursed of God, erratic and lawless rolling beyond the confines of creation with no song or star to light up its darkness and chase away its infernal vapors, rent with awful chasms over which the lost may walk and run and grope and stumble and fall and climb forever. It may have strange power over the lost answering to gravity which binds them to its surface and compels them to dwell there for all eternity." He said, "It may not be this. It may be a huge cavern, hollowing out the center of some blasted, shattered, and God-cursed planet in which the poison and stench of ages have gathered and, condensing, is still upon the walls dimly lighted by phosphorous torches held by grimacing and howling fiends whose sickly flickerings render the darkness and all the windings and pits and chasms but blacker; and where occasional blue flames break through the fissures overhead and lick along the arches, and bolts of thunder crash through the grottoes and roar along the labyrinth in which lost men and fallen angels may be driven from the judgment seat, the ponderous gates closing and locking behind them, the key fastened to the girdle of God and Divine Omnipotence installed as perpetual sentinel to guard the way.

"Or," he said, "it may be a huge lake of fire and brimstone surrounded by precipitous shores over whose surface beat eternal storms; the fiery waves lashing and dashing and groaning around all the shores, bubbles bursting on every wave and swell amidst fumes threaded with serpent flames in whose ascending volumes of lasting lightenings flash and cross while the unfettered thunders of God upon Hell's infernal drum roll the eternal bass in Hell's uproar and keep time with the ceaseless groans of the lost." He said, "Be it better or worse, let us not go there! Oh, let us not go there!" We don't have to go to Hell! He Who preached Hell in this text wept over the people and cried, "Oh, how oft would I have gathered thee unto myself even as a hen gathereth her chickens under her wings, and you would not! How can you escape?" Jesus said. And another said, "How can you escape if you neglect so great salvation?" So Jesus said, "How can you escape? I would have received you, but you would not! You rejected such great salvation." In another place, He said, "Ye will not come unto Me that ye might have life."

I believe we have a sovereign God and I believe in election. I agree with what Dr. Scofield said in his notes on First Peter 1, that election is determined upon foreknowledge is made clear. What there is in the foreknowledge of God which determines the election is not revealed. I believe in a sovereign God. I believe in predestination and election. I'm not as blue stocking as the old Presbyterian who fell down the stairs, got up and said, "Thank God, that's over!" While I believe in the sovereignty of God, I believe in the will of man. And the sovereign Saviour said, "I believe in the sovereignty of God, I believe in the will of man. And the sovereign Saviour said, "I would, but you would not!" And He said, "You will not come!" People who go to Hell intrude into the place, they're usurpers in Hell, God doesn't want them to be lost! "As I live, saith the Lord, I have no pleasure in the death of the sinner, but rather that he turn to Me." "Come now and let us reason together, saith the Lord, though your sins be as scarlet they shall be as white as snow; though they be red like crimson, they shall be as wool."

All through the Word of God, there is the invitation to come to Jesus. And in the last chapter, "the Spirit and the Bride say, Come. Let him that heareth say, Come. And let him that is athirst come, and whosoever will, let him take the water of Life freely." If you WILL, you may be saved! And people who go to Hell climb to get into Hell!

Climbing Over Childhood Influences

When you were a little child you went to Sunday School. You came home with a card in your hand. On that card was a picture of Jesus receiving little children. Underneath were the words, "Suffer the little children to come unto me, and forbid them not, for of such is the kingdom of heaven." The next Sunday there was a picture of the Saviour on a Cross, and underneath was the golden text, "For God so loved the world that he gave his only begotten Son, that whosoever believeth in him, should not perish, but have everlasting life." It was not easy for you, as a little child, to put those impressions aside. It was not easy for you to climb over those good impressions, to go over that little hill of good influence. Your feet were tender, your mind was impressionable, and your heart was tender. It was not easy to push conviction aside, but you walked over those influences, and you went on toward Hell. And God said, "I don't want to see that child lost. I'll put another barrier between him and the pit of Hell."

Climbing Over The Word Of God

And He reared up this blessed mountain, the Word of God, as Gladstone called it the "impregnable Rock of Holy Scriptures." It may lie untouched on a table or stuck back on a shelf, but it's the Word of God, and it brings conviction to the heart. You cannot look upon it without conviction. You may disclaim its authority; you may be skeptical about some of its teachings; but it's the authoritative, infallible, true Word of God! There is nothing so powerful as Truth!

A man asked me today, "What are the barriers that keep people from coming to Jesus?" I said, "The world, the flesh and the Devil." The sins of the flesh, the appeal of the world, and the subtle deception of the Devil, and people who are deceived voluntarily yield to that deception. "If thine eye be single, thy whole body shall be full of light." "If any man is willing to do his will, he shall know the doctrine." People who are in darkness choose the darkness for this is the condemnation that light came into the world but men would not come to the light that their deeds might be reproved. Men loved darkness rather than light because their deeds were evil. People climb over the revelation of God. This is His Word. Every word in the original manuscripts was inspired. You cannot destroy this

Book. Gladstone called it the "impregnable Rock of Holy Scriptures." It stands the test of time. Atheists have denied it, but there it stands. Skeptics have doubted it, but there it stands. Agnostics have questioned it, but there it stands. Infidels have forsaken it, but there it stands. Neo-orthodox teachers have watered it down, and New Evangelicals have compromised it, but there it stands. The impregnable Rock of Holy Scriptures! The tooth of time has gnawed upon it.

> Last eve I paused beside the blacksmith's door,
> And heard the anvil ring the vesper chime;
> Then looking in, I saw upon the floor,
> Old hammers worn with beating years of time.
> "How many anvils have you had," said I,
> "To wear and batter all these hammers so?"
> "Just one," said he, and then, with twinkling eye,
> "the anvil wears the hammers out, you know."
> "And so," I thought, "the Anvil of God's Word
> For ages skeptic blows have beat upon,
> Yet, though the noise of falling blows was heard,
> the Anvil is unharmed, the hammer's gone."

Where is the so-called "higher criticism" of thirty-five years ago? It's as dead as a door nail! Modernism failed, and its chiefest proponents confess it! Even Dr. Fosdick, who broadcast for so long on national hookup that a radio announcer inadvertently presented him as the "Prince of the power of the air!" wrote in his book <u>Successful Christian Living</u>, on page 163, "the modernistic movement has watered down the thought of the divine, and, may we be forgiven for this, left souls standing like the ancient Athenians before an altar to an unknown god."

You see, modernism passed into what theologians call "crisis," and "crisis theology" was born. Their churches and their coffers were empty, and they said, "We've got to go back toward the old orthodox position of our fathers. We've got to retrace our footsteps. The salt has lost its savor. We've got to get some fresh salt." They looked across the gap where the fundamentalists were packing them in, and they said, "We need to moderate our position." Mr. Hoover was with me in New York when we heard a brilliant man, a great pulpiteer and a great liberal preacher stand up and say, "We modernists have led this world astray. We have preached our humanism and our pacifism. We have taught that there will be no more war. We have preached peace, peace, when there is no peace. We stand with our hands dripping with the life blood of nations. We are responsible for the war through we have just passed. We need to

retrace our footsteps back toward the old orthodox position of our fathers."
But we [Dr. Parker & Mr. Hoover] held our tongues from saying "Amen,"
because we had heard him lecture before and we knew he would spoil it.
He said, "But shall we go back to that position? NO!" said he. "We
need to go back in that direction until we can strike a synthesis with the
fundamentalists. What we need," he said, "is a new modernism." I thought
of what old Dr. H.C. Morrison said to a group of students, "Blessed is
the man who does not play the fool, for verily, verily, I say unto thee, he
that playeth the fool two or three times close together becomes one."

The Word of God stands. All the philosophies and all the theories that
contradict it will die, but this Book will NEVER die as long as God lives,
for Jesus said, "Heaven and earth shall pass away, but my Word shall not
pass away." You've got to climb over it to get to Hell. It's authoritative.
I can support it. I could preach for hours on the subject, but I don't need
to. It speaks for itself. It will change your life! It'll lift you to God, and no
stream can rise higher than its fountain head. This Book lifted me to God;
it must have come from God.

You've climbed over the Word of God; you've climbed over good
influences of your early childhood. You say that there are heathen who've
never heard of the Word of God. This Book tells us that they are without
excuse, for they have natural revelation and they have conscience, and
they're condemned. They have enough light, but the tragedy is that they
turn from the flickering light of natural revelation. If they had the Love
Story of the Cross and the preached Word of God, they'd turn to Jesus
and be converted. So there will be heathen in Hell if we don't take the
Gospel to them, but they'll be in Hell without excuse.

Climbing Over The Prayers Of The Saints

Everybody who goes to Hell is an intruder there. He climbs over the
revelation and the call of God and he climbs over the prayers of the saints.
Literally thousands of people are praying for this campaign here. I've sent
out an appeal to everybody on our mailing list and many thousands of
pastors. I've got scores of letters and messages from godly friends all over
this country saying, "We're praying for the meetings in Indianapolis."
You're here tonight because somebody's praying. People in these
churches, along with many preachers, have spent hours on their knees.
Many of you have spent hours in prayer. I prayed half the night last night
for this service tonight. And somebody is here because of prayer. Maybe
because of the prayer of godly parents long since with Jesus. God never
forgets those prayers; He bottles them up in golden vials and occasionally
He opens the vials and smells the sweet odors, which are the prayers of

saints. That old mother who prayed for you years ago is already with Jesus, but God has not forgotten her prayer. And you've got to climb over those prayers to get to Hell.

If I had gone to Hell, it would have been in spite of godly parents. I was converted one Sunday morning reading the Word of God to a Sunday School class. I learned later that my mother had spent all night the night before, without sleep, that God would save her boy. My father had also prayed with her most of the night. And God answers prayer.

You've climbed over prayers. You've climbed over a mountain of good reason. You've gone down in valleys between the mountains; depressions, financial at times; hardships and sorrows. Many a man found God in a foxhole while the orchestra of Hell was playing on a battlefield above their heads.

Climbing Over Caskets

Years ago down in Pensacola, Florida, a young lady came forward to dedicate her life to God. She was a backslidden Christian. She went home with her testimony and came back the next night and said, "Pray for my husband. He laughed at me last night." I hear that plea all over America, "Pray for my husband. He's not saved. Pray for my wife. She's not saved. We have children. I want a Christian home." What must one be thinking of, to found a home and bring children into the world and not bring them up in the nurture and the admonition of the Lord? What must they be thinking?

We prayed with this young woman. She came back the next night and said, "He still laughs at me. Keep praying." And so we entered into a prayer covenant that God would convict him. The next Sunday afternoon, as I came out of the studio where I was broadcasting in the old San Carlos Hotel, I was called to the telephone. I was requested to come out to a certain address. It was about nine o'clock when I got there. Crepe was on the door, and people were out on the front porch. I went through the crowd into the living room and there was a casket. I looked into the casket and there was the body of the little woman who had asked me to pray for her husband. I stood there thanking God that she was ready, certain precious promises coming to my mind. "We sorrow not as those who have no hope." "Precious in the eyes of the Lord is the death of his saints." And I stood there thanking God that she was ready when I heard somebody sob.

I sat down with a young man. I said, "I know your heart's broken. But I'm so glad to tell you that Jesus cares. And your wife is with Jesus. I've talked with her three times in the last week. She was a Christian." He said, "Yes, I know it." "Well," I said, "do you believe that she's with Jesus now?" He said, "Yes, I know she is." "Well," I said, "you're not a Christian, are you?" He said, "No, I'm not, but she was." I said to him, "You know, she was praying that God would speak to your heart." He said, "Yes, I know." I said, "He's spoken to you, hasn't He?" "Yes, He has." I asked, "You have two little boys, don't you?" "Yes." "How old are they?" "Nine and eleven." I said, "They need a Christian father. Will you trust Jesus?" He said, "Not tonight." "Well," I said, "I don't know, but I believe God would tell her about it. Why don't you trust Him?" He said, "Not tonight."

He asked, "Preacher, will you conduct the funeral?" I said, "Of course I will, but I want you to be saved." He said, "We want a little service here at the home. Then we're going forty miles north of here to the old home cemetery up near the Alabama state line for the internment. We want the main service there at the grave." After the internment, we walked together back to the gate of the old country cemetery, and I said, "Now, before I leave you, will you trust Jesus?" He said, "Not tonight." "Oh," I said, "Now's the time." He said, "Not now. I'll be out to the service tonight." "Well," I said, "you may not feel like coming." He said, "I'll be there." So I said, "I'll be praying for you."

He came and sat in the back with his two boys. I preached and I prayed for him while I was preaching. I gave the invitation and down the aisle came a large number of people to the prayer room, but he did not come. I stood there and pleaded and he would not come. At the close of the service he came down and thanked me for my kindness and I said, "Won't you trust Jesus?" And he said, "Not now. I'll be back some other time." And I said to his boys, "How about you boys. Wouldn't you like to know your mother's Saviour?" And they looked at their father, and didn't know what to say. The father said, "We'll be back some other time." He took them by the hand and down the aisle they went and out into the night. My heart sank.

Some two years ago, I was in Macon, Georgia. A good brother and pastor from Pensacola was there and I asked him about that family. He told me that they were still without God. The boys are grown now and that man is old. His hair is covered with the snows of many winters and he's still without God. And when the man gets to Hell, and he'll go soon if he doesn't turn to Jesus soon, in a Lake of Fire, he'll rise up and say, "God is Love! He tried to stop me! He tried to flag my train, but I would not stop! I walked over a casket! I stepped on a shroud! I walked over the body of a little wife! I spurned the plea of the Saviour! I would not come to Jesus! I ought to be in Hell! I'm an intruder!"

Climbing Over The Cross

You may not have to go through that valley. You may not have to go over some of the mountains I may have mentioned, but there is one mountain I know you'll have to climb. It's not a very high mountain, but it's a very rugged one. It's in the shape of a skull. And on the brow of that skull is an old rugged Cross. On that Cross there's a bleeding Lamb. Nay, thank God, He's on no Cross, He's in no tomb. But He died on a Cross, and if you go to Heaven, you'll go by way of the Cross. But, my friend, if you go to Hell, you'll still go by way of the Cross. You'll go over the Cross to get to Hell. You'll walk over Jesus, you'll step on His heart, you'll trample in His blood, you'll spurn His love.

Down in Greenville, South Carolina, where I lived for some years, a young woman shot her father, killing him in cold blooded murder. I've known young people to kill their parents unintentionally. I've seen boys reach up with one hand and grab the gray hairs of an old Christian father, reach out with the other hand and take the heart strings of a Christian mother, and drag them down to an early grave. And so it was with one young man; he worried his mother to death with the life he lived. The night after the funeral, as his old father, lonely and blue, sat in front of the little open fireplace in the early Fall of the year, the young man came down the stairs and started out the door for an engagement. The old man asked, "Son, where are you going?" The boy said, "Father, I've got a date. I'm going out." The old man said, "Now, Son, don't leave me tonight. We just buried your mother and I need you, Son. I want to talk with you." The young man walked over and said, "Dad, cheer up. Mother's gone. There's nothing we can do. I'll see you in the morning. I've got a date. I can't break it."

The old man said, "Son, I can't allow you to go out tonight." The young man said, "Now Father, don't be foolish. I'll see you in the morning." The old man finally stood up and walked over to the door and said, "Son, you're not going out tonight. I won't allow you to go." The young man said, "Get out of the way, Dad! I'm going out." Finally, after a little struggle, the old man fell down on the floor and said, "My Boy, if you go out of this house tonight, if you go through this door, you'll have to walk over my body." The young man turned around and started to go for another door, but he said, "Get up, Dad!" The old man lay there. The boy said, "Get up!" The old man refused to move. Finally, with a curse on his lips, he walked over the body of his old father and went out to spend the night in sin.

You say, "he was a heartless wretch?" And he was. But, my friend, if you go to Hell, you'll walk over the crucified body of the suffering Son of God Who throws Himself between you and Hell, and begs you, in loving kindness and tender mercy, to stay back. You'll walk over the heart of Him Who suffered Hell for you so you would not have to suffer it. Suppose I should go out of this building tonight and get in the car and go for a drive. As I drive I see a house on fire. I stop the car and get out. I hear a woman scream. The siren is coming in the distance, but it seems so far away. So I rush into the burning building and up a winding stairway. I find there a woman afraid to come out through the fire and smoke. I seize a quilt and wrap it around her and bring her out to a safe place. Not a hair on her head is singed and there's not a scar on her body. But I receive scars that will go with me to my grave. The flesh is burned from my hands, and my face is all blackened and scarred. When I get out of the hospital, I stand before a congregation and people cringe with horror.

I go back to college and I'm unable to do my work. Suppose I become a tramp. I go from place to place begging food and ten years later I come back to Indianapolis. I go down a street and see a lovely home. While I've lost the practical use of my hands, I manage to work the brass knocker on the door. A lady answers the door. When she sees me, she shrinks back and says, "Who are you?" I say, "I'm just a plain tramp, Ma'am. I'd like a bite to eat, if you please, and a glass of water." "Oh," she says, "but where did you get all those scars?" "These scars? I got them here in the city of Indianapolis some ten years ago. One cool night in the early Fall, in the month of October, in fact it was October the 9th, I went down a street and I saw a house on fire. I heard a woman scream. I rushed into the house and up a winding staircase and wrapped a quilt around the lady." "Oh," she says, "stop! Come into this house. October the 9th, ten years ago, I'm the woman you rescued! You poor man. You'll not have to beg. Wait a minute."

(Knock. Knock. Knock.) Who is that knocking at your heart's door tonight? It's Jesus. "Jesus! Where did You get those scars?" "These scars? Put your finger here in this nail print. Put it here. Thrust your hand in here. Feel here, where the thorns tore My brow. Feel here where they plucked out My beard. Feel here, where thongs of leather tore my flesh. You can't feel the big scar. That's in My soul. I got these scars when I died for you." And, if you have any gratitude, if you have any appreciation in your heart, if you have any backbone, I don't see how you can walk on the Son of God Who died to keep you out of Hell. Don't climb over Jesus. Don't climb over this appeal tonight. Don't climb over the call of God's Holy Spirit in this service.

Let us bow for prayer.

GLEN SCHUNK

5

Man's Appointment With Death

BIOGRAPHICAL SKETCH

Glen Schunk
(1918 - 1978)

Born into a strong Roman Catholic family in Scales Mound, Illinois, on February 3, 1918, Glen Harold Schunk did not come to know the Lord as his Saviour until the age of twenty-four. It was during the Fall of 1942 that a Christian layman came almost daily to the restaurant where Glen worked as a cook and shared the gospel with him. In time, Glen trusted Christ as his Saviour.

Glen and Irma (Hartwig) were married on August 29, 1938, shortly before he joined the United States Army Infantry. He served in Italy during World War II and was awarded the Purple Heart for wounds received in battle.

After Glen's discharge from the Army, he sensed God's call to preach and enrolled in Bob Jones University in Greenville, South Carolina, to prepare for the ministry. While in college he conducted a number of evangelistic meetings, preparatory for a life of evangelistic ministry. During the school year he would commute to meetings enabling him to maintain all his daytime classes, then drive to and from the meetings, getting back home late at night. By the time he graduated in 1956, he had already conducted many such meetings.

After graduation, Brother Schunk spent the next twenty-two years of his life serving his Lord in more than 900 evangelistic campaigns all over America. His meetings were characterized by his fervent love of the Word and the ministry. In his love and encouragement for the pastor as well as young and upcoming evangelists, Glen Schunk was like a modern day

Barnabas. He also loved children and they loved to flock around him wherever he was.

His sermons were characterized by their abundance of Scripture. He felt, since God promised to honor His Word, he would give folks a good dose of the Scriptures. He purposely kept his messages brief, averaging 20-25 minutes.

He received an honorary doctorate from Central Baptist Seminary in Minneapolis, Minnesota, and also received a special Alumni Award from BJU. A special honor came when he was asked to consider serving as the president of Pillsbury Baptist Bible College in Minnesota, which he declined.

Dr. Schunk preached his last revival meeting at the Bethel Baptist Church in Schaumburg, Illinois in late May, 1978. Less than three weeks later he began to experience chest pains as he arrived at Pillsbury Baptist Bible College to be their convocation speaker. The pains worsened, forcing him to return home to South Carolina where he was admitted to the hospital. Two days later, on June 6, 1978, Glen entered the presence of the Lord he so dearly loved and faithfully served.

The sermon reproduced here is the last sermon preached by Dr. Schunk, and interestingly, deals with the all important subject of man's appointment with death and the necessity of being prepared to meet God. Indeed, he was. Are you prepared for your appointment? KWL

MAN'S APPOINTMENT WITH DEATH
Glen Schunk

Let's pray together before we preach.

"Our Father, thank you for all that's past, for a wonderful eight days, almost unbelievable how You've moved all these people who've been baptized, some we've come to learn to know and love. But now comes a different time. We come to preach and we're concerned because in this big of an audience, no doubt, there are several who do not know whether they'd go to heaven. We pray You'd draw them to Christ and make it easy to preach. Restore the backslider, speak to the disobedient, and make it easy to preach we pray in Jesus' Name, Amen."

Most of you know that there are four billion, and more people than that, in the world. But I wonder if you know this, that last year, 90 million people died. And in a 24-hour period 260 die by suicide, 600 die from accident, 1600 die from some kind of heart disease, and yet another 1,000 die from dreaded cancer.

Jack Clawson was his proper name. The fire bell'd rung down at the fire station and they'd say, "It's Lucky Jack again." And they'd get in their little vehicle, speed out to the house, apply the brakes in front of the house, run in the house and pick Jack up off the floor, put him on a cot, apply the oxygen mask to his face, and he'd revive. One hundred and seventy-two times! One hundred and seventy-two heart attacks! And the fire bell rang, and out they'd go. They'd say, "It's Lucky Jack again." Speed out to the house and screech the brakes in front of the house, run in, pick Jack up off the floor, put him on the cot, apply the oxygen mask-- but Jack's dead. The point is simple. You can have a hundred and seventy-two heart attacks, but you're going to have to die.

In fact, I read a story about a GI who'd survived a thousand barrages in battle. They pulled him off the front line, took him back to the rear eschalon, and some general pinned a medal on his chest for bravery. They sent him back to the rest camp and he went in and went to the doctors and said, "Doctor, my throat's a little raw. You got something for that?" Doctor looked in his throat and said, "Take these lozenges, but what you need is rest." So he went back to the barracks and said, "Tom, if I'm not up by chow time, give me a call." "OK." So chow time came, and he came into the barracks and hollered. When there was no movement down there, he went down and touched the twenty-year old boy on the shoulder and he fell off the cot dead. Wonder if you knew there are enough germs on the back of your tongue to kill you in the next 15 seconds if your body was not strong enough to ward them off.

Death Is A Surety

"What are you getting at, Brother Schunk?" Just as sure as you sit out in that seat, you're gonna have to die. You say, "I know that." But wait a minute. I want you to know from the pages of Scripture that death is a surety! In Isaiah 38:1 "Thus saith the Lord, set thine house in order for thou shalt die and not live."

Here it is in Romans 5:12; "Wherefore as by one man sin entered the world, and death by sin, so then death passed upon all men for all have sinned."

Mother brings the baby home from the hospital, puts him back in the crib, and the people come in to look at that little boy and say, "Isn't he a beautiful little child, just beginning to live." But he's beginning to die.

And all the time you've been sitting in your seats tonight in this church you've been dying, not living. In fact, in Ezk. 18:4 the Bible says, "The soul that sinneth it shall die." You drive with me across America. I go through nearly all the large towns, huge buildings stretching into the skies, dubbed wrong--they say "Life Insurance" when they oughta say "Death Insurance." Drive through the town and you see new memorial gardens going up, new funeral parlors. And death reaches out with her fingernails and scratches lines in your face, and, just as sure as you sit out in that seat, you're gonna have to die.

In Hebrews 9:27, the Bible says, "It's appointed unto men once to die and after that the judgment." In I Tim. 6:7, "For we brought nothing into this world, and it is certain we can carry nothing out."

The pastor knocked at my motel door one time and he said, "Brother Schunk, I wouldn't bother you 'bout this call 'cept I've been there three dozen times. This man's a lumber dealer. He's a great big fella, and he's a nice, pleasant man, but he just doesn't get saved. Seems like when I get down there to talk to him he kinda evades the issue. Maybe if two of us'll go..."

So I went down and knocked on the door, and from way in the back somebody said, "Come on in!" So we walked down those long rows of lumber and the pastor said, "Now he's evasive and you try to handle it." So we went in and he said, "Mr. Brown, I want you to meet Dr. Schunk. He's an evangelist and he's talked to hundreds and hundreds of men about their soul. And I want him to take the Bible and show you how to stay from screaming in hell forever." "OK," he said. So I opened the Bible and showed him every person on earth was a sinner including every lumber dealer. Unless there'd come a one-time experience in his life where he turned from every way that he thought was right, and turned to the only way that God taught was right, he'd die and go to hell. I got about that far and he said, "Excuse me. I have to get something out of the file."-- came back and said, "Go ahead. Finish what you were saying." So I started all over. I got half way through and he walked away again and came back and said, "I guess I really oughta be honest with you two preachers." He said, "Preacher, I'm for churches. I'm glad you got your church and I'm not against the Bible. I just don't wanna get saved. I don't want anything to do with your God, or your Christ, or your Bible, or your church." He said, "I keep this place open on Sunday and I'm gonna continue to do it. I wanna make money." He said, "That's the most important thing in life and when I die I'm gonna have my wife stuff my hands full of five dollar bills and put 'em in the coffin with me!" and he laughed. And we left. And three hours later he was dead. You say, "Heart attack?" No. The autopsy said that nothing killed him. But I'll tell you what killed him. God did! I believe that God got saturated with him saying, "No." I believe that God got sick and tired of him saying, "No, God! No, God!" And God said, "Take him outta this life."

What? In II Samuel 14:14, the Bible says, "For we must needs all die, for we are as water spilled on the ground." In Job 14:5, the Bible says, "Seeing the number of his days are determined, and the number of his months are with thee, thou hast appointed his bounds that he cannot pass."

Here's a true story of a man out in California worth many millions, and he comes into the doctor's office and he says, "Doc, I'm having that stomach trouble again." The doctor said, "Well, Bob, we're gonna have to take some X-rays." "X-rays, nothin! We're flying over to this island to do some huntin! I got no time..." "There'll be X-rays or I'm not your doctor!" "Well, get 'em over with!"

X-rays were taken. The doctor's hardly in his office the next morning when the phone's ringing. "Hey, Doc, what'd you find out in those X-rays?" "Well, Bob, we won't know for a while. I'll let you know."

Some days pass and the phone rings and Bob picks up the phone, "Oh, Hi Doc. What'd ya find out?" He says, "Bob, I'd like you down to my office as quickly as you can get here." Click.

The next scene you see is a nurse ushering a wearied looking man into the doctor's office and asking him to have a seat. And she leaves and the doctor comes in from another door and paces the floor a little bit. He says, "Bob, I might as well get right to it." He said, "You've got the worst kind of cancer known to mankind and you haven't even got thirty days to live. You better get your things in order." He said the man paced the floor, cursed and swore and yelled and hollered and said, "Don't you...I pay you good money to keep me alive...don't you tell me I'm gonna die!" Just before he went out and slammed the door, he yelled at the top of his voice, "I'm not gonna die!" But he did die!

Death Is Sudden

And just as sure as you sit out in that seat, you're gonna have to die! You say, "I already know that." I wonder if you know this: that when death comes, it comes suddenly and without warning. And ninety-five percent of all of us who sit in this building are going to die when we aren't ready. "What do you mean?"

In Proverbs 27:1, the Bible says, "Boast not thyself of tomorrow for thou knowest not what a day may bring forth." What's that mean? It means it doesn't make any difference about your age.

Here's a mother that raises a little girl. Now she does it by herself because her husband dies when that little girl was a baby. But she raises the little girl in defence. In other words, without discipline because she feels sorry for her. And she made the mistake of her life. The girl grew up to be a monster. By the time she was fifteen years of age she ran the whole house.

But revival came and mother went to the revival, got right with God, came back and got on that girl's back. And the girl said, "If you get off my back, I'll go to your stupid meeting one night!" And she did. And the gospel was preached and the invitation was given. She grabbed hold of the chair in front of her and the beads of perspiration broke out on her forehead and even the tears came. Mother begged her to go forward. "No." On the way home there were still tears and mother got her to promise to come again Saturday night.

The days passed swiftly and so did the conviction. Saturday night came and at the supper table mother said, "Let's hurry and get the dishes done so we can get to the meeting." "I'm not going. I'm going to the dance with Jimmy." "But you promised..." "Now, Mother, you get off my back and you go to your stupid revival. I'm going to the dance...!" Up the stairs she went to get ready and mother slipped over in the dark room where she'd gone often to weep before, and pray.

Time elapsed and the doorbell rang. It was Jimmy waiting for his date. She called up and when there was no answer she ran up the stairs and looked in the bedroom at the heap on the floor. The little girl was dead. Fifteen? Yes.

In James 4:14 the Bible says, "Whereas ye know not what shall be on the morrow."

November the twenty-second, nineteen hundred and sixty-three. Do you remember that date? Somebody handed the President of the United States a cowboy hat and said, "Try it on down in Dallas, Texas." And he smiled. I watched it on television. He said, "If you come by my office Wednesday, I'll try it on." And three hours later, he was dead.

Look at this. In Isaiah 55:6, "Seek ye the Lord while he may be found, call on him while he's near!" Oh well, I can hear somebody out in the audience say, "I'm gonna get saved on my deathbed." Are ya? Have you ever been to a deathbed? Most people that go to deathbeds, ninety percent of 'em go into a coma. A coma is death's own narcotic and when they go into that coma they never come out and die in that state.

I walked into a hospital and started to go into the room and the doctor said, "Uh, Reverend Schunk, would you...would you mind waiting in the waiting room? He's in a deep coma and it wouldn't do any good now anyway, and we're trying to do some things with him." So I went down there and read the newspaper, and old magazines, and three hours passed. I watched the doctor come in the room with that funny look on his face. "I'm sorry. I'm sorry, Mr. Schunk, but he's passed away." "But he was gonna get saved on his deathbed." "I'm sorry, but he's passed away."

In First Samuel twenty and verse three, the Bible says, "But truly as the Lord liveth, and as thy soul liveth, there is but one step between me and death." One heartbeat. One breath.

Here's a man that commutes to work. I guess they still do. But he gets in the car and his wife sits beside him. He drives down to the railroad station where he goes in to get his ticket and parks in a certain place. The wife moves over to the driver seat. He goes in, gets his ticket and rides on fifteen miles to work; every day, fifteen years, no different this morning. He gets in the car, the wife sits beside him, he drives down, parks in the same place. The wife moves over as he gets out and the truck, not seeing him in his blind spot, backs over his body and kills him. One step between you and death.

And it's dramatically described in the Bible in Luke twelve and verse sixteen. "The ground of a certain rich man brought forth plentiful. And he said within himself, what shall I do because I have no room where to bestow my fruits and my goods. And he said this to himself, This I will do. I 'll pull down my barns and build greater and there I'll bestow all my fruits and my goods, and I'll say unto my soul, Soul, thou hast much goods laid up for many a year. Take thine ease. Eat, drink, and be merry. But God said unto him, Thou fool. This night thy soul shall be required of thee. Then whose shalt these things be which thou hast provided?"

And look at this. In Proverbs 29:1, "He that being often reasoned with, and hardeneth his neck, shall suddenly be destroyed and that without remedy."

There's a church up in Austin, Minnesota that would cost $2 million dollars today to build. One night five teenage boys, came and sat in the last row. They didn't whisper and talk but they wrote notes and passed 'em back and forth. Then they'd laugh and write another one. The invitation was given and several came forward, but not one of those boys. All lost.

They got up the next morning and backed dad's car out of the garage without permission, crossed the wires to start the engine and said, "Let's go to the track meet." So they get in the car, push the acceleration to the floor and the big sign says "STOP." They said, "Stop, nothing--and plowed through the sign, hit the truck, killed the truck driver, killed four of those boys. That was twenty years ago. The other one is still alive. He lies there as a vegetable. Someday he'll die! And when he does, he goes straight to hell!

Listen to this. In Zephaniah 1:18; "Neither their silver nor their gold shall be able to deliver them in the day of the Lord's wrath, but the whole land shall be devoured by the fire of his jealousy; for he shall make a speedy riddance of all them that dwell in the land." Three hundred thousand last year died by accident. But you mark that down in a little black book somewhere, they weren't accidents at all. Many of them were planned by God in heaven. And I tell you, death is a surety and it oft times comes suddenly. And for the great masses of the people the world over, when death comes, it's sorrowful, and almost unbelieving. How?

In Hebrews 10:31, the Bible says, "It is a fearful thing to fall into the hands of a living God." I was down in Murfreesboro, Tennessee some years ago in a Bible conference. Many evangelists were there, six hundred preachers and their wives and some laymen. And we had seminars and we'd preach. And then at night, after it was all over, the preachers would go out and get coffee. One night we were talking about unbelievable things that happen in a revival meeting. We watched people have strokes and die in a revival. People get up out of their seats to walk out and keel over with heart attacks. You can't believe the things that happen.

Paul Levin was there and he said, "Let me tell you something that happened in a meeting I was in that's hard to believe. The pastor came to me and said, 'Brother Paul, there's a lady in the church that wants to go see this atheist she's been dealing with for eight years. Now, he's mean, rotten and cantankerous; I don't think we'll do one bit of good, and I don't believe he'll even listen. But I believe it'll help the morale of the lady if she knows somebody else went. OK?"

Paul said, "When we knocked on the door, it was a palatial, beautiful home, and when we went in, the man was real nice. We got to talking and I thought, 'he's congenial enough, I'll ask the question.' He said, 'Sir, if you died tonight, would you go to heaven?' He said, 'That's the question I've been waitin' for.' He walked out into the center of the room and Paul said, 'I could feel the hair begin to crawl on the back of my neck because I didn't know what he was gonna do.' Well, he got to the center of the room, lifted his fists up to the ceiling and said, 'I'm going to prove to you preachers that there is no God! And when I prove that I'm gonna go up and down these streets and ring the doorbells and tell everyone I made fools out of the preachers! Now you watch me.' And he lifted his fists up towards heaven and said, 'If there's a God up in heaven, I dare you to kill me!' and fell over on the floor dead!"

Now let me read you this. In Job 21:30, "the wicked is reserved unto the day of destruction; he shall be brought forth to the day of wrath."

In Isaiah 33:14, "Who among us shall dwell with devouring fire? Who among us shall dwell with everlasting burning?" And get this in Matthew 10:28, "... fear not them that are able to kill the body, and not able to destroy the soul, but rather fear him who's able to cast both soul and body into hell." Now that's not the power of the devil, that's the power of God.

Once more, in Proverbs 11:7, "when the wicked man dies, his expectations shall perish and the hope of the unjust man perishes in hell." Perishes! No second chance! No such thing as a purgatory. You make your decision to come to Christ while you live and breathe on this earth or you die and go straight to hell! And I tell you that death is a surety and it oft times comes suddenly. And for the great masses of the people the world over, it's a terrible and sorrowful thing in hell forever!

Death Can Be Serene

But, if that's all the Bible had to teach on the subject of death, I'd have stayed in the business world and never become an evangelist. But the reason I became an evangelist and the thing that drove me into full-time evangelism more than anything else is this last point. What's that?

Death can be serene. What do you mean? In Ezk. 33:11, the Bible says, "Say unto them, saith the Lord. I have no pleasure in the death of the wicked but rather the wicked turn from his way and live. Turn ye, turn ye, for why will ye die?" And a comparable verse in Psalm 116:15, "Precious in the sight of the Lord is the death of his saints."

(Knocking on pulpit several times) That insistent and loud knock stirred Dr. Reuben A. Torrey from his sleep and he reached up quickly and turned up the old gas lamp and slipped on his slippers, grabbed his robe and went to the door. There was a twenty year old young man. "Are you Dr. Torrey?" "Yes." He said, "Dr. Torrey, it's imperative that you come with me at this moment." Dr. Torrey said, "Son, it's one o'clock in the morning!" And the young man said, "Yes, I know, but it's a matter of life and death and..." And as he rattled on, Torrey said, "I didn't listen to his words, I watched his eyes. I could see in his eyes he really meant business. So I grabbed some clothes and put them on, got in his vehicle, and we sped across the city of Chicago and parked over in the southside somewhere where it was so dark you couldn't see. We ran up some steps and that boy knocked on the door. Strange knock. A woman with a painted face opened the door and nodded her head. We stepped in. I stopped abruptly because I could see the feet of some twenty women standing around. Then my attention was caught over here because I saw a light over the top of a bed. I slipped over in that direction and looked down in the face of a woman I thought to be thirty-two; she was nineteen...and dying. "Are you the Dr. Torrey that preaches over in these great halls that God loves everybody?" "Yes." "Well, did you mean when you said He loved everybody He could love the likes of me?" And Torrey took the Bible and showed her that if she'd call upon the name of Christ right there in the bed and receive Him in her heart that God would take every sin she ever committed and bury it in the deepest sea and make her as clean as any angel in heaven. And there quietly she received Christ and even through her pain, she smiled. "Now," he said, "I've got to leave but I'll be back early in the morning," and left.

He overslept, though he didn't mean to. He got up and stuffed his pockets full of tracts, grabbed his Bible and hailed a cab and sped across the city of Chicago where he parked over in the southside in the dark where now the rays of light were coming over the top of the buildings. He ran up those steps and knocked on the door. The same woman with the same painted face opened the door. "Oh, come in quickly, Dr. Torrey," she said with a smile. As he stepped in he saw twenty women sitting in seats. Then he turned to go to the bed and stopped abruptly and said, "Where's the bed?" "Oh," she said, "Dr. Torrey, in the early hours of the morning the young girl passed away. But wait a minute. Before she died she begged me to come over by the bed and accept Christ and I've done that. And then, one by one, all these twenty girls have all accepted Christ. We've all been saved and we want to know what to do next!"

Now listen. Dr. Reuben A. Torrey was standing in the middle of a house of ill repute. But don't you tell me the grace of God can't get there. Look at this. In Psalm 49:15, "God will redeem my soul from the power of the grave." And once more, in Ephesians 2:4 and 5, "God who is rich in his mercy for his great love wherewith he loved us, even when we were dead in sins hath made us alive in Christ."

I was preaching in that big First Baptist Church in Rockford, Illinois when the church was normal. It's not normal anymore. Normal is out knocking on doors, ringing doorbells, and bringing the lost into the church and people being saved Sunday after Sunday--that's normal. That church was on fire. You couldn't get a seat. If you came at 7:15 there weren't any seats. You had to stand!

One young man that worked in one of those big factories went and got his engineer boss there. He came and sat about three-fourths of the way back on the end of the row. He had red, high hair and was about six-foot seven. You couldn't miss him. So I preached that night and said, "Every head bowed--every eye closed," at the end of the sermon. He just kept looking at me. I said, "If you're out in that audience and you don't know whether you'd go to heaven or not, and you'd say 'pray for me,' put your hand up!" Oh, a couple dozen hands went up, but his went up first. I thought he was gonna reach the ceiling. And I continued to give the invitation. People were coming from every aisle, but not that big man. He never moved.

So, I was talking to a man and his wife whose teenager had been on drugs and gotten saved. And I saw that big man come down. He looked over at me and said, "Can I talk to you a minute?" "Sure." He said, "You noticed I raised my hand?" "Yes." He said, "You noticed I didn't come forward like the others did?" "Yes." He said, "Don't you wanna know why I didn't come forward?" I said, "Not unless you wanna tell me." Then he began to weep. "Well," he said, "the reason I didn't come forward like the others did 'cause I'm just not fit to have Christ in my heart!" "Oh," I said, "that's marvelous!" "What?" I said, "That's marvelous!" "Why?" I said, "The Bible teaches that Christ Jesus came into the world to save sinners and you sure qualify." He got down on his knees and was wonderfully saved.

You've gotta get to that place first; to know that you oughta go to hell. Then when you get there, then Christ can do the work. "What do you mean?" In I John 4:9, "In this was manifested the love of God towards us, because God sent his only begotten Son into the world that we might...-LIVE...ETERNALLY...through him."

Sure, we're gonna die. And it's gonna come before any of us expect it, almost. And when it comes, it's a terrible and sorrowful thing, and for some in this building it'll mean hell forever. But not for those who are willing to come to Christ. For them death can be serene.

I read a story in Southwest Pennsylvania. The government had come in there and built a huge dam. When they went back and inspected it, they found just a pencil point crack in the dam. But that was serious enough. So they went down in the village and put bulletins on all the boards they could find--a medium size village. They said, "The dam's not safe. You'd better move out." But only some three families moved out. They came back six months later to inspect that dam and found the crack had grown deeper. They didn't fool around now. They took government men and knocked on every door and said, "That dam's not safe! You'd better move." So they called a town meeting after the government men had left in the biggest hall they could find. They said, "The government's trying to take our property. We'll just stay right here." Oh, some twelve families moved out.

But one morning about eight o'clock, a man came riding down the middle of dirt Main Street on horseback. At the top of his voice he was crying. "The dam's burst! The dam's burst! Ya got thirty minutes to move out of the valley. Thirty minutes to move out of the valley!" But they didn't even have fifteen minutes. For in less than fifteen minutes 3800 people drowned in the Johnstown flood! See, you're gonna die, and it'll come suddenly and quickly when you weren't ready. And for the great masses of the people it's a terrible and sorrowful thing in hell. Only to those who are willing to come to Christ can death be serene. May we have every head bowed.

GIPSY SMITH

6

Repent Ye

BIOGRAPHICAL SKETCH

Rodney (Gipsy) Smith
(1860 - 1947)

Born in a Gypsy tent near Epping Forest (a parish not far from London), England, on March 31, 1860, Rodney Smith, later affectionately known as "Gipsy" Smith, was the fourth child of Cornelius and Mary Smith.

He was converted to Christ at the age of fifteen and soon after began preaching, even if it was only to a patch of turnips! Years later he would make references to his days as a Gypsy youth and would delight audiences with such quips as, "I used to be in the timber business--I sold clothes pins!" Once, when he said that, a lady in the audience was heard to quip back, "And good clothes pins they were, Gipsy. I've still got those you sold me!" He also spoke of the times when he and his family were the guests of the Prince of Wales; that is, when they would park their gypsy wagons on land belonging to the Prince!

Gipsy has been described as a "simple, straight-forward man who spoke from the heart." For several years he worked for General Booth's Salvation Army, until he was dismissed for a minor infraction of the Army's rules regarding accepting a "purse" given by a loving congregation.

In 1879 he married a young lady named Annie, and shortly was moved to Hull where large crowds gathered to hear him preach. He was warm, friendly, and sometimes quite humorous. Yet, at the same time, he took his work as an evangelist very seriously. He was extremely sensitive to the Lord's leading in his meetings and was not so structured that he "had" to preach. Author David Lazell writes,

"At one service the Gipsy did not even preach, because the people began to go into the inquiry room after the singing of the hymn. The Gipsy thought that many of the people had made up their minds to come forward even before coming to church. His comments on the service are certainly appropriate to today's evangelistic endeavors:

"'We are so apt to think that this must be done, and that that must be done, and that a certain fixed course of procedure must be followed, or else we must not look for results. Too often, I fear, our rules and regulations and orders of service simply intrude between men's souls and their God. We all need to be taught when to stand aside.'"*

In a rare, and autographed, autobiography of the Gipsy published in 1906, the noted English Bible expositor, Dr. Alexander McLaren writes the following in the Introduction: "He [the Gipsy] is not an orator, nor a scholar, nor a theologian. He is not a genius. But, notwithstanding these deficiencies in his equipment, he can reach men's hearts, and turn them from darkness to light in a degree which many of us ministers cannot do."

During his more than seventy years of evangelistic work, he made more than forty trips overseas including some thirty to America alone, where he was much loved and respected. In fact, it was on a boat trip to the United States that he suffered a fatal heart attack and died on August 4, 1947. A monument to his memory was erected near the place of his birth at Mill Plain in Epping Forest in July, 1949.

The sermon reproduced here is from a rare book of sermons published by the Gipsy in 1906, the same year as his autobiography referred to above. The picture of the Gipsy is taken from his autobiography so that both picture and sermon are of the same vintage. KWL

---

*GIPSY SMITH From The Forest I Came, David Lazell, Moody Press, Chicago, IL, 1973. p. 130.

REPENT YE!
Rodney (Gipsy) Smith

"Jesus came into Galilee, preaching,... saying, REPENT YE." (Mark 1:14,15)

The Bible, especially the New Testament, is the handbook of repentance. It commands it, urges it, enforces it, repeats it, drives it in everywhere. Over sixty times repentance is enforced. The great doctrine of repentance occupies a very prominent place in the teaching of Jesus Christ and His apostles. All the epistles were written to show men how to do it, because there is no such thing as vital communion, fellowship with God without it. And I want to speak plainly about Bible repentance, and I pray God to help me, for I have not anything pleasant to say. It is far easier to congratulate than it is to expostulate. My business is not to speak smooth things, but to say some things that you may resist, fight, get angry with; and you may get angry with me for saying them, but they are here, and it is my business to say, "Thus saith the LORD." There is no intelligent conversion without an intelligent understanding of these words. May the Holy Spirit breathe light upon these truths, and help us to see them! For it is my business to make you see what God means when He says, "Repent ye."

I am afraid that in our zeal to get people into the kingdom or the Church we have lowered the standard. These words meant far more when they were uttered than they do today with most people. I am afraid the familiar way with which we use them and the constant contact with them and with the daily handling of them, we have somehow allowed their edge to be worn off. They do not mean as much to us. The depth, the breadth, the height, the length of these mighty utterances do not search us and illuminate and startle, and thrill and overwhelm as they used to. But they do mean as much. If we have not eyes to see and ears to hear, if by long contamination with evil, and soothing the conscience with opiates from hell, if crying, "Peace" where there is no peace has brought a stupor upon us, that is our responsibility, not God's or His Word's. God means as much by these words today when He says, "Repent ye," as He did when they were first uttered. I am afraid we have brought them down, we have lowered them, we have pulled them from their heights down to the low levels of our own poor experiences. But that is not the way to climb with measured step the hills of light, and walk in unbroken fellowship with God. I am afraid that in our zeal to get people into what we call the Church we have been more anxious about heads than hearts. In order to capture, we have compromised and lost. We have been more concerned about filling our Church registers than we have about the kingdom. We have not sufficiently emphasized the greatness of coming to Christ, and we have said, "It is only a step." Who told you so? Only a step to Jesus? It is not true. It is not gospel. Only a step to Jesus? Then it is a very big step. We have made it a very little thing, and we have multitudes of people joining the Churches. It is child's play. It used not to be. When I came to Christ I came under the old Act. It was a conflict, it was a warfare, it was a pilgrimage, it was a struggle, it was cutting off the right arm and plucking out the right eye, it was being maimed if necessary. It meant sacrifice. There was a day in our calendar called Good Friday; there was a place called Calvary. It meant coming out, being forsaken, abused, slandered, rejected, despised, hated, persecuted, a fool for Christ's sake, sneered at, laughed at, misrepresented, suffering the cross. What does it mean now? A picnic. It is a "social," it is an entertainment, it is a guild, an ordinance; and with multitudes of people who call themselves Christians it means nothing more. We have made it too easy, but Jesus never made it so: He never deluded anybody. He never cried "Peace" when there was no peace. He knew the danger of saying "Peace" when the soul was in anarchy and the will in rebellion, and the whole man against God. He could not cry "Peace."

No, He never made it easy. We have said to anybody and everybody, "Only believe." The New Testament does not say so. The devil believes, and believes more than you do; in his heart he knows more about it. He believes; and if he says he does not, he is a liar, he is shamming. He believes far more than any of us, but he is not a saint. Jesus has never made it easy. There was one man who came and asked, "Are there few that be saved?" and He said, "Strive, struggle, agonize to enter in at the straight gate." He never made it easy. Here is another man who came and said, "Lord, I will follow Thee withersoever Thou goest." But Jesus knew he had not counted the cost, and said, "Foxes have holes, and the birds of the air have nests, but the Son of man hath not where to lay His head." Here is another who came and said, "Lord, what shall I do to inherit eternal life?" Jesus diagnosed the case instantly, and put His finger on the weak spot of his life and said, "If thou wilt be perfect, sell all that thou hast and give to the poor, and come, follow Me." He did not make it easy. Here is another man who came and said, "Lord, we know that Thou are a teacher come from God; for no man can do these miracles that Thou doest, except God be with him." Jesus said to him, "Ye must be born again." And to the multitude of people who listened to Him He said, "If any man will be My disciple, let him take up his cross and deny himself." He never made it easy; and the man who makes it easy to be a Christian preaches a mongrel gospel. Jesus said, "Repent." John preached repentance. He came to preach it. It had the first place in his sermons. It was first and last with John, "Repent, repent." You say it is too startling, sensational, vulgar; but remember, it was God's vulgarity. "Repent." No man who preaches as John did will be popular.

They put John in prison for preaching repentance, and so that the doctrine should not be silent, as soon as John was shut up Jesus began where John left off, and His first public sermon to the world was on repentance. He knew where to begin. "Repent ye," said Jesus. That is His first utterance, and if you care to go to His last before He left His disciples and was received up yonder in the clouds, He gave them the commission to go and preach repentance. So that in the first and the last utterances of the Son of God you have repentance enforced. And when He was back again on the throne, when angels and archangels had received Him with the shouts of triumph and welcome which He deserved, when He had been exalted as a Prince and a Saviour to give repentance, as though He knew that some of us would shrink from driving it in, as though He knew that some of us would be afraid to push it home, He said to Saul, "Saul, you go to the Gentiles, and make them--MAKE THEM--do works meet for repentance."

Jesus never made it easy. Let any man who ever tried honestly but one day in his life to serve God with all his powers, let him tell me if it was an easy thing to do. It is not easy. It is a struggle, it is a fight. Jesus Christ on Calvary is not a substitute for the life He means you to live, but the means by which you get the power to live the life. No, there is no salvation without repentance. This is the first step. First things first. And the man who misses repentance will miss everything. If your repentance is shallow your religious life will be shallow. If your coming to Christ does not mean everything you will not get everything. If your surrender is not complete you cannot receive. If your hands are filled you cannot take hold. It is only those who come empty-handed that can cling. It is only those who turn from darkness to light that understand God. It is only those who leave the devil who can receive God. No, we must repent.

Repentance Is Not Conviction

"Then," you say, "what is repentance?" Listen-- it is NOT CONVIC-TION. It is possible to be convicted without repentance. Why, it is hardly possible to meet and talk with anybody in these days but at some moment of their life's history they have been convicted of their need of Christ. It is hardly possible to meet with anybody who does not know what he ought to do and what he ought to be. You cannot meet and talk with any man that has not light about these things; but light is not life.

What brings you to a mission service? Deep down in your conscience, the soul of you, the man of you, back of everything, hid away that nobody else can see, there is a real cry in your soul for God. That is conviction. That is God-given; that is Holy Ghost-brought, that is the result of the light that flashes over the cliff-tops of eternity, that is the soul's awakening. It is one thing to be awake; it is another thing to get up. You have often heard your minister preach. Maybe you have been hearing him for years. Perhaps you sit in the gallery or away back in one of the pews, or near to him, and every time he preaches and you hear him, you go home and say, "My pastor is right; I ought to be a Christian, I know I ought," and you feel beneath the powerful pleadings of your own pastor, beneath the pleadings of the evangelist, you know God's claims, you admit them, you feel them. They are right, they are reasonable, and you ought to surrender. But it is one thing to be convicted and another thing to repent. Conviction is not repentance.

Repentance Is Not Sorrow

What is repentance? It is NOT SORROW. Sorrow for sin is one element of repentance, but you can be sorry without repentance. There is a kind of sentimental sorrow, a sorrow at the thought of coming retribution and exposure, which is mean, selfish, devilish, and is not healthy and life-giving. There is a sorrow that weeps at funerals and sentimental plays, and weeps beneath the ordinary preaching and the special preaching. There are multitudes of people who think they are not far from the kingdom because their tears come easily; they whisper all sorts of sweet messages to themselves because they can weep. They tell themselves they are not hard, and therefore there must be hope for them, and all the while they are holding on to forbidden things and walking in forbidden paths, and keeping company with those who are destroying them and leading them far from God. It is no good to cover God's altar with tears while your heart is in rebellion. It is no good to hold out one hand apparently to the Cross with the other holding on to a black hand behind you. You cannot hold Dagon in one hand and the Ark of the Covenant in the other. You cannot serve God and mammon. It is no good to sing on Sunday with your face towards the Cross and on Monday with your feet towards the beer shop.

I sat in a home a few days ago playing with a boy of ten. His face was bright as the sun. He looked as happy as any child in the home, calling me "Uncle." Presently his mother had missed something, and she came in and said, "Jack, have you taken so-and-so?" His head dropped. "Jack, have you taken so-and-so?" No answer. "Jack" -- and she came and put her hand on his shoulder -- "did you take --" "Yes, mother;" and he began to cry. Oh, he was sorry; he did look sorry; he sobbed as though his heart would break. What for? He was just as guilty five minutes before, and he knew he was. What made him sorry? Sorry that he had sinned against his mother? No. Sorry that he had sinned against God? No. Well, what was his sorrow? He was sorry because he was found out. And there are multitudes of professing Christians whose religious sorrow is no deeper. That is the sorrow that worketh death. There is a godly sorrow, sorrow because I have sinned against God. "Against Thee, Thee only, have I sinned, and done this evil in Thy sight ... For Thou desirest truth in the hidden parts, honesty where no eye but Thine can see, transparency where no light but Thine can penetrate." There is a sorrow that means death. There is a sorrow for sin that worketh life. Which is yours?

Repentance Is Not Promising To Be Better

What is repentance? Listen. It is NOT PROMISING TO BE BETTER. There are plenty of people who have been promising to be better ever since they can remember, from boyhood or girlhood. When God has laid His hand upon them, as He does in a thousand ways, they are ready to promise, and do promise. Where are you, you who have been making promises til your hair is gray and broken every one of them, and angels beholding your shattered promises have shuddered to the tips of their wings? You are further from God then ever you were in your life, with all your promises. Your psalm-singing and your hymn-singing, and your church-going, and your offerings, and all the rest of your religious paraphernalia, are so much mockery because you have not walked the straight and blessed path of obedience and trust.

It is not enough to promise. It means more than that. If it is not conviction, if it is not sorrow, if it is not the desire to be better and the promise to be better, what is it? What is repentance? Is it crying? No. Is it excitement? No. Is it emotion? Is it kneeling down and groaning? No. Is it going and hearing preachers? No.

What is it? Listen. Jesus Christ tells you in the beautiful picture in the fifteenth of Luke. It is a wonderful chapter. There are three cases in that chapter--the silver, the sheep, and the son. The sheep was lost out of the fold, the silver was lost in the house. The sheep was lost without any intention of being lost, but it was lost. The silver was lost in the house through somebody's carelessness, and it may be there is somebody lost in your house, in your pew in the church, through somebody's carelessness. God help you to find out who that somebody is! The son was lost, and it was his own fault. He was a prodigal before he left home. He was a rebel before he got a penny of his fortune. He was as bad in heart and in mind before he received a cent of the money as when he had spent it all. He was guilty the moment he said to himself, "I will demand the portion of goods that falleth to me." When the sheep went astray a man went after it. When the silver was lost a woman went after it. When the son went astray nobody went after him. How is that? Remember who told the story. Nobody went for him. How is that? Because he was a man, he was a moral agent, because he was accountable to God for his own act. Why did not the father gather his servants with the elder brother, why did he not gather his neighbors together, and say, "Look here, I may have lost my boy, let us go and find him and bring him back in spite of himself?" Why did he not? Because if he had brought him back again he would have been a prodigal still, he would have been a rebel inside the house as well as out of it, for no man comes till he returns; and heaven and the Bible, Christ and Calvary, the Holy Ghost and eternity stand absolutely defeated before the citadel of the human will. Do not forget it. Listen. The prodigal went astray, took every step from the homestead of his own deliberate choice, step by step away up into the far country, and he had to come to himself, he had to come back every inch of the way, and he did not send a letter home to his father and say, "If you will send the old chariot I will come home," and he did not ask anybody to give him a lift. He had to walk back every inch of his own self, step by step, with bleeding feet and aching head, and broken heart. He had to do it. "But," you say, "the father ran to meet him, did he not?" Yes, he did, and He will run to meet you when He sees you coming, but you must come.

Repentance Is Coming

Coming is repentance. It is the response of the will. Repentance is the response of the enlightened, redeemed man to the call of God, the "I will" of the soul. It is putting your hand on your heart and getting hold of what has been your curse, the thing that has chained you. It is getting hold of the thing that has made hell of earth for you, the sin of your heart--for I have discovered that there may be a dozen sins in a man's life, but there are not a dozen that predominate; there is one overmastering, predominating, all-prevailing sin that enslaves and damns, and if that sin goes everything goes. It is putting your hand in your heart and plucking that out by the hair of its head and saying to God, "That it is, and I will die before I will sin again." Have you repented in that fashion? Don't talk about Church membership, don't insult God by talking about the Communion until you have done this: this is the first thing and the others will not be expected until you have done this.

"Repent ye," make a full surrender to God.

Brother, listen to me once more. Repentance, when it is done, is such a beautiful thing that Jesus Himself said, "There is joy in heaven over one sinner that repenteth." Have you repented along that line? There are some of you who do not understand how it is you have no peace and no joy in your profession. I know just as well as if I lived with you, I know if you have no joy and no peace in your professed faith it is because you have never turned to God wholly. Some of you say, "I want peace." Never mind peace; do as you are told and peace will come. There are some people more concerned about nice feelings, happy feelings, ecstasies and joys, and all the rest of it, than they are about putting God in His place. You put God in His place, and you will have peace; you honor God, and you will have peace.

A dear fellow came to me when I was in South Africa, and he said, "Sir, I want to get relief from a guilty conscience," and he had an awful story to tell, a story that made me shudder. He unfolded a page in his history that I dare not tell you. Then he said, "Sir, I want God's pardon." I said, "Brother, how do you expect to get it?" He said, "By an honest attempt to undo the past." "Then," I said, "turn your face that way and wait for peace." "But," he said, "that will mean prison, and it may mean a lifetime in prison." I said, "Turn your face that way. It is no good to talk about peace while there is wrong to be righted, while there are stripes that need to be washed; it is no use to talk about peace till you get right with God. The kingdom of God is not meat and drink, but righteousness and peace." Righteousness, that means rightness, wholeness, harmony-- and then the music. There will be no music until the instrument is put in tune. You know where you have to yield; you know the point of controversy between you and God; you know the thing that has hindered you, you know the thing that robbed you, you know the thing that has darkened your sky, you know the thing that has come in between you and God, you know the thing about which you have persisted in having your own way and not God's. When you yield on that thing, you will repent.

Will you do it now? "But," you say, "I am a Church member." Never mind. You say there is someone near that knows you. Never mind. You say people expect better things of you. Never mind. Be honest. Put God in His right place. Turn from sin to God, from darkness to light-- and you can do the turning. The Spirit enlightens, the Spirit breeds tenderness, the Spirit coaxes, woos, tries to win. God the Holy Ghost is doing His work in your heart, but, brother, you must submit. When you submit wholly, that is repentance. God help you to do it!

HARRY VOM BRUCH

7

New Birth

BIOGRAPHICAL SKETCH

Harry Vom Bruch
(1892 - 1962)

Until November, 1995, the name of Harry Vom Bruch was completely unknown to me. Unknown, that is, until the day I went browsing through the old book section of a second hand shop in Northeast Philadelphia and ran across a copy of a book of sermons by him, entitled, Modern Prodigals and Other Sermons. Date of publication is unknown. I glanced through the book, reading a page here and there. Impressed with what I read, though knowing nothing at all about the author, I purchased the book for one dollar. What a blessing it turned out to be! In fact, the sermon reproduced here is the one that first impressed me in the second hand shop the day I found it.

It was not easy trying to research his life. I have only found three people who either knew of him, or who knew him personally. One was Evangelist Bob Shelton, who, as a young man, remembered hearing him preach in his home church; another was Dr. Bob Jones, Jr., who remembered him as a contemporary of his father, the famous evangelist. The one who knew him personally was Evangelist Phil Shuler. Brother Shuler relayed to me in a phone conversation that Vom Bruch was a close personal friend of Billy and "Ma" Sunday. After Billy's death in 1935, Ma Sunday gave Harry the right shoe from a pair of baseball shoes in which Billy, the Chicago White Socks baseball player, ran the bases (Home plate to Home plate) in the record time of 14.0 seconds! The next fastest time on record was by Mickey Mantle at a time of 14.7 seconds. Vom Bruch left that famous shoe in his will to Phil Shuler. It is currently on loan and can be seen in the Archives Room on the campus of Bob Jones University, Greenville, South Carolina.

Beyond that, the following tidbits are ones that I gleaned from reading his book of sermons.

Chicago, Illinois, was home to the Harry Vom Bruch family where he was born on March 23, 1892. His father died when he was just a young boy; a loss young Harry felt keenly. He later attended the Mount Hermon School for Boys in Northfield, Massachusetts, (which had been founded by D.L. Moody in 1881) as well as the Moody Bible Institute from August, 1913 through July, 1914.

He enjoyed sports immensely, including auto racing, once watching Barney Oldfield race against Ralph de Palma and Louis Chevrolet on the old circular track in Chicago. He was also a fisherman and an avid pilot who loved small planes and flying. As an experienced pilot, he used to love such maneuvers as loops, upside down flying, tail spins, barrel rolls, whip stalls, falling leaf, even the Emmelmann turn. In fact, he once quipped to a preacher who accused him of "tempting the Lord's hand" by doing such stunts, "I am not tempting God; I am just getting ready for the Translation!"

As an evangelist, Vom Bruch traveled from coast to coast and border to border, even occasionally crossing that border for ministry into Canada. While most of his meetings were in local churches, he did preach to larger crowds as well. One meeting in a large tent in Chicago was attended by more than five thousand people. He also preached to several thousand workers at the Curtis Aeroplane Plant in Buffalo, New York near the end of World War I. His ministry carried him through such difficult times in American history as World War I, the Great Depression and the days of Prohibition. You may observe in the sermon reproduced here more than one reference to "our saloonless nation." Would to God, we were still "saloonless!"

Harry Vom Bruch was a contemporary of such men as Bob Jones, Sr., Billy Sunday, and Gipsy Smith. His ministry spanned several decades. He died March 21, 1962. KWL

NEW BIRTH
Harry Vom Bruch

"There was a man of the Pharisees, named Nicodemus, a ruler of the Jews:

"The same came to Jesus by night, and said unto him, Rabbi, we know that thou art a teacher come from God; for no man can do these miracles that thou doest, except God be with him.

"Jesus answered and said unto him, Verily, verily, I say unto thee, Except a man be born again, he cannot see the kingdom of God.

"Nicodemus saith unto him, How can a man be born when he is old? Can he enter the second time into his mother's womb and be born?

"Jesus saith unto him, Verily, verily, I say unto thee, Except a man be born of water and of the Spirit, he cannot enter into the kingdom of God.

"For that which is born of the flesh is flesh; and that which is born of the Spirit is spirit.

"Marvel not that I say unto thee, Ye must be born again."

"Ye must be born again." You will find this a text that is seldom quoted in this day and age. It seems that modern teachers, instead of laying the axe to the root of the tree, are content with simply pruning its branches. Symptoms instead of diseases are being treated. We have been aiming our blows at the saloon, the dance hall, the tenderloin district, and evil here, there, and elsewhere, while God has decreed that we shall get a clean world when the hearts of the men and women of the world have been cleansed.

Now I am glad that we have today what is called a saloonless nation. I thank God we have the liquor crowd spitting cotton at last. Some say, "But they are getting it just the same." Yes, they are getting some, but they are paying freight on all they get too, and they will soon get tired of this stuff that is being passed out today.

Something More Than Reformation

While we have a saloonless nation, if statistics be true, we have already in the United States of America one and one-half million dope fiends, showing you that when men cannot satisfy the cravings of the natural man with one thing, they will soon turn to another.

Moral reform endeavors to remove the thing that the natural heart craves, longs for and desires, but what we need is, not to have something come in and remove the things the natural heart desires, but to have something come in and remove the DESIRE for those things from the natural heart. That is why Jesus comes on the scene and says, "Ye must be born again."

I do not know that I ever heard a preacher preach on the new birth, who did not, when he got this far, say that Jesus never explained the new birth, and that he would not either, as though God's Word were silent on the subject. I thank God it is not, and we can know what the new birth is if we dare ask God about it. I want to read just two or three verses of Scriptures:

II Peter 1:4 - "Whereby are given unto us exceeding great and precious promises: that by these ye might be partakers of the divine nature, having escaped the corruption that is in the world through lust."

Galatians 6:15 - "For in Christ Jesus neither circumcision availeth any thing nor uncircumcision, but a new creation."

Ephesians 4:24 - "And that ye put on the new man, which after God, is created in righteousness and true holiness."

II Corinthians 5:17 - "Therefore if any man be in Christ, he is a new creature: old things are passed away; behold, all things are become new."

From these Scriptures we can readily see, as from many other portions of God's Word, that the new birth is not reformation or education or baptism or imagination. It means a new creation with an impartation of the divine nature.

When God came to the crowning feature of the creation - man, He breathed into his nostrils the breath of life, and man became a living soul, different from the beasts of the field, from the fish or the fowl: he became a living soul. The animal has no living soul. Man was created in the image of God in righteousness and true holiness. He had affinity with God and fellowship with God. He could communicate with God. He was endowed with that heart faculty that could reach out and know God.

But there came the word back in Eden: "The soul that sinneth it shall die." Adam sinned against God, he fell from that high estate, and man is no longer a spiritual being. He is living down here in the realm of the flesh, in the human kingdom. I do not say animal, though sometimes I think he has fallen that far, and sometimes even farther. There are men and women tonight in the city of Chicago whose souls are dead. They are guilty of such immorality as no beast of the field was ever guilty of. You never saw a horse drunk. It is always men. Horses have too much horse-sense, and some men need a little horse-sense too. It would at least give them stable minds. You never saw a donkey chewing tobacco, and you never will. You may offer it to a donkey, and he will simply say, "I am from Missouri, and you have got to show me."

Now, brother, I tell you what, you can go out and take that dirty, vile wad out of your mouth and a lot of spit with it, and put it on the corner of North Avenue and Clark Street, and not a hog or donkey or a dog in the community will touch it. It will be there if you go back for it after a while.

We have on record but one case of a hog that was ever drunk. He passed by a distillery and saw some stuff oozing out. He sampled it and thought it tasted good. Before he knew it, he was full, and he went home and disgraced all the other hogs. The next day they called a council to see what to do about this member of their crowd that had disgraced them. They brought this hog in before the council and said, "You were drunk yesterday."

"I was."

"You disgraced all the rest of us yesterday."

"I did."

"What have you got to say for yourself?"

"The hog replied, "I simply have this to say: it was the first time I have ever been so, and, if you will forgive me, it will be the last time. If you will overlook it this time and pardon me, I promise you as long as I live I will never try to act like a man again."

Alas, men and women are guilty of things that even the beasts of the field are not guilty of.

That is not all. That is on the surface. If we dared tear back the roofs of the homes and houses, hotels and restaurants tonight and allow you to look in and see what is going on, you would wonder how man, created a spiritual being, could ever fall to such depths of sin and degradation. How can we account for it?

"The soul that sinneth, it shall die." It is accounted for simply on the basis that men today are dead toward right and righteousness; God and godliness. The soul has sinned, and death came because of sin, and death has passed upon all men, for that all have sinned in that they have come short of the glory of God.

Remember, I am talking about the soul. You have never seen me. You say you have, but you have not. I am destined to live forever and ever under some condition, but you only see my body. That is what my soul has to dwell in for a brief time, and then it is gone, but my deathless soul lives on. You can burn this body, but you cannot burn my soul; it lives forever. God has given me a wonderful body in which to house it for a few years.

Dead or Alive

God has given me ears with which to hear what is going on; He has given me windows through which I look, and when I want to express the thought in my heart and mind and soul to your heart and mind and soul,

God has given me lips, and a tongue, and vocal organs with which to express that thought in words and from the sensitive membranes of your ear, the sound travels to your brain, and you know what I am thinking. That is the way I have of communicating with you. I have never seen you, and you have never seen me. We are souls, and we are destined to live forever. Our bodies may die, but our souls live on. You may drown the body, but not the soul; you may destroy the body, but not the soul; you may cremate the body, but not the soul. The soul that sinneth, it shall die. Jesus said, "She that liveth in pleasure is dead while she liveth." "The wages of sin is death." "Ye are dead in trespasses and sin." That is God's portrait of the human race, and all because of sin.

"Well," you say, "brother, we are very much alive, yet you preach that we are dead. How can we be both?"

Very easily. There are many things in this world that some folks are alive to and other folks are dead to. There are a great many things which I am alive to and a great many I am dead to. I do not know much about grand opera, but what little I do know of it, I can assure you of the fact that I am dead to it. I heard it once, and it sounded to me like the little girl who heard it on the victrola. When the record was ended she said, "Mamma, the hen laid an egg."

I heard a fellow say in the Y.M.C.A. not long ago (they were playing a piece of what is called "jazz"), "If jazz is music, then a dime novel is literature." Yet the world has gone crazy over it. I have never heard but one definition of it, and that was given by John Philip Sousa. He said, "Jazz is prostituted music, and the sooner we get rid of the stuff, the better for our boys and girls." This lad had heard a piece of this jazz on the phonograph as I also had, and I heard him say, "That stirs my feet."

I want to tell you, when I came into this Tabernacle and heard this choir and audience singing the old songs, I lifted up my heart and said, "That stirs my soul." Thank God, I am alive to that.

In one place where I held a meeting, a little woman used to come and look into my face night after night. Not until the closing meeting did she come up and shake hands with me. I said something to her, and she passed on. Another woman standing by said, "She did not hear what you said. She cannot hear a word you say."

"Why did she come to the meetings?" I asked.

"Oh, she likes your preaching."

"My preaching! She doesn't know what I am talking about if she cannot hear."

The lady said, "You would be surprised how little of your sermon she fails to get."

She was dead to sound but alive to sight. She read my lips.

I had a friend who went through the Art Institute. He took three courses and graduated with honors. He said to me one day, "Before I leave the city, I am going to give you a trip you will never forget. I am going to take you through the Art Institute."

I shall never forget it. That was the longest day I ever put in in all my life, standing there looking at daubs of paint. He would stand there and rave about them and say, "Isn't that marvelous, superb, exquisite?" All those great big words, but I didn't see anything to it.

I was almost as bad as the farmer that came to review a masterpiece. The crowd passed by and raved about it. He did not say anything until some one nudged him and said, "What do you think about it?"

"Think about what?"

"Why that masterpiece, that painting?"

"What is it?" he asked.

"Why that is a sunset. What did you think it was?"

He said, "It looked to me like a fried egg."

That fellow and I are dead to art. You may be alive to it.

In the Graveyard

I was down South holding some revival meetings in the churches. I remember during my campaign in a certain church I used to get up in the morning a little later than some of the rest of the crowd. The preacher was always gone. Now I do not want you to get the impression that I slept long because I did not get up as early as the rest of the folks. It was not because I slept long, but because I slept slowly.

As I said, the preacher was always gone, and I did not know where he was. He was not around the house. One day I said to the wife, "Where is your husband?"

She replied, "Up in the graveyard."

"Where was he yesterday?"

"In the graveyard."

"Is that where he goes?"

"Yes, every morning in his life, the first thing after he wakes up he goes to the graveyard."

"What does he do up there?"

"Go up and see; I don't know."

I went up, and there he was sitting on a tombstone. He had a few flowers around him, but he was just sitting there.

I said, "Preacher, what are you doing?"

"I am studying nature."

I said, "What?"

"Why, don't you ever study nature?"

"Well, I study human nature."

"Don't you ever go out and study the wonderful handiwork of God? I come out here every morning and hear the birds sing and look at these flowers. Let me show you something, will you?"

He went over and got a flower, and what do you think he picked? Not a lily of the valley, not a daisy, not a southern honeysuckle or a violet. He picked the blossom of a burdock. He brought it back and said, "Sit down. I want to show you how wonderfully God constructs this thing, and when you have seen the wonderful work in this, then I will show you something even more beautiful and wonderful."

By the time he had picked that thing to pieces and preached a sermon about God's work in nature, my soul was born to the fact that the heavens declare the glory of God and the firmament showeth his handiwork, and from that hour to this, I have loved the flowers just as much as any other person. I had been blind to this beauty, dead to the construction of the handiwork of God, but I was born anew. The light of nature broke upon my darkened mind.

Spiritual Paralysis

A man comes home, and he says, "Wife, you remember my telling you something about that strange sensation? Well, that has crept up now into this limb until at last it has reached my hip."

She said, "Husband, you go and visit a physician."

The doctor says, "When did you first feel it?"

"It was weeks ago."

"Why did you not come then?"

"Why, doctor, it surely is nothing serious?"

"Man, it is one of the worst things that could come on you."

"Do you know what it is? It is creeping paralysis. If that thing is not checked, there could be nothing worse."

I had a little chum. We used to swim together. One night at the Y.M.C.A. he dived. The water was not shallow but he struck his head on the pavement at the bottom, and he became paralyzed from the neck down. One of the most pitiful sights in the world was to look into the face of that boy, unable to move a finger. It is a horrible, dreadful thing to be paralyzed, but to feel it coming on bit by bit must be the keenest agony. Is there anything worse? Yes, there is one thing worse.

Here is a man who goes out of the Tabernacle. He is silent for two or three blocks. Finally his wife says, "Well, what did you think of the last meeting?"

"Oh, it was all right, all right - pretty good speaker."

"What did you think of the message?"

"Oh, it was all right."

"What did you think of the folks that went forward?"

"Oh, that was all right if they see it that way. But, do you know, wife, it doesn't move me any more. It doesn't move me."

God pity you tonight, if that is true, that it doesn't move you. Brother, there was a time when you were moved; there was a time when emotion after emotion swept over your soul and the tears reddened and enflamed your eyes and trickled down your cheeks, and you went home dispirited and distressed and spent restless, weary, sleepless nights, and you could hardly work the following day. What did it mean? God was calling to your soul, and it was alive to the voice of God. But now you can say, "It doesn't move me." Take care. That is spiritual paralysis, and tonight you are dead to God.

I used to hear in the olden days about a sermon preached by Jonathan Edwards, entitled, "Sinners In The Hands Of An Angry God." And you would hear how, while Jonathan Edwards preached that sermon, men and women would leave their seats. They would not wait for the invitation, but they would leave their seats and go down to the front and cry out for mercy. They would tremble under the preaching of that man of God with his message, and they could not wait for the invitation to be given. So did they tremble in the early days under the preaching of that man of God.

They used to call the Society of Friends, "tremblers," and then they nicknamed them Quakers.

You do not find folks trembling and quaking today. I wanted to read that sermon if I could. Finally I secured a copy, and read it. It was plain; it was tame. I have heard students preach sermons as good, of course, allowing for the fact that the Spirit of God was there. But folks trembled, folks cried, folks were stirred, folks were moved, folks wept, and yet I have heard one of the strongest evangelists of America preach on the unpardonable sin and I wondered how the people could sit there in their seats. I did not see how they could wait for the close of the meeting without crying out to God for mercy, but when the invitation was given, there was no response. They sang three or four songs, but there was no decision. Then he asked the congregation to bow their heads, and, if any needed prayer, to raise their hands. No hand was raised for prayer. How do you account for it? SPIRITUAL PARALYSIS.

Listen to me. If the Word of God does not stir your soul in these days as it did in the days gone by, search your own heart, and maybe you will find that spiritual paralysis is there. If at the close of this message tonight, when the invitation is given, you find the slightest response in your heart, if there is the slightest desire to say, "Yes," to God, do not quench that desire - it is heaven born. There will come an hour when you will not have it. Spiritual paralysis will have done its work.

"Well," you say, "if that is the condition that exists today, if this paralysis has settled down on the hearts and souls of men and made them dead, why preach? A dead man cannot act."

Come Forth!

There is only one thing a dead man can do, just one. Lazarus was so long dead that his sister said, "Lord, by this time he stinketh." But Jesus standing at the grave of Lazarus calls, "Lazarus, come forth," and, in response to the call of Christ, Lazarus comes forth from death to life. And that is the only thing a dead man can do, but thank God, he can do that if he wills it. And that coming forth at the call of Christ, out of death into life, out of darkness into light, out of sin into salvation, that coming forth at the call of Christ from death to life is the new birth. "Ye must be born again."

Necessary Because of Sinfulness

Now stop a few minutes and consider. It is necessarily demanded for two reasons. First, because of the sinfulness of man. Man, by nature, does not love God. It is easier to curse than pray; it is easier to hate than love; it is easier to profane than to praise. Men, by nature, do not love God nor the things of God. If they did, there would be no need of police, lawyers, lock-ups, penitentiaries, and reform schools. If men, by nature, loved God, these things would not exist. There would be no theatres, no dance halls, no pool rooms, no card parties. If men, by nature, loved God, you would not have enough churches in the city of Chicago to accommodate the crowds that would come to worship God in the beauty of holiness. You will find the places of worldly pleasure, sin and shame jammed to the doors and in the churches a scattered handful. Why? Men, by nature, do not love God. They love sin, and that is why God makes every appeal possible for men to forsake sin, and until man forsakes sin, he is lost, he is doomed, he is damned. How can man forsake sin? How can he be rid of sin, be free from sin? I may sever my finger from my hand, but I cannot thereby get away from sin. I may sever my hand at the wrist, but I cannot thereby get away from sin. I may offer my neck to be chopped from my body, but I cannot thereby be freed from sin. Sin is not in the flesh, in the ligaments, in the bone, joint and marrow. Where is it? Sin is in the heart, in the will. That is why God says, "My son, give me thy heart." "Whosoever will may come." "They will not come to me that they might have life."

Do you read your Bible? If you do, you will be thoroughly convinced of four things:

First. The fountain of humanity back in Eden was poisoned by the virus of sin.

Second. The stream flowing through the generations to this present day remains unchanged.

Third. The mind, the flesh and the natural heart are at enmity against God.

Fourth. The new birth is absolutely necessary to sonship.

"Well," you say, "you do not know the weakness in my life - my sinful tendencies. You did not know my father; you did not know my mother. I am ashamed of it, but I have to acknowledge it. It was born in me and it has developed all down through these years. I am wedged to it. It is there, but I am not to blame. It was born in me."

I know it was, but I thank God tonight, I do not care what your weakness is, your sin, your shame, your ambition, your lusting, your desires that were born in you. They can be born out of you, and that is why the new birth is demanded - that the sin born in might be born out.

Holiness of God

In the second place, not only because of the sinfulness of man is it demanded, but because of the holiness of God. Hebrews 12:14 - "Without holiness no man shall see the Lord." Now, the average church member is as afraid of that word "holiness" as a tramp is of water. But the Scripture teaches that without holiness no man shall see the Lord. Here is a man who comes to me and says, "I am all right." He is a good man, a self-righteous, moral man, benevolent, honest, clean. He says, "I do not need to be born again because I am not a great sinner."

Suppose, for the sake of illustration, you were no sinner at all - although you are. Suppose in your life there could be found no sin - although there can be. Suppose you could prove to this intelligent audience beyond any reasonable doubt, that your life were absolutely sinless. Still you are apart from the kingdom of God. Why? God demands more than sinlessness. He demands HOLINESS without which no man shall see the Lord, and that must be imparted. You cannot find it in yourself.

No Affinity

Why did God make a demand like that? We are told in the Scripture, "That which is born of the flesh is flesh; and that which is born of the spirit is spirit." There is no affinity between the two. What do I mean by affinity? Here is a pile of shavings, steel, brass, lead, copper, gold, and silver. I take a magnet and run over that pile. The brass, the gold, the silver, the lead, and the copper will not adhere to that magnet, but the steel and the iron will. Why? Because between those two is found what is called magnetic affinity. You can take a glass half full of water and half full of oil and shake it up and let it stand a moment, and you will find a mark of division. They will not mix. Why? There is no affinity. The specific gravity of water is heavier than that of oil, and the oil rises to the top. But take the glass and pour it full to the brim with water and bring a chemist in, and into that glass filled with water he can pour in and pour in chlorine gas. Why? Because there is chemical affinity between water and chlorine gas.

Ye must be born again because flesh is flesh, and spirit is spirit, and there is no affinity between the two. "God is a spirit; and they that worship him must worship him in spirit and in truth." You cannot worship God who is a spirit in spirit until you are born of His spirit that there might be spirit affinity.

You take the natural man out of Chicago, with his natural heart, natural ambition, natural inclination, natural impulses, natural desires, and natural mind, and put him in heaven, and heaven would be hell to that man. Why? There would be no affinity. You take some of the men of Chicago, and without any change of heart and nature, and mind and relation to God, and put them in heaven, and by next Saturday night they would be hunting around for a hooker or two. They would have a desire for something that heaven could not give. I will leave it to any man who has ever been a drunkard. An unsatisfied desire is hell in itself.

Take some of the people out of the churches of Chicago who have never been born again, who have never had a change of heart, and put them in heaven with a natural heart, and heaven would be hell, and by next Wednesday night they would be trying to run a card party or a dance. They would desire to do things which they would not be permitted to do. They would have longings that could not be satisfied.

Prepared Place

Heaven is a prepared place for a prepared people, and the preparation for that prepared place is the new birth, that there affinity might be changed from the things which are sensual and sinful, to things that are of God and eternal. The natural heart in heaven would find heaven hell. There are dear friends and people looking into my face tonight who, if you should ask, "Whither bound?" would say, "Heaven," yet they will acknowledge to you that they are living for pleasure. They will say, "I can see no harm in it." They care little for the Church, little for the Bible, little for prayer, little for Christian songs, and yet they expect to be at home in heaven.

Listen, if you ever expect to be at home in heaven, to talk heaven's language, sing heaven's songs and enjoy heaven's joys, you had better start talking heaven's talk, and singing heaven's songs and enjoying heaven's joys down here, or there will be no affinity for you over there. That is what I mean by affinity. You let a soul die that has never passed from death unto life in response to the call of Christ - that soul cares nothing for God or godliness. He cares nothing for the Church or prayer meeting. There are men in this audience tonight who hate a prayer meeting and never go. Brother, let me tell you something. If you hate a prayer meeting, you do not want to go to hell, for it will be one eternal prayer meeting, calling on God. You let a natural man die with the natural hate and ambition, inclinations, desires, impulses, and there is not enough power in heaven to take that soul up to heaven when the body releases its grip. Why? Its affinity has been for sin, and the wages of sin is death, and when the body releases its hold upon the soul, the soul goes to its own affinity. But you let a child of God - I don't care whether he has been saved for forty years or forty minutes - you let a man or woman that is born of the Spirit of God die, and there are not enough demons in hell to drag that soul down to the pit. That soul is borne on up to God because of its affinity. Sinlessness is not enough. Holiness is demanded, because God is holy. God is holy, and we are sinful, and there is no affinity between holiness and sinfulness; so one or the other must be changed, and God says you must be changed. Sin must be born out and holiness must be born in, that being born of the Spirit you might have affinity with God who is Spirit; and when the body releases its grip upon the soul, the soul goes to that for which it has affinity.

Now listen! If you die tonight - church member or not, you know what you have lived for, you know what you long for, what you delight in, what you hate, what your ambition in life has been, whether for things of sin and sinfulness or things of God and godliness - if you die tonight, your soul goes to its own affinity. Where is your affinity tonight?

Sin Born Out

Just this, and I am through. Ye must be born again. It is the impartation of a new life, a new nature, a divine nature that is given when you, in response to the call of Christ, step forward from death to life. The new birth is demanded that sin might be born out and God's Spirit born in, that the affinity might be changed from darkness to light, from death to life, from sin to salvation, and from things temporal to things eternal.

How may I obtain this new nature and enjoy this joy of heart, this joy of affinity? Hear me, and I will put it in one statement. When a man, believing in the claims of Jesus Christ, receives Him to be all that He claims to be, that moment that man is born again. I repeat it! When a person believing in the claims of Jesus Christ receives Christ to be all that He claims to be, that moment he passes from death to life; that moment he is born again.

Once more! When a person believing in the claims of Christ receives Christ to be all that He claims to be: What did He claim to be? Two things - Son of God; Saviour of sinful men. The moment a person believes in the claims of Christ and receives Christ to be all that He claims to be, Son of God and personal Saviour, that moment that soul is born again, and that can be RIGHT NOW if you are willing to say yes.

Will you put this question to your own heart? "Has my affinity yet been changed from the natural to the supernatural?" If not, will you say, "I will take Jesus Christ as the Son of God to be my personal Saviour that it might be changed, that my soul might go to its heavenly affinity at the release from the body, for destiny depends upon affinity."

Part Two

Voices From The Present

NEIL CADWELL

8

The Fear Of The Lord

BIOGRAPHICAL SKETCH

Neil Cadwell
(1940 -)

Robert Neil Cadwell began his earthly journey in Atlantic, Iowa, the 10th of April, 1940. The first fourteen years of that journey was spent moving from town to town as his father outran the bill collectors. One day his father left and just did not come back. At that point Neil, his mother and two brothers moved to Harlan, Iowa, where God brought Neil to Christ through the influence of the Bethel Baptist Church. His conversion took place at a summer Bible camp in June of 1954.

In 1965 he graduated from Pillsbury Baptist Bible College with majors in Bible and Evangelism. While in college he served two years as president of the European Prayer Band, conducted evangelistic crusades, worked as a youth pastor and pastored two churches.

He met his wife, Peggy while at college and they have one daughter, April.

Dr. Cadwell has traveled in vocational evangelism for twenty-eight years conducting nearly 900 crusades. He has also traveled to mission fields to conduct crusades for twenty of those twenty-eight years. He has traveled to nearly sixty countries on six of the seven continents.

Since 1990 he has traveled almost exclusively to the former U.S.S.R. Most of that travel has been in the Ukraine where, as of February, 1996, he has seen the beginning of the Slavic Baptist Institute.

Dr. Cadwell served as an assistant pastor and pastor for three and a half years before entering evangelism. He has been preaching for thirty-seven years.

In recent years he has been highly involved in missions conferences, and spent a great deal of time in the C.I.S. where he has literally seen thousands of professions of faith. Also God has used this local church evangelist to plant many churches in twenty-eight years of evangelism.

For relaxation he enjoys books, golf and fishing. His greatest joy is serving God and seeing folks saved.

Dr. Cadwell and his wife, Peggy, make their home in Muncie, Indiana.

Evangelist Neil Cadwell
4304 West Petty Road
Muncie, IN 47304

THE FEAR OF THE LORD
Neil Cadwell

"God is greatly to be feared in the assembly of the saints, and to be had in reverence of all them that are about him." (Psalms 89:7)

"Having therefore these promises, dearly beloved, let us cleanse ourselves from all filthiness of the flesh and spirit, perfecting holiness in the fear of God." (2 Corinthians 7:1)

Our Father, we come into thy presence, poor and needy this evening. Father, we come, even though we're poor and needy, as a child of thine; knowing that we have the privilege to ask you for those things that we do need. Father, we need a moving of thy Spirit. We need a meeting of thy presence. We need a discernment of thy Word; we need an understanding of thy Word. Father, this evening, in Jesus name, I claim this service for You, asking Father, that you might save that soul that's nearest the brink of Hell. Warm that cold heart. Encourage that one that's discouraged. Strengthen the weak. And Father, for those that love you tonight, that they might leave this place loving you more. And Father, we're looking forward to your blessing, because we ask it, and we pray it in the sweet name of Jesus. Amen.

Several years ago I was challenged by hearing about a certain evangelist who read twenty-five chapters a day in his Bible. I received a challenge in my own life, and I began to set out to read twenty-five chapters a day in the Word of God. Now if you read twenty-five chapters a day, you'll get through the Bible seven times a year. I began in 1970. I suppose I've averaged around five times a year getting through the Word of God. When I began to read the Bible and began to consume that much, which was considerably more than I had at any prior time, the Bible began to take on a panoramic view like I'd never seen before. One week I'd be reading over here and the next week in just a matter of days, and yet several hundred chapters, I'd be further down the Bible. Things began to dovetail together and connect like I'd never seen before. As I began to read that many chapters a day--God, of course, pointed out several things to me in my own mind and I kept seeing a phrase: *"The fear of the Lord..."* *"The fear of God..."* *"The fear of the Lord..."* God began to impress upon my mind that phrase was there for a definite, specific reason. So I went to my library, my study, and I went through all of the sermon books that I had. I went through all of the magazines, all of the periodicals. I had *Sword of the Lord's* going back into the 50's; the early 50's. I had a 36 volume set of Charles Haddon Spurgeon's sermons. I went through everything that I had in my library trying to find a message on "The Fear of the Lord." In one little devotional booklet I found a brief synopsis, or resume concerning the fear of the Lord. To this day, I can never remember hearing a message on "The Fear of the Lord." Yet the Word of God is literally saturated with that theme. So I began to study it in the Word of God. I began to ask myself questions: "What is the fear of the Lord?" "Who does the fear of the Lord apply to?" "Why is it unmentioned, basically, in preaching?" God began to challenge my life about many things. I began to preach a message on "The Fear of the Lord." A dear friend of mine was pastoring in Minneapolis at that time and I preached the message in his church and he became stirred by the same thought. Every time our paths would cross, he would say "Brother Neil, have you got anything new on the fear of the Lord?" "Have you got a better definition on the fear of the Lord now?" We'd talk about it; we'd converse about it. He'd say, "Now here is what I believe the fear of the Lord is." I'd say, "Well, I believe that this is what the fear of the Lord is." Of course we agreed, though we may have come in a different door to try to explain it. I laid the message aside for, I guess, three or four years and didn't preach it. This summer I picked up a book that I had bought, by John Bunyan, on "The Fear of the Lord." As I began to read through the book, he had some thoughts and some definitions that I had not thought about. One of the definitions is a definition that I'd like to give to you tonight on what the fear of the Lord is. The definition reads like this:

> *"Man crumbles to dust at the presence of God. Yea, though He comes to us in the robes of salvation."*

Now I like that definition, because it's a Bible definition. Would you take your Bibles please, this evening, and turn with me to the book of Genesis, chapter 28. We find in verse 10 that Jacob has gone out from Beersheba and gone toward Haran. Lord willing, in about a week and a half, I'm going to see some of these places. This meeting closes next Sunday night. Lord willing, on Tuesday of the next week I'm going to get on a plane and take off for the Bible lands. I tell you, I'm so excited about it that I can hardly stand it! I've been trying to get to go for several years and I thought that I'd start advertising myself as the only evangelist in America that has never been to the Bible lands. But, my father-in-law took pity on me and he's making sure that I'm getting to the Bible lands this year; that's the kind of father-in-law to have, I guess. I'm looking forward to it and I can't wait to see some of these places. I believe that it's going to make the Bible come alive. Dr. Parker used to say that a tour, or trip to the Bible lands is worth one year in graduate study. I'm looking forward to it.

> "And Jacob went out from Beersheba, and went toward Haran. And he lighted upon a certain place, and tarried there all night, because the sun was set; and he took of the stones of that place, and put them for his pillows, and lay down in that place to sleep. And he dreamed, and behold a ladder set up on the earth, and the top of it reached to heaven; and behold the angels of God ascending and descending on it.

Now in this particular scripture we find that Jacob has rested for the night. God brings a vision to Jacob. He sees a ladder, angels descending and ascending this ladder which reaches into Heaven and brings Jacob a special revelation and promise during that dream. After the dream has passed, the vision is gone, been completed notice what Jacob says in verses 16 and 17:

> And Jacob awaked out of his sleep, and he said, Surely the LORD is in this place; and I knew it not. And he was afraid, and said, How dreadful is this place! this is none other but the house of God, and this is the gate of heaven.

Now I want you to see that Jacob says *"How dreadful is this place!"* Now he didn't say it was an awful place to be in the sense that he'd never want to be there, because he says "This is the house of God; this is the gate of heaven." He was not saying it's awful to be in the house of God; it's a fearful thing to enter into the gate of heaven in the sense that it's something he did not anticipate. Rather, he's saying that it's a fearful thing, because he'd been in the presence of God. He'd been in the presence of Holiness and it had wrought a tremendous fear within the heart of Jacob because he was nothing but man and he'd been in the presence of God. Daniel chapter 10 please, verses 16 and 17.

> And, behold, one like the similitude of the sons of men touched my lips; then I opened my mouth, and spake, and said unto him that stood before me, O my lord, by the vision my sorrows are turned upon me, and I have retained no strength. For how can the servant of this my lord talk with this my lord? for as for me, straightway there remained no strength in me, neither is there breath left in me.

Now God came to bring Daniel some special and pertinent instructions and revelation and Daniel said, "How can this, the servant of the Lord talk with my lord?" He said that there was no strength left in him. He said, "My breath has gone from me." Why? Because he had been in the presence of a Holy God!

Once again, Revelation chapter one. I believe that there are few portions of Scripture in the Bible that describe the majesty of our Savior like Revelation chapter one. Let's begin reading in verse 12.

> "And I turned to see the voice that spake with me. And being turned, I saw seven golden candlesticks; And in the midst of the seven candlesticks one like unto the Son of man, clothed with a garment down to the foot, and girt about the paps with a golden girdle. His head and his hairs were white like wool, as white as snow; and his eyes were as a flame of fire; And his feet like unto fine brass, as if they burned in a furnace; and his voice as the sound of many waters. And he had in his right hand seven stars: and out of his mouth went a sharp two edged sword: and his countenance was as the sun shineth in his strength. And when I saw him, I fell at his feet as dead. And he laid his right hand upon me, saying unto me, Fear not; I am the first and the last:"

When John knew that he was in the presence of the God-man he knew that he was in the presence of the Lamb that had been slain before the foundation of the world. When he knew that he was in the presence of the Holy Savior, Jesus Christ, the Bible says he fell as one who was dead! I want to ask you tonight, can you honestly say before a Holy God in Heaven, that you have a fear of God? The definition that Mr. Bunyan gave us is that *"Man crumbles to dust at the presence of God. Yea, though He comes to us in the robes of salvation"* and that is exactly what takes place in every one of these illustrations. Jacob had a fear of God even though God came with a special promise that He was going to bless his heritage and that He'd promised him that he'd inherit that land one day. Daniel said, "No strength remains in me; I have no breath," though God came to bless him and give him special information. The same thing was true in the life of John. God came to give John a special message for you and I to have even today. God didn't come with a whip. God didn't come with a battering ram. God came in the robes of salvation! He came in the garment of love! He came with a special revelation. But the truth is today that we do not have a fear of God today in America! My friend, unless we come to the place where the children of God walk and live and have a fear of God, you and I have no right to expect the unsaved to have a fear of God. This world that you and I live in tonight does not have a fear of God! They're brazen. They're crass. They're braggadocios. In their rebellion against God, they're brazen in their sinful acts and they act as if there is no God to answer to one day. My friends, you mark it down. The Bible says that one day that God shall have them in derision. The Bible says that God shall mock; he shall laugh at their calamity, he shall mock when their fear cometh. There is no fear of God. We can blame our Congress. We can blame our politicians and we can blame everyone that we want to point our finger to, but the truth is that the reason that America is in the chaotic condition it's in tonight is because Fundamentalist Christianity has failed in its responsibility to a Holy God! There's no way in the world why we should expect a president or a senator or a congressman or a governor or a mayor to have a fear of God who is not saved when even the saved people do not have a fear of God. We cannot expect it. The truth is, it does not take much time looking at the average church member today to see that he has no fear of God. The man who stands up and says he has a fear of God and does not live like it is giving every evidence of everything but a fear of God. If tonight, I were to close this service and tell my wife in the trailer afterwards, "Honey, that's the last message I'm going to preach. I'm going to leave the ministry. I'm going out into the secular world and get a secular job," I would fear for my life, because I do not think that I would get twenty-five miles down the road before God would kill me. Now I mean that. You say, "That must be awful to serve a God like that!" My friends, it's not awful to serve a God like that; it's a privilege to serve a God that loves you so much that He'll chasten you if you get out of line! The Bible says that He will chasten them who He loves!

I remember that my father used to make me bend over after I'd done something wrong. He'd double up the razor strap and he'd always say these two things. First of all, he'd always say, "Neil, now I want you to know that this is going to hurt me more than you," and I knew that was a lie. There's not a way in...I mean I wasn't going to be able to sit down when he got done. Then he'd say this, "Now Neil, I want you know that I love you." I thought, "Man, if that's love, I don't need any--I've got all that I can stand!" But you know, when I have to discipline our little eleven year old girl, it breaks this dad's heart and I pick her up and I say, "Now April, honey, I want you to know that I love you and I do it because I love you." I tell you friends, the reason that a lot of folks profess to be saved and live like the devil and never have the chastening hand of God come upon them is an indication that they just flat have never been born again. I got saved when I was 14 years old. I went back to my home church after that Bible camp. Now I didn't realize, because it was all new to me...I

figured that when you went to camp and made a decision, when the Spirit of God spoke to you that you're supposed to mean business about it. Man I went back and I wanted to tell everybody about Jesus. I wanted to tell them how to get saved. I wanted to live for God. But I found that the kids still went out on the back roads and necked. They still told the same dirty stories. They still disobeyed their parents. They still had the same dirty mouths. It wasn't long before I got a bad case of rebellion. I just didn't have any time for spiritual things. One night, ninety miles an hour on a back road, God put me in a car accident. It was my junior year in high school. When I climbed out of that mangled mass of metal and climbed up on to that road I said, "Oh God, I'll be whatever it is that you want me to be." You know what happened on April 17th, 1957? God got out His razor strap. The very fact that God disciplined me that night is an indication that I was saved. God loved me so much that He wanted His child to go straight; to do right. He said, "Neil, this is going to hurt me more than it's going to hurt you. I want you to know that I love you." And then, Zap. Now just between you and I and a fence post, I don't care for God to get out His razor strap too many times. I'd just as soon enjoy the blessing instead of the heartache. Now, I want you to see the pro and con of this thing of the fear of the Lord. Take your Bibles and turn with me to Psalm chapter 36. I want you to notice there verse one.
"The transgression of the wicked saith within my heart, that there is no fear of God before his eyes."
The very fact that a man transgresses and sins against God is a proof and an indication that there is no fear of God before his eyes.
Romans chapter three please, beginning in verse ten.

> *"As it is written, There is none righteous, no, not one: There is none that understandeth, there is none that seeketh after God. They are all gone out of the way, they are together become unprofitable; there is none that doeth good, no, not one. Their throat is an open sepulchre; with their tongues they have used deceit; the poison of asps is under their lips:"*

An asp is a small, poisonous snake found in the Middle East. One of the four most poisonous snakes in the world. And the Bible says that "...*the poison of asps is under their lips. Whose mouth is full of cursing and bitterness: Their feet are swift to shed blood: Destruction and misery are in their ways: And the way of peace have they not known: There is no fear of God before their eyes"*
You remember the story of Nadab and Abihu. They offered strange fire to God. In other words, they were offering up a false sacrifice to a false

god. They were doing that which was contrary to God's teachings. They had no fear of God before their eyes and God had to bring severe judgment, because they did that which was contrary to God. Remember the story in the Bible about the man by the name of Uzzah who laid his hand against that ark, and God struck that man with death because he defiled the principles of a Holy God. There was no fear of God before his eyes in the very indication that he deliberately disobeyed God. In Acts chapter five, Ananias and Sapphira were to sell their land and to bring back to the temple, back to the men of God to distribute it to the cause that they were working for. As they were asked the question, "Did you sell your land for so much?" They said, "Yea Lord," but they were holding some back for Social Security. They wanted to make sure that they had something to retire on. They were saving some for a rainy day, you see. They really couldn't trust God for the rainy days; it was all right for the bright days, but not the rainy days. God brought judgment into their lives because that they lied to God because there was no fear of God before their eyes. Now friend, you can count on it. You go contrary to God's will in your life and there's going to be a reaping; there's going to be a reckoning. God will bend, break or bury the disobedient child of God. If you're here tonight and you're not saved, my friends, I pray that God will place a fear of God in your heart. You say, "Why?" Because no man ever got saved but what he had a fear of the Lord. No one ever got saved, but what he had a fear of the Lord.

Now, I want you to notice another thing of this aspect of the fear of the Lord. Take your Bibles please and turn to Proverbs chapter three verse seven. *"Be not wise in thine own eyes: fear the LORD, and depart from evil."*

Effects of the Fear of the Lord

Now if you do not fear God you can plan on judgment. If you do fear the Lord, you can plan on separating from sin, because a man who fears God is going to trust and obey. He's going to be surrendered. He's going to be submissive. He's going to be yielded. That means he's going to depart from evil! A man who is sold out to God is not going to hold hands with the devil's crowd. You don't want to. You don't like to. You're offended by sin. I wonder just how much we're offended by sin today as the children of God? I wonder how much sin really grieves our hearts? Friends, if God has convinced me of anything in the last two or three years in evangelism, it's that we need to preach on sin like never before. Now you hear me. I'm not talking about just getting up and saying, "Brethren, sin's wrong," and someone getting up and saying, "Amen." I am talking about saying that sin is wrong and naming sin. If we ever need a dictionary that explained and defined and told what sin was, we need it today. You didn't use to need it because people had a fear of God. They kept their hearts and lives in the Word of God and they based everything they did, geared according to the Word of God. You see, what we do today we do because of personalities; we do because of prejudice; we do because of programs; we do because of philosophy; we do because somewhere along the line we've been influenced by worldly, materialistic ideology and we've gotten contrary to the Word of God! That's why we've got an ERA amendment today! It's not based according to Bible principles; it's based upon man-made philosophy! God bring us back to the place, where today in America, we stand upon the Word of God and what we believe, and how we act, and where we go and what we do is according to Bible principles, instead of saying, "Well you know I just can't accept that...I don't believe..." Listen friends, it's still true whether you believe it or not. God's Word has not gotten out of date! The truth is, we've gotten out of date with God. We need to realize the truth of Jeremiah chapter six where it says that we need to go back to the old paths. You say, "Well, Brother Cadwell, that's not contemporary. That's not relevant." Hey, you're right. But I don't care. I'm not here to satisfy a wicked world! This world's not my home, I'm just passing through. I'm not going to drive any tent stakes here! I'm not interested in building a mansion here! I've got the greatest architect of the universe working on one for me and that's the one that I'm going to enjoy in glory! I'm not worried about a retirement here; I'm laying up one over there in glory. I'm not worried about vacations here; Blessed be His name, I'm going to have an eternal vacation one day. I'm going higher some day.

Hate Evil

Now notice Proverbs chapter eight verse 13. The Bible says, *"The fear of the LORD is to hate evil:"* Let me ask you a question tonight. "You been hating any sin lately?" Hey, I'm not asking if you're hating your neighbor's sin down the street from you. I'm not asking if you're hating the wino's sin or the bartender's sin or the harlot's sin or the drug addict's sin. I'm asking you tonight my friend, "Have you been hating any sin that's in your life?" One of the things that I try to pray daily in my life is "God, help me to hate sin." The Bible says, *"The fear of the LORD is to hate evil:"* The man who says he has a fear of God and goes month after month after month after month and never opens the Word of God and never prays does not have a fear of God in his heart. The Bible says in Psalms chapter one "...that his delight is in the law of the Lord." A man that does not have an affinity for the Word of God, you ought to have serious reservations about whether you've ever been born again or not. A man that's more interested in reading his sports page than his Bible; a man that's more concerned about his funny papers than having his private devotions is a man that needs to get on his knees before God and say "Oh God, I need a revival. I need a reworking. I need a change in my life." A man that will constantly cuss, take God's name in vain, keep up with the dirty habits, keep the cheap, filthy things in his life he ought not to do does not have the fear of God. Listen, if the Bible teaches something friends, and you and I know it's true and we deliberately disobey God, you mark it down there's a lack of the fear of the Lord in your life. The fear of the Lord is not only the aspect that God is gonna, if you please, "blister your bottom" if you get out of line, but the fear of the Lord is that which magnetizes, which draws you and I closer to God. It'll draw you closer. You see, the fear of the Lord is going to be a motivating force for you to walk closer to Him. The man who walks away from God, the man who walks far from God has no fear of God. I pray tonight that God will give us a supercharging of the fear of the Lord, if you please. That God would shake our very foundations. I have a pastor friend...whenever we get together, he falls completely prostrate on the floor, just as flat as he can get. Not because he's trying to be more spiritual, not because he's trying to have a "holier than thou" attitude. He doesn't walk around with a little halo on top of his head. He's saying, "Oh, God, I want you to know that I realize that I'm a wretched worm. I deserve hell, but I'm coming into your presence; I'm coming humbly and contritely with the fear of the Lord in my heart." Now I'm not saying that you have to do that. I believe that you can be just as sincere when you're praying standing up as lying down, but I think it's an attitude of the heart which he's showing. Now I'm saying that very few of us have that kind of the fear of the Lord. If you had to get on your knees to pray, some of you would go without praying. If you had to lie flat out, if you had to become nothing, some of you just wouldn't do it! That's the reason why some of you don't do it. That's why you don't do it.

Depart From Evil

Notice Proverbs chapter sixteen please, verse six. The Bible says, *"By mercy and truth iniquity is purged; and by the fear of the LORD men depart from evil."* Not only would we ask the question tonight "Have you been hating any sin?" but, "Have you been running from any sin?" You see, a lot of people are willing to confess that they've got sin and a lot of people are willing to name that sin, they're willing to confess that sin, but very few folk are willing to forsake it. The Bible says that we need to confess and forsake. When we ask God to forgive us our sin, we confess our sin, you'd best be ready to forsake it at the same time. If you hate it enough, you will. By the fear of the Lord, men depart, men flee, men run from sin! The Bible says "Flee youthful lusts," and that's not only for young people. Mom and Dad need to flee youthful lusts. The same lustful desires that teenagers have, Moms and Dads have and they need to be conquered and challenged and committed to God just as much as anyone else. Now my friends, we tried tonight to briefly show you what the fear of the Lord is; we tried to show you the positive and the negative, the pros and the cons of the fear of the Lord. Let me say this tonight also, that the fear of the Lord is going to result in salvation. It's gonna result in salvation.

Persuade Men

Take Your Bible and turn to 2 Corinthians chapter five where we were this morning and I want you to read a verse there with me that we didn't read, verse eleven. We read verse ten this morning. I want us to notice verse eleven. The Bible says, *"Knowing therefore the terror of the Lord..."* I believe you'll find in your Scofield Bible that word "terror" is translated "fear." *"Knowing therefore the fear of the Lord we persuade men; but we are made manifest unto God;"* He's saying because we know the fear of the Lord we persuade men, we win men, we convince men, we bring men to Jesus Christ. A man who has a fear of God is gonna be a soul winner. Not he might be or he's gonna try to be, but a man who has a fear of God is going to be a soul winner. Now, and in that sense, I can say the fear of the Lord results in salvation, but I want to say also the fear of the Lord results in salvation because as I said earlier, the unsaved that have a fear of the Lord results in salvation because as I said earlier, the unsaved that have a fear of God will come to salvation. No man has ever been saved without the fear of the Lord. Take your Bibles, turn with me to Psalms chapter eight-five please. By the way, sometime take your Bible and go through and study all the verses on the fear of the Lord. We have touched just a mere pittance; we haven't even come close to covering the topic. Listen, go through, take your Bible and study the fear of the Lord on the provisions, on the blessings that God gives to the one that has the fear of the Lord. I tell you, they're tremendous. God promises you protection, God promises provision, God promises abundant life, God promises so much to those who have a fear of God. Now notice in Psalms chapter eight-five, verse nine. The Bible says, *"Surely his salvation is nigh them that fear him;"* I believe that when I got saved in 1954 it was because I had a fear of the Lord even before I got saved. I had a fear of the Lord because I'd been taught a fear of the Lord in my own home. Now my Dad was not saved; since then he's been saved. My mother was not saved; since then she's been saved. But they had a fear of God; there was a fear of God in that family. Their homes before them had a fear of God. You don't have to be saved to have a fear of God, but I tell you, if you're going to be saved, you're gonna have to have a fear of God. Now notice Acts chapter ten; would you turn there with me. Here I believe is one of the most perfect illustrations of exactly what we're talking about this evening. Acts chapter ten and verse one. The Bible says, *"There was a certain man in Caesarea called Cornelius, a centurion of the band called the Italian band, a devout man, and one that feared God with all his house,"* By the way, take your Bible sometime and go to the book of Deuteronomy and study how often the fear of the Lord is to be taught by the parents to their children. The reason we've got rebellion and riot and revolution, disrespect and sassing and back talking and disobedience in the homes today in America is because we've tried to raise our children of Spockism instead of Mom and Dad raising them on the fear of the Lord as it's taught in the Word of God. God bring us back to the place, where...now of course, when Dad goes out boating on Sunday and is not in God's house, it's kinda hard to teach the fear of the Lord. When Mother says it's all right for you to study for your test on Wednesday night instead of being in prayer meeting, it's kinda hard to teach the fear of the Lord. When you go home and criticize and bad-mouth and destroy the testimony of your preacher before your children, it's kinda hard to teach them the fear of the Lord. When you say it's more important to stay home and watch TV on Thursday night instead of going out on visitation, it's kinda hard to have the fear of the Lord. Now that's gotta be taught to the children. It's got to be taught in the home. The trouble is, we've left off the teaching to the church and to the school today and that's the reason we've got chaos today in America. God brings us to the place...but notice, He said, *"...A devout man, and one that feared God with all his house..."* I mean, even before they were saved. *"...which gave much alms to the people, and prayed to God always."* Now here's a religious man, here's a devout man, here's a faithful church-going man, but he's not saved yet. He's not saved until later in this chapter, and yet he feared God. The Bible says that *"...salvation is nigh unto them that fear God."* I'm saying if you're here tonight and you're not saved, that Jesus Christ can save you; He wants to save you and He will save you if you'll by faith receive Jesus Christ as your personal Savior. Now here's the last verse tonight.

Keep His Commandments

In Ecclesiastes 12 and verse 13 the Bible says, *"Let us hear the conclusion of the whole matter: Fear God, and keep his commandments: for this is the whole duty of man."* "Let us hear the conclusion of the whole matter: Fear God...keep his commandments! People come to church and say "Oh, how I love Jesus..." Do you? Do you? Then keep my commandments. It's one thing to say you love Him, it's another to do it. If you love Him, you're gonna keep His commandments. *"Fear God, and keep his commandments: for this is the whole duty of man."* The one-hundred percent responsibility that you have as a child of God is to obey Him; to fear God and keep His commandments.

All right, what have we said tonight? The fear of the Lord is that *"Man crumbles to dust at the presence of God. Yea, though He shows Himself to us in the robes of salvation."* What happened when Jonathan Edwards preached the message *Sinners in the Hands of an Angry God?* I believe they stood in the presence of God. Here was a man who stood and read his message like this. He could not see but just a few inches...I mean it was just as dry as dust, if you please, as far as personality and oratory, but he had the one thing that we lack today in America; he had the power of God and as he preached that message they stood in the presence of God and folk fell on their knees and cried out to God, because they "crumbled to dust in the presence of a Holy God." Oh that God would be so pleased to meet with us in such a way that the flesh could be set aside and that tonight we could see God that we might crumble to dust; that we might be willing to walk right with Him, that we might hate evil-- to depart from evil. To live in such a way to bring glory to His name. The Bible says, "It's a fearful thing to fall into the hands of a living God." Do you have a fear of the Lord tonight? Can you say the way you act in your home, the way you act on your job, the way you act when some crazy driver pulls in front of you and about makes you wreck; can you say the life you live is an indication that you have the fear of the Lord? The friends you run with, the things you say, the way you dress, the way you talk, the way you act? Let's bow for prayer please. Will you quit looking, in your mind, at your neighbor and at somebody else you're thinking about. Will you ask yourself tonight, "Is it me, Oh Lord, standing in the need of prayer?" Is it me? Not my brother, not my sister...Is it me?"

> *Our Father, I would ask in Jesus name tonight that you'd meet the need of every heart and every life. Lord, I pray tonight for that one that may be here unsaved. Lord, they have a fear of the Lord in their heart. Lord, help them*

tonight to be willing to receive Christ as their personal Saviour; to be able to walk with confidence and assurance that they're Heaven bound. Father, for those Christians that are here tonight, who know that they are deliberately grieving the Spirit of God. They're not walking in the fear of the Lord. They have been disobedient and blatant in their sin against you. Father, I pray in Jesus name that you'd speak to their hearts. That one who doesn't win souls has no fear of God. That one who doesn't read his Bible or pray has no fear of God; not as it ought to be. Lord, I believe that there are so many needs that need to be met; there's some Moms and Dads here that never have family devotions in their home. No fear of God; they're not teaching it to their children. Oh God, break their hearts about that matter. Father, we just ask now that you'd be with this invitational part of the service. God, it's so mighty important. Homes could be rearranged; lives could be changed. God, we anticipate and we expect your blessing, because we ask it and we pray it in the sweet name of Jesus. Amen.

RON COMFORT

9

The Rapture

BIOGRAPHICAL SKETCH

Ron Comfort
(1938-)

Ron Comfort was born into a Roman Catholic home in Elmira, New York, on September 14, 1938. Between the ages of seven and fifteen, he sang on radio, television, stage, and in small night clubs. It was at the age of fifteen that he was saved in a city-wide crusade in Ashville, North Carolina. He immediately felt God's call to preach.

Ron entered the Bob Jones Academy, in Greenville, South Carolina, as a sophomore in high school. Through opportunities there, he began to develop leadership abilities. He was elected president of both the high school student body and the inter-society council.

While in the University, he was twice named to Who's Who in American Colleges and Universities. He served as both president and vice-president of the university's ministerial class of one thousand students. He was also elected president of the university student body.

After working to pay his own way through seven years at Bob Jones Academy and University, Ron graduated in 1961 and immediately entered full-time evangelism. He has continued this ministry for more than thirty-five years conducting more than 1,000 crusades in forty-five states and numerous foreign countries.

In 1973, Maranatha Baptist Bible College honored him with the degree Doctor of Divinity. That same year he was also honored by the Bob Jones University Alumni Association for "Outstanding Work in the Field of Evangelism."

Ron and Joyce were married in 1963 and have been blessed with three daughters. Joyce serves the Lord as part of the team's musical ministry playing the piano and vibra harp. She also conducts children's meetings and serves as team secretary.

In 1989, Dr. Comfort founded the Ambassador Baptist College, located in Shelby, North Carolina, and became its first president. The college was founded for the express purpose of training men and women for full-time Christian service and has experienced a steady growth since its inception.

Evangelist Ron Comfort
900 S. Post Rd.
Shelby, NC 28150

THE RAPTURE
Ron Comfort

All right, First Thessalonians chapter four and verses thirteen through eighteen tonight is our text. Paul says, "But I would not have you to be ignorant, brethren, concerning them which are asleep, that ye sorrow not, even as others which have no hope. For if we believe that Jesus Christ died and rose again, even so them also which sleep in Jesus will God bring with him. For this we say unto you by the word of the Lord, that we which are alive and remain unto the coming of the Lord shall not prevent them which are asleep. For the Lord himself shall descend from heaven with a shout, with the voice of the archangel, and with the trump of God: and the dead in Christ shall rise first: Then we which are alive and remain shall be caught up together with them in the clouds, to meet the Lord in the air: and so shall we ever be with the Lord. Wherefore comfort one another with these words."

In First Thessalonians four we have the first real clear passage in the Bible on what is called the "rapture." Dr. H.A.Ironside made this statement, "One may go through Matthew, Mark, Luke, and John and he will only find one Scripture that deals with the rapture. That's John chapter fourteen and verse three." I'm not sure whether or not that's true. I suspect it probably is. But I do know that in First Thessalonians chapter four we have the first real clear passage in the Bible on what is called the rapture.

Now, there may be folks in the building tonight who have been saved for a long time and you're not aware that the Second Coming of Christ is in two phases. When He comes for those of us that are saved, His feet will not touch the earth, but we will be raptured to meet Him in the air. That's the rapture.

Now, somebody says, "Where do you find that word in your English Bible?" It's not in the English Bible. Let me tell you where we get that word. It is what is called a transliteration. That is a fancy word for saying that we take a foreign word and make it an English word. And it comes from the Latin word, "rapto," r-a-p-t-o, "rapto." So therefore we derive the English word, "rapture." Rapto. First Thessalonians four seventeen, "caught up together with them in the clouds," "rapto," rapture.

Now, after the rapture, there will be seven years when all hell breaks loose on earth called the Tribulation. Now, ladies and gentlemen, tonight I am preaching on Act One of the drama. So, there is the rapture, when we meet Him in the air; seven years of Tribulation; then when He comes back to earth, that is called the revelation.

Now, as far as I can tell, there are only two Scriptures in the New Testament that mention both phases of the Second Coming in the same verse. For instance, Second Timothy 4:1 - "I charge thee therefore before

God, and the Lord Jesus Christ, who shall judge the quick and the dead at his appearing (that's the rapture) and his kingdom (that's the revelation). Again, Titus two thirteen: "Looking for that blessed hope (that's the rapture) and the glorious appearing (that's the revelation) of the great God and our Saviour, Jesus Christ." Now, what we are primarily concerned with tonight is the rapture. I want you to notice several things with me tonight about the rapture.

IT IS A SURE EVENT

Number One, it is a SURE EVENT.

I Thessalonians 4:16 - "For the Lord himself SHALL descend from heaven with a shout." It's a sure event.

I Corinthians 1:7,8 - "So that ye come behind in no gift waiting for the coming of the Lord Jesus Christ."

I Corinthians 4:5 - "Therefore judge nothing before the time until the Lord come."

Phillippians 3:20 - "For our citizenship is in heaven from whence also we look for the Saviour, the Lord Jesus Christ."

Philippians 4:5 - "Let your moderation be known unto all men, for the Lord is at hand."

James 5:8,9 - "Be ye therefore patient, stablish your hearts: for the coming of the Lord draweth nigh . . . behold, the judge standeth at the door."

Colossians 3:4 - "But when Christ, who is our life, shall appear, then shall ye also appear with him in glory."

Hebrews 9:28 - "So Christ was once offered to bear the sins of many; and unto them that look for him shall he appear the second time without sin unto salvation."

Hey, what could be plainer than that? He's coming the second time! Do you know, ladies and gentlemen, the day that they hung Jesus Christ on Calvary's Cross, there were thirty-three Old Testament prophecies fulfilled in one day. I was in Okinawa for meetings and the pastor asked one of his military men who worked with computers to find from the computer what the chances were that thirty-three could be fulfilled in one man in one day. And do you know what the man replied? He said, "Pastor, the computer read out that the chances that thirty-three prophecies could be fulfilled in one man in one day were less than 1 in 87, with 92 zeroes after it. Think of it!"

But, do you know, my friend, that in the life, the death, and the resurrection of Christ, there were more than three hundred Old Testament prophecies fulfilled! Are you aware that for every one promise in the Bible on the First Coming of Jesus Christ you will find twenty promises on the Second Coming?

In the New Testament there are seven thousand nine hundred and fifty-nine verses. Do you know that no less than three hundred and thirty verses in the New Testament speak of the Second Coming of Jesus Christ? Why, my dear friend, more is said about "King" Jesus than is said about "baby" Jesus. More is said in this Book about Jesus on a Throne than even Jesus on a Cross! Now let me ask you a question. Doesn't it stand to reason to any logical mind that if all of the promises concerning His First Coming were fulfilled, that, as surely, all of the promises concerning His Second Coming are going to be fulfilled? And, ladies and gentlemen, they are.

Now, I want you to follow me. Do you realize that every chapter in First and Second Thessalonians speaks of the Second Coming of Christ? Every chapter. Please follow me.

I Thessalonians 1:10 - "...and to wait for his Son from heaven, whom he raised from the dead, even Jesus, which delivered us from the wrath to come."

I Thessalonians 2:19 - "For what is our hope, or joy, or crown of rejoicing? Are not even ye in the presence of our Lord Jesus Christ at his coming?"

I Thessalonians 3:13 - "To the end he may stablish your hearts unblamable in holiness before God, even our Father, at the coming of our Lord Jesus Christ with all his saints."

I Thessalonians 4:16 - "For the Lord himself shall descend from heaven with a shout, with the voice of the archangel, and with the trump of God: and the dead in Christ shall rise first."

I Thessalonians 5:23 - "And the very God of peace sanctify you wholly; and I pray God your whole spirit and soul and body be preserved blameless unto the coming of our Lord Jesus Christ."

II Thessalonians 1:7,8 - "And to you who are troubled rest with us, when the Lord Jesus shall be revealed from heaven with his mighty angels, In flaming fire taking vengeance on them that know not God, and that obey not the gospel of our Lord Jesus Christ."

II Thessalonians 2:1,2 - "Now we beseech you, brethren, by the coming of our Lord Jesus Christ, and by our gathering together unto him, That ye be not soon shaken in mind, or be troubled, neither by spirit, nor by word, nor by letter as from us, as that the day of Christ is at hand."

II Thessalonians 3:5 - "And the Lord direct your hearts into the love of God, and into the patient waiting for Christ."

Ladies and gentlemen, there it is and any preacher that denies the Second Coming has to rip those two books right out of his Bible.

I was preaching in Pittsburgh and a lady came up to me and said, "Brother Comfort, I went to my Presbyterian preacher and asked him if he believed in the Second Coming." She said, "He told me that he didn't believe it but that it didn't matter whether you believed it or not." Now, what do you think about that? I wish that woman would have had enough backbone to say, "Listen, preacher, I don't care whose seminary you've been to, it DOES matter whether or not you believe it." Do you know what she said? "Brother Comfort, I've been in that church since I was knee-high. I can't leave that church now." I said, "God pity a woman who loves her denomination more than she loves the Word of God!" Now, I'll tell you what. We had ladies at the Ladies' Luncheon today who are married to a denominational tag. They love their denomination more than they love the Word of God!

Hey, I'm talking to people in this building tonight who may be married to a denominational tag. You've gone to a church where, in all of your life, you've never one time heard a preacher preach on the Second Coming of Christ. You say, "Well, I don't know whether he believes it or not. I've never heard him say." Well, my dear friend, if he's never said it, he doesn't believe it. And if he doesn't believe in the Second Coming, he doesn't believe in the verbal inspiration of the Word of God, either! If he doesn't believe in the Second Coming, he probably doesn't believe in the Virgin Birth, either. My friend, you need to get outta that church and you need to go to a church where they believe and preach the Second Coming of Jesus Christ!

Now, most of you know that I was not reared in an independent Baptist home. I was reared in a Roman Catholic home. Ladies and gentlemen, for the first seven years of my life I was a Roman Catholic. For the next eight years of my life I was a Southern Baptist. When I was fifteen, I was born again. Then I became an Independent Baptist by conviction. But, I'm gonna tell you somethin', friend. I love this Book a lot more than I love the tag "Independent Baptist." And, if the time ever comes when Independent Baptists are known for their denial of the Second Coming, Preacher, I'm gonna call myself by another name! I am NOT married to a denominational tag! And, God pity you if you love your denomination more than you love the Word of God.

It Is A Sudden Event

All right, notice, number two, it is a SUDDEN EVENT. I Thessalonians 4:16 - "For the Lord himself shall descend from heaven with a shout." It's a sudden event. Hey, that word for "shout," in the Greek language, means "a military command." He is coming and He is shouting a military command. What is it going to be?

You remember His command to Noah was, "Come in." His command to Lot was, "Come out." His command to you and me who are saved is going to be, "Come up!" And every child of God is going higher. Revelation 4:1 says, "And the first voice which I heard was as it were of a trumpet talking with me; which said, Come up hither." Get it. One day Jesus is coming in the air and He's shouting, "Come up hither!" And I'm climbing an invisible stairway to be with Jesus Christ.

First Corinthians 15:51,52 says, "Behold, I shew you a mystery; We shall not all sleep, but we shall all be changed, In a moment, in the twinkling of an eye, at the last trump: for the trumpet shall sound, and the dead shall be raised incorruptible, and we shall be changed." And, my dear friend, it is all going to happen in a moment, in the twinkling of an eye. Someone said, "That's as quickly as you can bat your eye." No, my friend, it's quicker than that.

An atom is the smallest unit of matter. May I say that the word "twinkling" is the same Greek word from which we get the word "atom." And that Greek word "twinkling" means the smallest unit of time. It's not the "blinking of the eye;" it is the "sparking of the eye." That is less than 1/1,000th of a second. Think of it. Can you imagine that? In less than 1/1,000th of a second I'm changed from a body of mortality into a body of immortality! From a body sown in weakness to a body raised in strength. From a body in corruption to a body in incorruption, all in less than 1/1,000th of a second! Hallelujah!

Science tells us today that light from the farthest star has never reached the earth. They "guesstimate" that the light from the farthest star is 500 million light years away! What does that mean? You know that light travels at the speed of 186,000 miles per second, not per hour, but per second! And it would take 500 million years going at the rate of 186,000 miles per second for the light from the farthest star to reach the earth. Question. Where is heaven? Heaven is beyond the farthest star. Where is Jesus? Jesus is in heaven. Well, my dear friend, it's not going to take Jesus 500 million light years to come back and get His little children! He's coming in a moment, in the twinkling of an eye!

You know, when Jesus Christ was on earth, He told His disciples He was coming again. He never told them when, but He intimated He may come in their lifetime. Did you know that? For instance, in John 14:3, He said, "And if I go away and prepare a place for YOU, I will come again and receive YOU unto myself that where I am there YOU may be also." Again, in Luke 12:40 - "Be ye therefore ready also: for the Son of man cometh at an hour when ye think not." Again, Mark 13:35,36 - "Watch ye, therefore: for ye know not when the master of the house cometh, at even, or at midnight, or at the cock crowning, or in the morning: lest coming suddenly he find you sleeping."

You know what I believe? Every disciple in the New Testament was looking for Christ to come in his lifetime. I do not believe the teaching of the New Testament is that you and I are to look forward to dying! Did you get that? Hey, I'm looking forward to cheating the undertaker. We are not to look for the undertaker, we are to look for the upper taker! Peter was. First Peter 5:4 - "And when the Chief Shepherd shall appear, ye shall receive a crown of glory that fadeth not away." John was. First John 2:28 - "And now, little children, abide in him; that, when he shall appear, we may have confidence and not be ashamed before him at his coming." Jude was. Jude, verse 14: "And Enoch also, the seventh from Adam, prophesied of these, saying, Behold, the Lord cometh with ten thousands of his saints." And, ladies and gentlemen, you and I are to live in constant expectation of the Second Coming of Christ.

I was talking to a lady in Indiana who was elderly. She said to me, "Now, Brother Comfort, you're a young man." Now, she did have a measure of discernment, I'll grant that. "Now," she said, "you're a young man; I'm an old lady. Jesus may come in your lifetime, but I don't believe He'll come in my lifetime." You know what the Bible calls that, friend? Three letters, S-I-N. And I believe the teaching of the Word of God is that we are to get up in the morning looking for the Second Coming of Jesus Christ. We are to go to bed at night thinking that, before we ever arise, the Son of Righteousness may dawn the eastern sky.

Dewitt Talmadge said, "I never lay my head on my pillow at night but what I think that, before I awake, the Son of Righteousness may dawn the eastern sky and call me Home with Himself. I never begin my day's work but what I think that Jesus may interrupt my work and begin His own work in me. And my constant theme is, 'Perhaps today.'" And that's the way you and I should live. And, may I say, the Second Coming of Jesus Christ is not put in the Bible to entertain you. It is put in the Bible to do something to your life. It'll produce two things in your life. Number one, it will produce the inward look of preparation.

Now, I want to show you something. Take your Bible and turn to First John chapter three. Do you know that every time in the Bible you have a prophetic utterance, you have a practical application that accompanies that prophetic utterance? All right, notice First John 3:2,3 - the inward look of preparation - "Beloved, now are we the sons of God, and it doth not yet appear what we shall be: but we know that when he shall appear, we shall be like him: for we shall see him as he is." All right, that's the prophetic utterance. Notice the practical application in verse three: "Every man that hath this hope in him purifieth himself, even as he is pure."

You listen to me, teenager. There is not a saved teenager in this building today who is looking for the Second Coming of Christ who feeds on rock music. That's an impossibility.

I was preaching in Memphis, Tennessee. The last night of the meeting a lady brought a great big bag of rock records to the pastor. She said, "Pastor, I am not a teenager but I want this garbage out of my house." Listen to me. If you let your children listen to rock music, parent, you're not right with God! Did you get that? Underline it and mark it in red. If your children listen to rock music with your knowledge, you're not right with God!

So, the lady said, "Pastor, I want you to break these things." So the pastor, before breaking the records, turned over the record jacket on top and he read the inscription. Listen to what it said. "In the beginning, man created God. In the likeness of man made he God." And as he read that, there was a groan all over that auditorium. You know what one phoney in that Christian day school said? He said, "I don't know why my preacher's breaking those rock records. I wish he'd give them to me. I could put 'em to good use." That young man was in no way looking for the Second Coming of Jesus Christ. No way!

Now, my dear friend, if you are looking for the Second Coming of Jesus Christ, how in the world can you allow R-rated videos to come into your house? How in the world can you let HBO come into your living room, if you are looking for the Second Coming of Christ? It is to clean up our lives so we will not be ashamed when He comes again. If He came right now, would you be ashamed to have Him see the things you have around your house? It'll produce the inward look of preparation.

Number two: it'll produce the outward look of occupation.

Luke 19:13 - "And he called his ten servants, and delivered them ten pounds, and said unto them, Occupy till I come."

Romans 13:11,12 - "And that, knowing the time, that now it is high time to awake out of sleep: for now is our own salvation nearer than when we believed. The night is far spent, the day is at hand: let us therefore cast off the works of darkness, and let us put on the armour of light."

Now it seems to me like the closer we get to the Second Coming, the more that God's people would be involved in getting others to Jesus Christ. Doesn't that seem logical? But I want to ask you, is it that way today? I believe the greatest paradox in the Bible is Matthew 24:12. It says, "And because iniquity shall abound, the love of many shall wax cold." Doesn't it seem that when iniquity is abounding, the love of many would wax hot? But, is it that way today? There has never been a day in the history of the Church of Jesus Christ when we have been taken up by materialism as we do today! And God says, the closer we get to the Second

Coming we oughta realize that material things are only a vehicle for doing the will of God.

You know I preach six hundred times a year, an average of twice a day. And I'm honest with you, ladies and gentlemen, many times I get up in the pulpit and my mind is spinning a hundred miles an hour. Brother Brubaker, on two occasions after a service, has fainted with exhaustion. There have been many times I've preached with a 103 degree temperature. And, my dear friend, do you know why we do that? Because I believe that we don't have much time and this is an urgent message. And, brother, we're fiddling while Rome is burning! Why in the world, if we are looking for the Second Coming of Christ, are we taken up with a material world? You know what I find, Pastor, in every country to which I go? The closer that country is like America, the less results we have in that country. Now, what do I mean? The more they get taken up with the material world, the less results we have. And, brother, we have more people saved when we go to the primitive countries. That's where people are hungry because they have not been lulled to sleep in a material world. And I'm convinced of this with all of my heart: the reason why we are not getting more young people to go to Bible college from our Christian schools and go out into God's service is because we parents have showered everything materially upon our children. Man, they've got radios, they've got VCR's, they've got video games, they've got motorcycles, they've got automobiles. What in the world interests them spiritually?

I remember preaching in Garland, Texas, and there was a young man in that school who would not listen to anything I said. I tried every way in the world to get him to look at me. If I stood on my head and gargled peanut butter, he still wouldn't look at me. After the service was over, the pastor came to me and said, "Ron, do you know why he doesn't listen to you or anybody else who preaches in our chapel?" He said, "His parents gave him a brand new BMW automobile on his sixteenth birthday. And there is nothing spiritual that interests that young man." I believe with all of my heart that if those parents are saved, one day they are going to rue the day they ever gave him that BMW automobile. And, my dear friend, we need to be teaching our children that there is nothing more important in life than serving Almighty God!

A young lady came forward in Tuscon, Arizona and her Christian mother said, "Honey, I am so disappointed in your decision tonight. You've given your life tonight for full-time Christian service. What a waste. What a waste." She continued, "Now, you know Mother always wanted a career for you. These Bible colleges are so inferior and I'm so disappointed with your decision tonight." God pity that Christian parent!

Now, I mean this. If my daughters married the President of the United States, Ron Comfort would be disappointed. Why? I'm not rearing my daughters to be the wife of the President of the United States. I am rearing my daughters to serve God Almighty! And I am praying constantly, "God, keep my three daughters morally and spiritually pure until one day three preacher boys come along and marry them." And I mean this: I would rather see my daughter in a grass hut living in the jungles of Africa in the will of God than to see my daughter married to a business executive out of the will of God and see my grandchildren every week-end of my life. Parent, I want to ask you, when is the last time you got down on your knees and said, "Oh God, call my children into your service."

Do you know why the day of fearless gospel preachers is gone? Because the day of praying mothers has long since gone. And I challenge every parent in this building tonight to say, "Dear God, on June 25, 1986, I am going to begin praying for You to thrust my children into the fields of God."

Hey, when we were in Kenya, Africa, the missionary said, "Brother Comfort, I've been here thirteen years and I have never had one door close in my face in thirteen years. I have never seen a person refuse a gospel tract. Why, last year alone, our local church distributed five million tracts. You go down the streets of Nairobi, or any other place in Kenya, take a handful of tracts, throw them out the window and the Kenyans will swarm to them like flies swarm to sugar." He said, "You talk about liberty. I can go in the junior high, the high school, the grade schools. I can preach, give an invitation and there are no strings attached."

I'll never forget the second time we were there. Mel Reed, a pastor from Canada was with us. We were having a meeting there in Nairobi and some men from the military came and said, "Would you have a service for our military men?" I said, "Well, we'd be glad to. Is there any time you could schedule it, except the time when our services are going on?" They said, "No, we're sorry, it has to be on a Thursday night." I said, "Brother Mel, you're not preaching in the meeting. Would you go?" He said, "I'd be glad to go."

That night I have never seen Mel Reed so excited in all my life. Mel Reed is a fellow who's never at a loss for words. But, when he came back from that service, he couldn't stand still and he couldn't talk straight. I said, "Mel, what in the world is it?" He said, "Wha...wha...I'm not an evangelist. But I preached tonight and over one hundred, over one hundred, received Jesus Christ as their Lord and Saviour!"

The military men came back to us and said, "We've got to have another service at the military base." So, the next week we went and they said, "Now, there won't be as many there. Many of them have gone home for the weekend. But, we've got to have another service!" Do you know that night I preached to about four hundred military people. At least seventy-five adults came that night to get saved! A hundred and eighty-five adults in two services! What am I saying?

Time after time we would go into a grass hut out in the boon docks. Here was a mud and manure floor. I would get down on my knees and lead a black man to Jesus Christ and there would be a cow, or a goat or a calf come walking beside me. I'll tell you what, teenager. You can take your Trans Am automobile. You give me a grass hut in the will of God any day! Any day! And what I am saying is that it is a shame that the work of Jesus Christ is limited by money and by manpower! If Jesus is coming again soon, we oughta say, "Here's my life, Lord. I'm gonna invest it in Your service."

It Is A Separating Event

All right, number one, it's a sure event. Number two, it's a sudden event. Number three, it's a SEPARATING EVENT. Please go back to First Thessalonians, chapter four and the latter part of verse sixteen. It says, "for the dead (underline this) IN CHRIST shall rise first, then we which are alive and remain shall be caught up together with them in the clouds." There's a qualifying phrase, two words, those who are "in Christ." Are you "in" Christ tonight, ladies and gentlemen?

The first seven years of my life I was in the Roman Catholic Church. For the next eight years of my life I was in a Southern Baptist church. But I was as lost as a Southern Baptist as I was as a Roman Catholic. Do you know that I went all over North Carolina singing for a Southern Baptist evangelist in his revival meetings? If Jesus had come during those eight years, I'd have been left behind. I was not in Jesus Christ. Are you "in" Jesus Christ tonight?

I preached in Kansas City, Kansas, and a man came to me and he said, "Brother Comfort, three years ago on Easter Sunday morning when you were here, I was saved." He said, "Let me tell you my story. I had been a deacon in this fundamental Baptist church for fifteen years, but as an eleven year old boy I made a profession to get my mom and dad off my back. For fifteen years the folks in this church did not know that I was an unsaved deacon." He said, "Don't you think it took a lot of swallowing my pride to come down an aisle and tell them that for fifteen years I had been an unsaved deacon?" I believe with all of my heart that if the rapture came tonight there would be people left behind in this building whose parents would be appalled as they went up and their children were left behind. There are kids in this school who think you're gonna hang on to your mom and daddy's coat tail when the rapture comes. You're not gonna do it. You're not gonna do it.

Hey, here's a man and his wife in bed together. Jesus may come in the middle of the night. The wife's saved and the husband's not. All right, what happens? The wife goes to meet Jesus. The next morning he gets up and sees her bed clothes lying unnaturally behind. So he goes to the kitchen, "Honey, are you in there?" She's not there. He goes to the living room, "Honey, are you in there?" She's not there. Why? She's with Christ. She's gone. He's not. He's left behind.

Perhaps the most often asked question about prophesy to me is this: "Will there be any saved in the tribulation?" Now let me answer that question. Take your Bible and turn to II Thessalonians chapter three please, verses nine through twelve. First of all, let me say that Romans 11:26 and 27 says that all Israel will be saved. And then Revelation 7:9-17 says through the preaching of the Jews, a multitude of Gentiles which no man can number will be saved. But let me tell you something, friend, it won't be anybody in this building tonight. You know why? You've had a chance. You're not gonna have a chance in the Tribulation Period.

You'll find this principle in the Word of God. Before God sends the judgment, He always sends a prophet along to announce that judgment is coming. Now listen. When the judgment comes, nobody who has had a chance to repent before the judgment has a probationary period during this judgment. Did anybody have a chance to repent when the floods came on the land? No, sir! Did anybody in Sodom and Gomorrah have a chance to repent when God almighty sent fire and brimstone? No, sir! When God rained plagues in the land of Egypt, did anybody have a chance to repent? No, sir! And you will not have a chance in the Tribulation. You've had your chance now. Now let me back that up with Scripture. II Thessalonians two, verses nine through twelve, speaking of the Antichrist: "Even him, whose coming is after the working of Satan with all power and signs and lying wonders, and with all deceivableness of unrighteousness in them that perish; because they received not the love of the truth, that they might be saved. And for this cause God will send them strong dillusion, that they should believe a lie; that they all might be damned who believed not the truth, but had pleasure in unrighteousness." Don't you see what that means, friend? If Jesus comes tonight and you are left behind, your eternal destiny's already set. You have a chance now. You'll not have a chance then.

Let me ask you a question. Who was the oldest man that ever lived? Anybody? (audience response: "Methuselah") How long did he live (audience: "969 years") Nine hundred and sixty nine years. Do you know, ladies and gentlemen, that it was Methuselah who was the oldest man that ever lived and that he lived exactly nine hundred and sixty-nine years? Let me give you the background for that.

You see, many times when a man had a child, he would name that child as a direct revelation from God and his name carried a message for the people of the day. And I believe it was like that in the life of Methuselah. Do you know what the name Methuselah means? Listen. It means, "When he is dead it shall be sent." You know what God was doing? He was giving his people a sign. He was saying, "Keep your eyes on that little baby boy, Methuselah, because when he dies, the flood's coming and all hell's gonna break loose on earth." It would seem to me that anybody in their right mind would have watched Methuselah. And when Methuselah got a little sniffle, it would have started a world-wide revival. But they didn't watch Methuselah.

All right now, get it. A man by the name of Enoch had a son, and he named him Methuselah, "when he is dead it shall be sent." When Methuselah was one hundred eighty-two years old, he bore a son whose name was Lamech. Now, listen. When Lamech was one hundred eighty-seven years old, he bore a son whose name was Noah. How much are one hundred eighty-two and one hundred eighty-seven? Three hundred sixty-nine. My friend, do you know how old Noah was when God told him to get into the ark? Are you ready? He was exactly six hundred years old. How much is three hundred sixty-nine plus six hundred? Nine hundred sixty-nine years. It was my contention that the very day that Methuselah died God said unto Noah, "Get into the ark! Get into the ark!". God kept the door open for seven more days. Hey, isn't God so long suffering? And some blasphemer says, "Well, I don't believe a loving God would send a soul to hell!" Well, get it. He gave them nine hundred sixty-nine years to repent, and now he gave them seven more days to see that Methuselah was dead and the judgment was coming. Hey, did anybody get into the ark during the seven days? No, sir. Who was it that closed the door after those seven days? It was not Noah. It was God. And my dear friend, if Jesus Christ comes tonight during the service and you are left behind, God is going to close the door, your eternal destiny is already settled.

It Is A Sublime Event

It's a sure event, it's a sudden event, it's a separating event. In closing, number four: It's a SUBLIME EVENT. Will you notice, please, I Thessalonians four, verse seventeen. It says, "Then we which are alive and remain shall be caught up together with them in the clouds to meet the Lord in the air, and so shall we ever be with the Lord." It's a sublime event.

Here's an interesting thing. There are two Greek words for the word "air." A man can go to Mt. Olympus and stand on that mountain and point upward. The Greeks have a word for "air" that means "above the mountain tops." He can stand on that same mountain and he can point downward. The Greeks have a word for "air" that means "below the mountain tops". Now get this. Do you know where Jesus is coming to get his little children? He's not coming in the air above the mountain tops. He's coming in the air below the mountain tops. You say, "Why is that important?" Ephesians 2:2 says, "The Devil is the prince of the power of the air." You know what air he's the prince of the power of? He's the prince of the power of the air below the mountain tops. We sing the song, "He's got the whole world in his hands." I'm sorry, God doesn't have this wide world in his hands. And this is not the kingdom of God. I John 5:19 - "The whole world lies in the hands of the wicked one." This is the kingdom of Satan, but get it. One day King Jesus is going to invade Satan's domain. He's gonna snatch away his little children, and so shall we ever be with the Lord.

It's going to mean three things. Number one, it'll mean the reunion of loved ones. Many years ago my wife carried a baby for over ten months. She had previously had two miscarriages. So we were very apprehensive. I thought the baby was going to be born deformed, and, if it were, I thought I ought to be home at that time to comfort my wife. So, I canceled my next meeting, stayed home all week, and the baby still wasn't born. The next week I had a meeting that had been scheduled for four years north of Grand Rapids, Michigan. I knew I had to honor that commitment, so I went to the meeting. Sunday night, after the service, my mother-in-law called me. She said, "Ron, Joyce is going to have the baby, but the baby cannot live. The doctor says the top of the baby's head has not been formed and the baby cannot possibly live." She said, "I think you oughta try to get here before the baby is born to comfort Joyce at that time of grief." So, immediately, I took off and started driving all night long. I got home at six o'clock in the morning. The baby was born at three o'clock in the morning. May I say that, after ten minutes, little Rachel Jan went on to ornament heaven. Do you know my wife carried Rachel Jan for ten and a half months? She never got to touch her, she never got to see her, she never got to hold her. I stood by the grave of my little daughter, Rachel Jan, and my pastor read First Corinthians 15:51 through 58. It never meant as much to me in my life as it did that day, Brother Smith. As I stood there I said in my heart, "Rachel, honey, I love you with all my heart. I've never seen you before, but, on the way up when Jesus comes, I'm gonna tell you I love you."

You know, one of the greatest relaxations of my life was when my daughters were little. We'd go back to the trailer after I'd get through preaching and they'd put on their bedclothes and run and jump at me and they'd say, "Daddy, it's love time! It's love time!" And they'd all three jump on me together and we'd hug and kiss and slobber all over each other and they'd say, "Daddy, I love you." And I'd reciprocate and say, "I love you." I used to look forward to seeing Robyn, when she was a three year old waddler, waddle out of the nursery. I'd be standing at the front of the auditorium and I'd see that little three year old waddle down the aisle. And I knew what she was going to do. I knew she'd come up to me and grab a hold of my knees (now I'm just about to the place where I'm gonna have to grab a hold of hers!), and she'd look up into my face, and she'd say, "Daddy, I WUV OU!" And, I'll tell you, when she said that, I'd tingle all over. I mean that.

I wish you could listen to our trailer before we go to bed at night. Sounds like the Walton's. That's right. When Rhonda was home, she'd lead it off and she'd say, "Daddy, I love you. Mommy, I love you. Good night everybody." Then Robyn would say, "Daddy, I love you. Mommy, I love you. Good night, everybody." And then Rebecca would say, "Daddy, I love you. Mommy, I love you. Good night, everybody." And then, sometimes they'd say, "All right, let's do it again!" So, they'd go through it again. "Daddy, I love you. Mommy, I love you. Good night, everybody." After going through it the second time, sometimes they'd say, "All right now, on three, all together. One, two, three. "Daddy, I love you. Mommy, I love you. Good night, everybody." And do you know what, friend? Never one time in all of my life have I ever been tempted to say, "Would you shut up and go to sleep?" Never one time. Oh, I love it. I love it.

And that day, as I stood by my little daughter's grave, I said, "Rachel, honey, on the way up, I'm gonna tell you I love you." When we lived in West Virginia, every time I was home from meetings, I would go by that cemetery out in the country. Our bank was out there, and I mean this. I never went by that cemetery but what I said in my heart, "Rachel, honey, it's not going to be too long now." The reunion with our loved ones.

Number two, it'll mean the redemption of our bodies.

First Corinthians 15:49 - "As we have born the image of the earthy, we shall also bear the image of the heavenly."

Philippians 3:21 - "Who shall also change our vile bodies that it may be fashioned like unto his glorious body."

Romans 8:23 - "And we ourselves, groan within ourselves, waiting for the adoption, to wit, the redemption of our bodies."

I'm aware that many of you in this building tonight have not had a good eight hour a night's sleep in years and years. Your pastor is in constant pain, whether you know it or not. I heard him say the other day, as he spoke to the young men, "I very, very seldom ever sleep more than four hours at a time." And only God knows how many of you go to bed at night taking aspirins to soothe your arthritis. You go home and have a migraine headache. Let me tell you something, friend, the moment you see Jesus you're going to realize, "Hey, I'm living in a body that is totally incapable of experiencing any type of pain." A body just like Jesus, all but the nail prints, and they belong to Him.

Many years ago I preached at Calvary Baptist Church in Normal, Illinois, for the first time. I'd heard so much about Marilyn Weniger, the pastor's wife, who contracted MS in her late 20's. And I'd heard what a tremendous testimony she was. When I came to the meeting for the first time, I would watch Marilyn come in each night with a walker. And I never watched her come in but I watched her face grimace with pain with almost every step. I'd look at her night after night and I'd say in my heart, "Marilyn, if Jesus Christ comes tonight, that walker's gonna be in the past."

The second time I was there, she did not come in with a walker; she could not even come every night. She came about half the time and she had to be wheeled in in a wheel chair. And, honestly, I never saw Marilyn Weniger wheeled into that building but what I thought, "Marilyn, if Jesus Christ comes tonight, that wheel chair is going to be history."

The third time I was at Calvary Baptist Church, Marilyn could not come to the services at all. She couldn't come with a walker, couldn't come in a wheel chair; she was confined to bed. She'd be laying in that bed just wasting away like a vegetable. But, do you know what? Every night I would preach, Marilyn Weniger would have the phone by her ear listening to the services over the telephone. And I never preached but what I thought, "Marilyn, if Jesus Christ comes tonight, that MS is all going to be in the past and you're going to have a body just like Jesus."

Finally, number three, it'll mean the revelation of Jesus Christ. Years ago I was preaching in Indiana. The pastor got up ten minutes before I was to preach and he said, "Folks, I want some testimonies. Why are you looking forward to going to heaven?" And I remember, as though it were last night, a big, burly man stood up and said, "Ladies and gentlemen, I'm looking forward to going to heaven because I've got a praying mother that's in heaven tonight. She prayed for years for me to be saved and went to be with the Lord before I ever got saved." He continued, "When I get to heaven, I'm gonna run down the streets of gold, I'm gonna wrap my arms around my mother's neck and I'm gonna say, Thank you, Mother, for praying for me." He sat down. A woman stood up and said, "Pastor, nobody in this building knows the vacuum in my life since God saw fit to take my child. You remember standing at the grave side of my little baby and the most important reason why I wanna go to heaven is to see my little baby again and be reconciled to that baby." She sat down. A man stood up and said, "Pastor, you know that Wednesday night after Wednesday night, I've asked prayer for my prodigal son. And only God knows how many times I've gone to bed weeping and tossing and turning over my prodigal son." He said, "Pastor, to me, the most wonderful thing about heaven is that there'll be no heartache there, there'll be no more sorrow there, there'll be no prodigal sons there." But, honestly, as I sat there on the platform, I sat there with a heavy heart. You know why? In ten minutes, nobody stood up and said, "I wanna go to heaven because I wanna see Jesus!" Nobody said that. My friend, I don't care about the fine mansions! I don't care about the streets of gold! I wanna go to heaven because I wanna see Jesus!

Fanny Crosby, the greatest songwriter the church has ever known, was blinded at the age of six months. She never liked to be reminded of her blindness. One day, D.L. Moody was talking to her. She was well into her 90's, and he said, "Miss Crosby, if you had one desire of your life fulfilled before you breathed your last breath, what would it be?" He said that he knew with all of his heart she'd say, "Mr. Moody, I would just like to see a ray of sunshine." But she didn't say that. You know what she said? She said, "Mr. Moody, if I had one desire of my life fulfilled it would be this: that I would remain blind until I breathed my last breath so that the first person to gladden my eyes would be the Son of God, Himself." No wonder the songwriter could write:

> I want to see my Saviour first of all,
>   Before on any others I would call.
> And then, for countless days,
>   On His dear face I'll gaze.
> I want to see my Saviour first of all.

> (Singing):
> When my life work is ended,
>   And I cross the swelling tide,
> When the bright and cloudless morning I shall see;
>   I shall know my Redeemer
> When I reach the other side,
>   And His smile will be the first to welcome me.

> I shall know Him, I shall know Him,
>   As redeemed by His side I shall stand;
> I shall know Him, I shall know Him
>   By the print of the nails in His hand.

Do you know who wrote that song? Fanny Crosby. Let's bow our heads as we pray.

LIN CROXTON

10

What A Change

BIOGRAPHICAL SKETCH

Lin Croxton
(1943 -)

A Virginian by birth on January 27, 1943, Linwood Marvin Croxton made a profession of faith at the age of eleven years during a revival meeting in a country church near his home. Shortly after his profession of faith he was baptized and surrendered to preach. However, he struggled in his Christian life as a teenager. It was after his Junior year of high school that he received the assurance of his salvation, and yielded to the Lord. He left home to finish his senior year of high school at Bob Jones Academy in Greenville, South Carolina.

He graduated from Bob Jones Academy in 1961 and went on to the University graduating in 1964 with a major in Bible and a minor in Greek. He then received his M.A. degree in Bible in 1967.

While a student at Bob Jones University, he held various offices in Chi Alpha Pi Literary Society including president. Lin was also active in week-end extension ministries including a Christian Servicemen's Center in Augusta, Georgia. In fact, this author had the joy of traveling with him and some of the other students on those week-end trips to Augusta, though my extension ministry was not in the servicemen's center but in a nearby country church. Some of Lin's other extension ministries included leading the street meeting ministry in Anderson, South Carolina, and serving as an interim pastor for Fellowship Baptist Church in Anderson, South Carolina.

For six and a half years he served as Pastor of the First Baptist Church in Frederick, Maryland, where he saw the church attendance more than double. While there, he edited a weekly column in the local newspaper in addition to a monthly church paper which went to every boxholder in the county. He also conducted a weekly radio broadcast and saw the church through a major building program with a new 300-seat auditorium.

In January, 1974, Lin entered the ministry of full-time itinerant evangelism. Since that time he has conducted more than five hundred crusades in some thirty-six states and several foreign countries including Canada, Mexico, Antigua, Haiti, Puerto Rico, and Brazil.

Although busy as an evangelist, Lin was used of God to direct the Bible To Youth Camp in Mt. Union, Pennsylvania, for more than six years. In 1992, he accepted a temporary position as Assistant Pastor at his home church, Calvary Baptist Church in Simpsonville, South Carolina, while continuing to take a limited number of meetings. After three years, he re-entered the ministry of evangelism on a full-time basis in 1995.

He has a great burden to help missionaries and small works throughout America as well as foreign countries.

Lin has memorized more than three thousand verses of Scripture. His wife, Carol, also a graduate of Bob Jones University, travels with her husband and conducts special children's classes. The Croxton's have three children and make their home in Simpsonville, South Carolina. KWL

Lin Croxton
798 Powderhorn Drive
Simpsonville, SC 29681

WHAT A CHANGE
Lin Croxton

Turn in your Bibles to Romans 6 and I want to read Romans 6:11-18 but will be considering primarily one verse -- verse 17. The message is entitled "What A Change" and Romans 6:17 talks about the change that takes place in a person's life when they come to Christ as Saviour, but we want to read that verse in context, so we'll read beginning with Romans 6:11. Romans 6:11 "Likewise, reckon ye also yourselves to be dead indeed unto sin, but alive unto God through Jesus Christ, our Lord. Let not sin, therefore, reign in your mortal body, that ye should obey it in the lusts thereof. Neither yield ye your members as instruments of unrighteousness unto sin: but yield yourselves unto God, as those that are alive from the dead, and your members as instruments of righteousness unto God. For sin shall not have dominion over you: for ye are not under the law, but under grace. What then? shall we sin, because we are not under the law, but under grace? God forbid. Know ye not, that to whom ye yield yourselves servants to obey, his servants ye are to whom ye obey whether of sin unto death, or of obedience unto righteousness? But God be thanked, that ye were the servants of sin, but ye have obeyed from the heart that form of doctrine which was delivered you. Being then made free from sin, ye became the servants of righteousness." Romans 6:17 is a tremendous verse in the Bible, I believe. I want us to examine that verse and notice three important facts I believe this verse expresses to us. First of all, would you notice with me that praising God is encouraged.

Praising God Encouraged

Praising God is encouraged. The verse begins by saying "But God be thanked..." But God be thanked. Oft-times of course, at Thanksgiving, we remember to give God thanks but everyday should be a day of believers giving thanks to the Lord. The Bible tells us we ought to give thanks, we ought to praise the Lord, we ought to exalt the Lord, we ought to extol the Lord.

I want you to hold your place there in Romans 6, if you would for a moment, and turn back to the Psalms and I want you to notice with me the last few Psalms. Find Psalm 144 and I want you to notice just the beginning of each one of these Psalms, Psalm 144 through the end, and notice how the Bible wants God to be praised, exalted, extolled, thanked.

The writer gives an expression of adoration to the Lord. For example in Psalm 144:1 -- The Bible says "Blessed be the Lord my strength, which teacheth my hands to war, and my fingers to fight:" Psalm 145:1-2 -- "I will extol thee, my God, O King; and I will bless thy name forever and ever. Everyday will I bless thee; and I will praise thy name forever and ever." Psalm 146:1-2 -- "Praise ye the Lord. Praise the Lord, O my soul. While I live will I praise the Lord: I will sing praises unto my God while I have any being." Psalm 147:1 -- "Praise ye the Lord: for it is good to sing praises unto our God; for it is pleasant; and praise is comely." Psalm 148:1-5 -- "Praise ye the Lord. Praise ye the Lord from the heavens: praise him in the heights. Praise ye him, all his angels: praise ye him, all ye hosts. Praise ye him, sun and moon: praise him, all ye stars of light. Praise him, ye heavens of heavens, and ye waters that be above the heavens. Let them praise the name of the Lord: for he commanded and they were created." Psalm 149:1 -- "Praise ye the Lord. Sing unto the Lord a new song, and his praise in the congregation of saints." And then Psalm 150 -- "Praise ye the Lord. Praise God in his sanctuary: praise him in the firmament of his power. Praise him for his mighty acts: praise him according to his excellent greatness. Praise him with the sound of the trumpet: praise him with the psaltery and harp. Praise him with the timbrel and dance: praise him with stringed instruments and organs. Praise him upon the loud cymbals: praise him upon the high sounding cymbals. Let everything that hath breath praise the Lord. Praise ye the Lord." I sort of get the idea that God wants to be praised and I think we ought to come with praise and thanksgiving and exaltation. The Bible here in Psalm 148 talked about the heavens and the waters and the stars and the sun and the moon praising the Lord. But Psalm 150 ended by saying "Let everything that hath breath praise the Lord." Very simply, if you have breath, praise the Lord! If you don't have breath, don't bother doing it. I don't think you'll be around very long if you don't have any breath. Let everything that hath breath praise the Lord. Let God be thanked or praised.

I read in the New Testament where the Bible talks about praising God or being grateful or being thankful. For example, in Romans 1 -- the indictment against the human race, Paul records and says about people in Romans 1:21 -- "...neither were they thankful..." neither were they thankful. 2 Timothy 3:2 tells us one of the characteristics of the last days before Jesus comes is that people will be unthankful. The Bible tells us in Philippians 4:6, when we pray, to be careful for nothing or don't worry about anything, but in everything with prayer and supplication, with thanksgiving, let your requests be made known unto the Lord. God wants us to come and ask for things but he also wants us to praise him and to thank him for what He has done.

But when I think about praising the Lord, I think about some verses over in the last book of the Bible, especially in Revelation chapters 4 and 5 where the Bible describes the scene in heaven and Christ sitting on the throne. Let me share with you just a few verses from those two chapters how the Lord wants to be praised and adored, thanked and exalted. For example, Revelation 4:8-11, the Bible says "And the four beasts had each of them six wings about him; and they were full of eyes within: and they rest not day and night, saying, Holy, holy, holy, Lord God Almighty, which was, and is, and is to come. And when those beasts give glory and honour and thanks to him that sat on the throne, who liveth forever and ever, the four and twenty elders fall down before him that sat on the throne, and worship him that liveth for ever and ever, and cast their crowns before the throne, saying, "Thou art worthy, O Lord, to receive glory and honour and power: for thou hast created all things, and for thy pleasure they are and were created." Chapter 5:8-14 -- "And when he had taken the book, the four beasts and four and twenty elders fell down before the Lamb, having every one of them harps, and golden vials full of odours, which are the prayers of saints. And they sung a new song, saying, Thou art worthy to take the book, and to open the seals thereof: for thou wast slain, and hast redeemed us to God by thy blood out of every kindred, and tongue, and people, and nation; And hast made us unto our God kings and priests: and we shall reign on the earth. And I beheld, and I heard the voice of many angels round about the throne, and the beasts, and the elders: and the number of them was ten thousand times ten thousand, and thousands of thousands; Saying with a loud voice, Worthy is the Lamb that was slain to receive power, and riches, and wisdom, and strength, and honour, and glory, and blessing. And every creature which is in heaven, and on the earth, and under the earth, and such as are in the sea, and all that are in them, heard I saying, Blessing, and honour, and glory, and power, be unto him that sitteth upon the throne, and unto the Lamb for ever and ever. And the four beasts said, Amen. And the four and twenty elders fell down and worshipped him that liveth for ever and ever." The Bible pictures a scene in heaven and it pictures the angels; it pictures the redeemed; it pictures all creation giving praise and honour and glory and thanks and worship to the One who sits on the throne. I think sometimes as fundamental Baptists we don't praise the Lord like we ought and one of the reasons, or excuses we might have, is because we see some of the crazy things Charismatics and other people do and their supposed praise to the Lord but, yet today, we need to realize as Christians, saved people, we need to have grateful hearts. We need to praise the Lord. We need to thank God for what He has done for us and have a grateful heart. So here in Romans 6, we see first of all that praising God is encouraged. It begins by saying "But God be thanked." But God be thanked.

Past And Present Condition Contrasted

But notice the second thing, if you would, and I want to dwell on this for a while. Not only is praising God encouraged but, secondly, our past and our present condition is contrasted. <u>Our past and our present condition is contrasted.</u> The verse continues after it says, "But God be thanked" by saying, "that ye <u>were</u> the servants of sin, but ye have obeyed from the heart that form of doctrine which was delivered you." The Bible says you were the servants of sin and that's in the past tense. I read over in 1 Corinthians 6 and the Bible tells me in verses 9, 10 and 11 those that will not inherit the Kingdom of God. The Bible says, "Be not deceived: neither fornicators, nor idolaters, no adulterers, nor effeminate, nor abusers of themselves with mankind, Nor thieves, nor covetous, nor drunkards, nor revilers, nor extortioners, shall inherit the kingdom of God." But 1 Corinthians 6:11 is one of my favorite verses because it says "such <u>were</u> some of you" such were some of you but now you are washed, and sanctified and justified. In other words we are cleansed from those sins. Some time in the past we were the servants of sin and thank God for that change that takes place when a person does trust Christ as personal Saviour.

Now I want you to hold your place in Romans 6 and I want you to turn to another one of my favorite chapters in the Bible, Ephesians chapter 2. Now if there are any verses in Ephesians chapter 2 you already know, it's probably verses 8 and 9 and they are tremendous verses. There are other wonderful verses in Ephesians 2 besides those two verses and I want you to notice with me in Ephesians 2 the contrast we're talking about between the state we're in before salvation and what we're like after we're saved. In Ephesians 2, I have underlined four phrases; four phrases that speak about the same thing. It speaks about our condition before salvation. Here are the four phrases. In verse 2, I have underlined the phrase "in time past." And then in verse 3, I've underlined the phrase "in times past." And then down in verse 11, I've underlined the phrase again "in time past." And, then in verse 12 "at that time." Four phrases are used -- "in time past" "in times past" "in time past" "at that time", the Bible is speaking about our condition before salvation. Now how does it describe that condition before I was saved? Let's go back and examine it.

Beginning with verse 1, it says before salvation, we are dead. "dead in trespasses and sins." Verse 2 further describes "we walked according to the course of this world." That is, we follow after things that are wicked, things that are wrong. The verse elaborates -- "according to the prince of the power of the air." That's Satan; we follow after his leading. "The spirit that now worketh in the children of disobedience." Another characteristic; we're disobedient as unsaved people. And verse 3 further elaborates when it says when we walked in times past in the lust of the flesh -- our conversation or our behavior was in the lust of the flesh. It was after the desires of the flesh. We are children of wrath, even as others. Look at verse 11, the Bible pictures us as "Gentiles in the flesh." We're uncircumcised. Verse 12 tells us further, we were without Christ, we were aliens, we were strangers, we had no hope, we were without God in this world. What a terrible description of unsaved man. Dead in our sins, following the prince of the power of the air, following the lust of the flesh, telling us we're aliens, that we're without Christ, without God and therefore, we were without hope. Now if that were all we talked about today, that would be a terrible description.

Notice something else in Ephesians 2. There are two phrases I have circled. For example, in verse 4 I've circled the first two words. It says, "But God." And then in verse 13 the first few words, "But now." What a wonderful change that makes when God does come into a person's life. "But God;" "But now." What is our condition when we trust Christ as Saviour? We've seen a description before salvation let's notice what it's like in the matter of salvation.

I mentioned earlier that if there were any verses you know in Ephesians 2 it was probably verses 8 and 9 which say, "For by grace are ye saved through faith; and that not of yourselves: it is the gift of God: Not of works, lest any man should boast." I thank God for his grace. Some people define grace as God's unmerited favor. I believe it goes much further than that. Not only is grace God's unmerited favor but it's the fact that I deserve to receive condemnation and separation from God in hell but God shows me that mercy, that grace and saves me in spite of my sin, saves me in spite of my wickedness; God changes my life.

But you know, there's something better than the grace of God. Now, don't get excited. I want to share something with you. There is something better than the grace of God. Hold your place in Ephesians 2 and turn back to Romans 5 for a moment and notice something better than grace. Romans 5:17 speaks of it. Romans 5:17 says "For if by one man's offense death reigned by one; much more they which receive abundance of grace..." I said there is something better than grace and that is "abundance of grace." That means God never runs out of it. There's an abundance of it. Thank God you can still preach to people today and still tell them the grace of God will still save them.

But will you notice something else? There's still something better than the abundance of grace. Back in Ephesians 1:7, the Bible says this "In whom we have redemption through his blood, the forgiveness of sins, according to the riches of his grace." You see I can have an abundance of certain things but I may not be rich in those things. Sometimes at Christmastime there is an abundance of food, the only problem is it can run out, it can spoil. But thank God, God's grace is always there abounding but also we have the riches of his grace. But, that's not the greatest yet. Notice with me something yet to come.

Go back to Ephesians 2 and look at verse 7. We have experienced his grace, we see the abundance of his grace, we're redeemed through the riches of his grace, but notice verse 7 "That in the ages to come he might show the exceeding riches of his grace." Listen you haven't seen anything yet. You've experienced his grace in salvation. We experience the abundance of it and the riches of it but the Bible says in the ages to come, when we're with the Lord, he will give us the exceeding riches of his grace in his kindness toward us through Christ Jesus. Thank God for his grace. Thank God for salvation.

Look further in chapter 2, notice the change that does take place when a person is saved. We saw that we're dead in sins but according to verse 1 God quickens us or God makes us alive. We come to verse 4, the Bible says that "God is rich in mercy." And then the Bible tells us in verse 6, not only does he quicken us but he raises us up together. You see the wonderful truth of the Word of God is that when you trusted Jesus Christ as your personal Saviour, the Bible in Romans 6 pictures you as dead with Christ, but it pictures you here as having been quickened or raised but not only that, the Bible says that we sit together in heavenly places in Christ Jesus. Verse 13 says, "we are made nigh by the blood of Christ." Verse 16 says that we are reconciled to God. Verse 19 says that we are no longer strangers and foreigners, but fellow citizens with the saints. What a wonderful change takes place when a person is saved. Our past and our present condition is contrasted.

Before salvation, the Bible says, we are servants of sin. Do you realize something important today? Everybody in the world is a servant. The question is, who's servant are you? How do you determine that? Verse 16 of Romans 6 gives you the criteria. Verse 16 says, "Know ye not, that to whom ye yield yourselves servants to obey, his servants ye are to whom ye obey; whether of sin unto death, or of obedience unto righteousness." There are some who are still servants of sin. Some are still in that unsaved state -- still lost in their sin. But thank God as we come to Christ, we become the servants of righteousness. Let me ask you today, whose servant are you? Verse 16 says the one that you yield yourself to obey. In fact, five different times in Romans 6, the Bible uses the word yield and says we are to yield ourselves to the Lord. Everyone of us here knows what it means to yield. When you drive down the road and you come to a yield sign you know what it means. You don't obey it but you know what it means anyway. It means to give your right over to somebody else.

And as a child of God I am to yield my rights over to Christ and surrender to him to be an effective servant of the Lord.

Verse 17 goes on to say "That ye were the servants of sin, but ye have obeyed from the heart." You have obeyed from the heart. What does that mean? 2 Thessalonians 1:8 says the Lord is coming in flaming fire taking vengeance on them that know not God and have not obeyed the gospel of our Lord Jesus Christ. You obey the gospel -- understand you are a sinner, trust Christ as Saviour, then are redeemed, made right as we obey from the heart. And, by the way, it must come from the heart. It's not just an acknowledgement from the head. It's to believe with our heart the truths of the gospel. Romans 10 talks about the resurrection and we're to believe with our heart that God raised him from the dead. I'm concerned because I believe there are people even in fundamental churches that have given doctrinal assent or acknowledgement of certain creeds and doctrines that perhaps have never been born again.

Sometimes you can talk to people and you ask them "Have you received Christ? Do you believe in Christ?" They respond by saying, "Oh yes, I believe in the Lord." The problem is that some of them believe in the Lord like they believe in George Washington. I think of 3 types of faith, if you want to call it that. You might call one an earthly faith; that is, you give just head knowledge or assent to certain truths. Or there's a second kind; that is, a temporal faith. If someone is driving down the highway and they see a big tractor trailer coming toward them about to crash into them, most anyone would call upon the Lord and ask the Lord to help them or to save them. There have been people when I was a pastor that I visited in the hospital. I had often wished after I had visited them in the hospital that they would keep their promises to the Lord they made while they were in the hospital. Sometimes you talk to people in the hospital and they know they're about ready to die, or they think they are and they call upon the Lord and ask the Lord to save them and then they get well and then they come home. Oft-times they don't think about the Lord anymore until they get sick again. That's just a temporal belief, just a crutch to lean on, just something at the moment that they did not really mean with all their heart. But then there's real saving faith. That's acknowledgment to God that I am a sinner but I turn from my sin to Christ, an act of repentance and faith in Christ. I trust him as my Saviour. We believe in our heart. As the verse says "We obeyed from the heart that form of doctrine (that form of teaching)." By the way, understand this; doctrine is important. There are some people today who say doctrine is not important. I've heard people say what is important is that we just love everybody and be one in the spirit. The Bible says "how can two walk together except they be agreed." And we need to realize that there are certain doctrines that are essential to our salvation. Without them we have no salvation whatsoever. We have to obey from the heart that form of doctrine and notice, "which was delivered you," and that brings us to the third thing in this verse. Not only is praising God encouraged, not only is our past and our present condition contrasted, but would you notice with me that proclaiming the gospel message is implied in this verse.

Proclaiming The Gospel Message

Proclaiming the gospel message is implied in this verse. Now, the Bible says "the form of doctrine which was delivered you." Now understand there is a certain sense in which we have been delivered over to the gospel when we trust Christ. We cast ourselves on him. We believe the message of the gospel but it says here "the doctrine which was delivered you."

I want to show you something very important. Hold your place in Romans 6 and turn to one other Scripture; 1 Corinthians 15. Paul, in Romans 6, talked about the doctrine, the gospel that was delivered you or delivered to you. In 1 Corinthians 15, Paul talks about that gospel, that message, that truth. By the way if you ever looked at a definition of what the gospel is, you'll find it here in 1 Corinthians 15. There's only one Bible definition of the gospel. There is no such thing as the full gospel or the empty gospel, it's either the gospel or it's not the gospel and Paul describes for us in verses 3 and 4 what the gospel is. He says that Christ died for our sins according to Scriptures, that he was buried, and that he rose again the third day according to the Scriptures. That is the gospel. The death of Christ according to Scriptures, his burial, his resurrection according to the Scriptures. That is the gospel. That is the full gospel. That is the complete gospel and Paul says if anybody preaches any other gospel, he is to be accursed. So it's pretty important that we know the gospel here.

Notice what Paul said about the gospel in the first few verses. Here's a good outline to use sometimes. Verse 1 Paul says "I declare unto you the gospel which I preached unto you." Paul said I preached it to you. Secondly, he said "ye have received it." And, thirdly, he says "wherein ye stand." And in verse 2 he says you're saved by it. Concerning the gospel, Paul says, I preached it, you received it, you stand on it, and you're saved by it. But then what does Paul expect those people to do once they have received the gospel? And this is the important application now of Romans 6:17 -- verse 3 "For I delivered unto you first of all that which I also received." Now get that phrase in your mind. "For I delivered unto you first of all that which I also received." Paul said, I received the gospel. And then Paul said, I delivered to you the same gospel that I have received. And that's what it's talking about in Romans 6:17. The form of doctrine which was delivered you. In other words, today if you're saved, you have received the gospel. That's the only way you can get saved. Nothing else saves, other than the gospel of Christ. There is no other salvation and so if you're saved, you have received the gospel. My question to you is this. What are you doing with what you have received? Paul said I received it and now I deliver it unto you. Paul said, I received it, I gave it to somebody else. What should you do once you received it? You should deliver it to someone else.

2 Timothy 2 has a great verse in the Bible that Sunday School teachers and anyone that teaches the Word of God ought to be familiar with. Paul wrote in 2 Timothy 2:2 "And the things that thou hast heard of me among many witnesses, the same commit thou to faithful men, who shall be able to teach others also." You see I'm afraid sometimes in our fundamental churches there are those who come to church and they hear, they take in the Word of God, the Bible says that those things they have heard, they ought to commit to somebody else. Paul said, what I received I delivered to someone else. What kind of delivery service do you have? Probably at Christmastime more people complain about the postal service more than any other time of the year but I'll tell you what will help cure you about complaining about it. Go to a foreign country for a while and live there and you'll come back and be grateful that things get there just a few days later rather than never arrive and, of course, I'm not saying the postal service always delivers. I don't work for the postal department but I am saying this. There is something that they have received from you, you put a stamp on it, you sent a letter, you sent a package, you have entrusted the care of that to them and you've delivered that to them and you expect them to receive that and then deliver it to someone else. Do you know what God expects of us? God gave us a message. Something more important than anything you have mailed in the mail. You've received the gospel of Christ. You know what God wants you to do? God wants you to deliver it to someone else. You have received something. You have received the gospel. Are you delivering that? What kind of delivery service are you from the Lord? Do you complain about the postal service, or about some other people not delivering like they should? I wonder what kind of delivery boy, what kind of delivery woman are you? God has given you a message and God wants you to deliver it to someone else.

Let me close with this illustration that excites me when I think about it. I know a family that had two little children -- one was about five years old and the other one about two years old. They moved from the area where I live to the New England area. On the way to New England, they stopped in New Jersey to visit relatives. The previous summer their daughter, five years of age, attended a children's Bible club and she heard the wordless book story. The wordless book is a book with different colored pages. One page is black and that pictures our sin. Another is red which pictures the blood of Christ, that cleanses from sin. Another page is white which is a picture of our heart made white as snow. This little girl learned the wordless book story. When they went up to New Jersey to visit relatives there were many relatives who were unsaved, adult relatives. And this little girl one day was sitting in the living room with some of her uncles. And she said to one of her uncles, "Can I tell you a story?" What does an adult say when a little girl of five years of age wants to tell you a story? You say "Of course, you can tell me a story." Except this unsaved man didn't know what he was in for. And she began to tell him the story of the wordless book. That his heart was black with sin, then she explained that the red was the blood of Christ and it cleanses the heart from sin and I thought to myself as I heard that story. Here's a five year old girl who heard the gospel message -- whether she really understood much about salvation at that age or not, I don't know -- but I thought to myself, if she can share with a grown uncle the gospel message, why can't we as an adult get the gospel message out as well. What are you doing with what you have received? Realize God has entrusted to you a gospel message and if you're saved, you've received it. But how many deliveries are you making?

Our verse Romans 6:17 says, "but God be thanked that ye were the servants of sin but ye obeyed from the heart that form of doctrine which was delivered you." We have talked about praising God being encouraged, we have talked about our past and present condition being contrasted, we have talked about proclaiming the gospel being implied in these verses.

Let me ask you several questions. First, do you have a grateful heart? Do you express your thanks to God on a regular basis? Secondly, as we read in Ephesians 2 about the those in times past; are you still in that condition? Are you still in your sin, still dead, still after the course of this world, still separated from God, still lost in your sin, or have you been quickened and are now in Christ Jesus? You've experienced his grace. You've experienced his compassion, and now you're made nigh to the blood of Christ, now you're reconciled to God, now you're a fellow citizen of the saints. Which one of those conditions describe you? Are you still the servant of sin? Or are you a servant of Jesus Christ? If not, would you bow your head right now and ask the Lord to save you and he will. Thirdly, if you have been saved, are you delivering to others the message you have received? May God help us to do it.

BILL HALL

Bill Hall

11

Better Never Born

BIOGRAPHICAL SKETCH

Bill Hall
(1933 -)

Evangelist Bill Hall is a native of Memphis, Tennessee where he was born on July 27, 1933. He was converted to Christ at the age of seventeen under the ministry of Dr. H.C. Walton. A year later he surrendered to the call to preach while attending Memphis State University. Within one week of his conversion, he preached his first sermon. The following summer he conducted his first revival meeting in a rural community church. Even while pursuing his studies in college, he pastored churches and conducted numerous evangelistic meetings.

Brother Hall is a graduate of Bob Jones University, Greenville, South Carolina, receiving both a B.A. and B.D. degree. He was later honored with an honorary degree of Doctor of Divinity from BJU. Dr. Bob Jones, Sr., founder of the university and one of the foremost evangelists of this century, has left the influence of the "old time" revivalists upon Dr. Hall. He makes no apology for being a "fighting fundamentalist" or for being an outspoken foe of liberalism and compromise.

Dr. Hall is widely known as an evangelist and pulpit speaker, having preached throughout the nation as well as abroad. He has conducted more than 1,000 crusades since 1952 reaching and winning thousands for Christ. Having planted two churches (and pastoring one of them), he has a burden for the local church. Being from a broken home, he has a special burden for the family and its needs. He deals with the problems of every age group and every level of society, both from the pulpit and in personal counseling.

Though Bill and his lovely wife, Shirley, have no children, Bill has become affectionately known as "Grandpa Hall" to the many children who flock around him in their meetings. The Halls currently make their home in Eads, Tennessee, a suburb of Memphis. KWL

Evangelist Bill Hall
100 Waterford Cove
Eads, TN 38028

BETTER NEVER BORN
Bill Hall

Mark, chapter fourteen, beginning in verse seventeen and reading through verse twenty-one: "And in the even he cometh with the twelve. And as they sat and did eat, Jesus said, Verily I say unto you, One of you which eateth with me shall betray me. And they began to be sorrowful, and said unto him one by one, Is it I? and another said, Is it I? And he answered and said unto them, It is one of the twelve, that dippeth with me in the dish. The Son of man indeed goeth as it is written of him: but woe to that man by whom the Son of man is betrayed! good were it for that man if he had never been born."

The Lord Jesus is in the upper room at the Love Feast with His disciples, and He makes the startling announcement that one of the twelve will betray Him! Instead of all the apostles pointing an accusing finger at Judas and saying, "That's the scoundrel!" everyone of them said, "Could it be me? Is it I?" Judas was a very successful hypocrite. He knew all the language, he had the appearance. I mean, you would have thought he was a wonderful Christian, a fine follower of Christ. But he never had been born again. And no one suspected the hypocrite, Judas.

And Jesus said, "It's one of the twelve that dippeth with me in the dish." Now He said, "The Son of man is going to be betrayed, even as it has been prophesied." But, He said, "Woe to that man by whom the Son of man is betrayed, good were it for that man if he had never been born." One day, as I was reading over that Scripture, it seemed the phrase, "better never born," leaped from the page of my Bible and latched on to my heart. "Better never born!" That's our subject tonight.

I wonder, have you ever, in a fit of self-pity, said, "I wish I'd never been born." Maybe you didn't exactly use those words, but I suppose the great majority of folks here tonight are so maladjusted that at some time in your life you probably made such a silly statement as this! Later, after the crisis is over, and the outlook is brighter, you said, "Why in the world did I ever say anything like that?"

Job Said It

I want to show you something back in the book of Job, chapter three. You remember Job lost his children, he's lost his property, and he has lost his health. He has boils from the top of his head to the soles of his feet. His own wife has said, "Curse God and die!" (Now that was an encouragement, wasn't it?) He has three friends to come and comfort him, and with those kind of friends you don't need any enemies. Instead of comforting Job, they said, "The reason you are suffering so is because you have so much sin in your life. Deep, hidden sin somewhere." And so, in the midst of all that misery, listen to what Job says in verse three, "Let the day perish wherein I was born, and the night in which it was said, There is a man child conceived. Let that day be darkness; let not God regard it from above, neither let the light shine upon it. Let darkness and the shadow of death stain it; let a cloud dwell upon it; let the blackness of the day terrify it. As for that night, let darkness seize upon it; let it not be joined unto the days of the year, let it not come into the number of the months." Then, you look on down in verse eleven, "Why died I not from the womb: why did I not give up the ghost when I came out of the belly?" You know what he's saying? "I wish I never had been born."

I mean, this is the same man of faith who later says, "I know, even though some day I will die and my body will decay, yet in my flesh I will see God." This is the same man of God who later said, "I know that my Redeemer liveth." Yet, here he is, in a fit of despondency, discouragement, and self-pity, saying, "I wish I had never been born."

Jeremiah Said It

There was another man similar to that in the book of Jeremiah, chapter twenty. Jeremiah lived in a day when God's judgment had been pronounced upon his nation. His own loved ones thought he was crazy. His persecutors threw him into a dungeon and did all kinds of terrible things to him. Then we find Jeremiah getting discouraged. Jeremiah twenty, beginning in verse fourteen, "Cursed be the day wherein I was born: let not the day wherein my mother bare me be blessed. Cursed be the man who brought tidings to my father, saying, A man child is born unto thee; making him very glad." He even cursed the fellow who made the birth announcement! Verse eighteen: "Wherefore came I forth out of the womb to see labour and sorrow, that my days should be consumed with shame?"

Why do I point this out? I'm not excusing Job or Jeremiah; I just want to show you that they were men of like passions as we are. And, they faced discouragements and disappointments, bad times, and storms in life just as we do. And they responded like we do many times! "Better never born; I wish I never had been born." Do you know, Christian, it's a sin for us to indulge in self-pity? I mean, we know the source of Life! Christ said, "I am come that they might have life and that they might have it abundantly." He said, "I am the way, the truth and the life..." We came to the Father through Jesus Christ, and, in so doing, we receive life. "He that hath the Son hath life, and he that hath not the Son of God hath not life," according to First John, Chapter five. If we have the Lord Jesus

Christ, why would we ever say, "I wish I never had been born?" He has given us exceeding great and precious promises to encourage our hearts. He said, "I'll never leave you nor forsake you." "Casting all your care upon Him, for He careth for you." He says, "It's expedient that I go away and I will send the Holy Spirit to comfort your hearts." He's the "Balm in Gilead." He says, "Fear thou not for I am with thee: be not dismayed for I am thy God; I will strengthen thee, yea, I will help thee; yea, I will uphold thee with the right hand of my righteousness." Oh, the exceeding great and precious promises to encourage our hearts in even the darkest days, and the most terrifying experiences.

Men Who Never Said It

However, as I look through the Bible, I see some great men of faith that I never hear say, "I wish I had never been born."

Joseph

I'm thinking right now of Joseph. Now, there was a man who faced adverse circumstances. His own brothers sold him as a slave into Egypt because they were jealous of him. Then they lied to their daddy about him and broke his heart. When Joseph gets down to Egypt, I never hear him complain; I never hear him say, "I wish I never had been born." No, he's sold to a man by the name of Potiphar and he is such a faithful man, so diligent in his business, that it isn't long before Potiphar makes him the foreman of the ranch - head of the whole farm. In the meantime, Mrs. Potiphar set her eyes on Joseph and she sought to have an affair with him; but he refused her flirtations, ran from the house, and you know what he got for it. That conniving woman lied about him to her husband, and her husband had Joseph thrown in prison.

Now, had that been some of us, we'd have said, "That's what you get for trying to live for the Lord. I just wish I had never been born." I don't hear Joseph saying that. He gets to prison and he just keeps on fellowshipping with the Lord and faithfully serving Him wherever he is. He's so faithful there in the prison, that it isn't long until he is the head trustee at the prison. A couple of Pharaoh's servants are put into the prison and on an occasion Joseph has the opportunity to interpret their dreams by the power of God. One of these servants is restored to his original position and he remembers Joseph to Pharaoh when Pharaoh had a dream. Joseph was called to interpret Pharaoh's dream and he saw in him the wisdom to lead a people and he made Joseph the Prime

Minister of the land of Egypt. Better never born? Not when you know the Lord. Not when you walk with the Lord.

Daniel

I think of Daniel. Ah, he was brought into captivity as a teenager. A godly young man. And when they tempted him with the things from the king's table he refused and the Bible says, ".....Daniel purposed in his heart that he would not defile himself with the portion of the king's meat, nor with the wine which he drank..." God blessed Daniel and he became a leader and served under many kings, until finally he served under a king that passed a decree that everyone was to pray to the king alone for thirty days; and that if anybody prayed to any other god, they would be thrown into the den of lions. Well, Daniel didn't disobey the king just for the sake of disobedience; he just had a regular habit of talking to the Lord every day. So he went to the Lord in prayer and the "Watergate Committee" had bugged his room! They listened and he was talking to God! So they went running to the king and said, "O King, according to the law of the Medes and the Persians, which cannot be altered, you must throw Daniel into the den of lions; he's facing back toward Jerusalem and praying to his God!" And so the king, though he liked Daniel, and realized he'd been tricked into passing an unjust law, nevertheless, had to keep the law. So he had Daniel thrown in the den of lions. Now, don't get the idea that Daniel was some kind of an angel with wings and wasn't like us. He was made of the same kind of flesh we are and when he looked down into that pit and saw all those drooling lions, I can imagine his knees began to knock and a lump came up into his throat. But I never hear him say, "I wish I never had been born."

When they threw him into that den, do you know every one of those lions lost their appetite! I can imagine Daniel saying to one of them, "What's the matter with you boys? Aren't you hungry?" One of them says, "we don't like preachers." And so he says, "Well, if you are not going to eat, I believe I'll go to sleep. I'm tired; it has been a long day." One of the lions laid down and Daniel pillowed his head on that lion and slept like a baby. The next morning the king, who had not slept but spent a sleepless night, concerned about his friend, came to the edge of the pit and said, "Daniel was your God able to deliver you?" And Daniel said, "Live forever, O King, My God was able to deliver me!" And they drew him up out of the den, threw the enemies in and the lions got their appetites back! But better never born? Ah, you may have to go to a den of lions and you may not be delivered, but it's still better to go there with Jesus than to be without Him.

Shadrach, Meshach, and Abednego

Have you considered Daniel's three friends, Shadrach, Meshach, and Abednego? Now, according to the king, when the denominational orchestra plays, everybody's to bow down before the ecumenical shrine. Shadrach, Meschach, and Abednego had the law of their God so they just couldn't bow down before that shrine, that idol, that the king had made. So someone came and told the king about their refusal to bow and they brought Shadrach, Meshach, and Abednego before the king and he said, "Boys, I'm plenty mad about this, but I'll tell you what, we'll just forget about it. You seem like pretty good boys and I want you to be good leaders. If you'll just bow down when the orchestra plays the next time, we'll just forget about the incident. However, if you don't, we'll throw you into the furnace of fire." Shadrach, Meschach, and Abednego showed some of the most unusual courage you read about anywhere in history. They said, "O King, if you throw us into that furnace of fire, God may not deliver us. If God wants to deliver us, He can deliver is; He can do anything. But if God chooses not to deliver us, we want you to know, O King, that we still will not bow down before your idol because the word of our God forbids us to bow down before any idol."

And so they took Shadrach, Meshach, and Abednego and threw them into the furnace of fire. "I wish I never had been born!" No, I never hear them saying that. They're walking in the fire. What? They're walking around in the fire! And the king's looking in, and he says, "Didn't we throw three men in there? I don't see three, I see four, and the fourth is like the Son of God!" Huh? You say, "Preacher, do you believe that?" Absolutely! I say, if you're walking with Jesus, it's better to walk in a furnace with Him than to walk outside a furnace without Him. Better never born? Not for the child of God. Jesus said, "Blessed are ye when men shall persecute you and say all manner of evil against you falsely for my sake. Rejoice, and be exceeding glad for great is your reward in heaven."

I like the fifth chapter of Acts. After they had beaten the apostles and commanded them not to preach anymore in the name of Jesus, instead of the apostles going out and bathing in self-pity, it says, "they departed from the presence of the council rejoicing that they were counted worthy to suffer shame for his name. And daily in the temple and in every house they ceased not to teach and preach Jesus Christ." You just couldn't shut them up! They had such a message inside, it was like a fire shut up in their bones, and they had to let folks know about it. A holy necessity was laid upon them and they would not keep their mouth shut.

Paul

Then, there was Paul. What a Christian! Every place he went he faced persecution, and yet, I never hear him bathing in self-pity. In one city, they'd run him out of town. Another place they'd beat him. Another place, they'd throw him in jail; in fact, it seemed that in most cities, they'd throw him in jail because he preached Christ. At Lystra, they stoned him and left him for dead. He was in the jail at Philippi with his preacher partner, Silas, down in a dungeon with their legs in stocks. Now and then, in the shadows of that vermin infested dungeon, a rat would run out of a corner and across their legs. Perspiration runs off the back of their necks and down into the raw wounds on their backs. And, do you know what they were doing, at midnight? "I wish I never had been born!" You know what they're doing? They are singing! I don't know what they were singing. If "Amazing Grace" had been written at that time, I believe they would have been singing that. But they were singing praises to the Lord and talking to Him. I say this reverently. Evidently the Lord enjoyed the song so much, He patted His foot and it caused an earthquake causing the jail doors to come open! The old jailer, realizing that it would mean his job and probably his life, started to commit suicide, but the prisoners cried out, "We're all here, do thyself no harm!" The jailer came running in and asked the great question, "Sirs, what must I do to be saved?" And they answered, "Believe on the Lord Jesus Christ and thou shalt be saved and thy house." Better never born? Not when you can get somebody saved. I don't care what you have to go through. So I'm saying, if you know the Lord we ought never to say, "I wish I never had been born."

Men Who Might Have Said It

Bartimeaus

But, I can understand why some folks would say, "I wish I never had been born." I'm thinking now of blind Bartimeaus. Bartimeaus lived in Jericho. He had never seen a lovely sunset or looked upon a beautiful rose. He's never seen his mother's face. He was blind. And, to add to his misery, the only way he could even live was to beg. So he sits outside the gate of Jericho and begs. Don't you know there were times in his continual midnight that he'd cry out, "I wish I never had been born?"

People began to talk about somebody called Jesus, and some were even saying He was the Messiah, heir to the throne of David. One day, he heard a crowd buzzing with excitement, and somebody said, "It's Jesus, He's in Jericho. Some say He's the Messiah." Bartimeaus, perhaps, had been taught as a little boy, that, one day, the Messiah would come. And he figured, if Jesus is really the Messiah, He'll love a blind man like me. He'll have compassion on me. And so, as the crowd got nearer, and he figured Christ must be in the midst of the crowd, Bartimeaus cried, "Jesus! Thou son of David! Have mercy on me!" And somebody said, "Shut up, blind man!" But he wouldn't be denied and he cried out the louder, "Jesus, Thou son of David! Have mercy on me!" There never has been anybody that has cried out to Jesus but that Jesus heard them. Jesus stopped and said, "Bartimeaus, come here." Somebody said, "Bartimeaus, He's calling you." Bartimeaus felt his way through the darkness toward that voice. And, when he got to Jesus, Jesus opened his blind eyes, and the first face Bartimeaus ever saw was the face of Jesus. Better never born? Not when you meet the Master.

The Demon Possessed Man

Remember the poor demon possessed man in Mark 5. No one could tame, control, or help him. For the safety of his family and community, the elders of the city had to put the man out in the mountains among the tombs and caves. Some nights, when he was more sane, he must have sat in a cold lonely cave remembering his loving wife and the warmth of his home. He may well have cried, "Why am I like I am? Why can't I be better? I wish I had never been born!"

Then Jesus passed by and cast the legion of demons out of the man into a heard of swine and now we see the man sitting at the feet of Jesus, clothed and in his right mind, Mark 5:15. Jesus told him to go home and tell everybody what great things the Lord had done for him.

When he gets home I can imagine his wife saw him coming and ran to the door shouting, "Go away, I'm afraid of you." But he says, "Honey, I've met Jesus Christ and He's cast the demons out. I'm not like I was, I'm different now." He is so convincing that she, maybe for the first time in months, embraces him and welcomes him home. If there were children, they come from behind doors or under the beds and hug their Dad and welcome him home. Better never born? Not when you meet the Master.

The Woman At The Well

I think of the woman in John, chapter four. Now, here's the news about her. She's been married five times and is presently living with a man she has not married. When the respectable people see her on the street, they pass over to the other side. About the only glances she ever gets are the lustful glances of wicked men. She had tried marriage after marriage, but she is still empty and love is unknown to her.

One day, at noon time, she comes to Jacob's well for water. Now most people came either in the morning or in the evening, but she didn't want to come when everybody else came; she didn't want to face the people. And, as she approached the well, this Samaritan woman sees a Jew sitting at the well. She thinks to herself, "Oh no, not one of those self-righteous Jews. Well, I'll just ignore him." She starts drawing water from the well and the kindest voice she ever heard said, "Would you give me a drink?" She snapped at him, "Jews have no dealings with Samaritans! Why are you talking to me?" His voice, so unperturbed, said, "If you knew Who talked with you, you'd ask of Him and He'd give you Living Water." That aroused her curiosity. "You have nothing to draw with and this well is deep. What are you talking about, living water?" And Jesus went on to explain to her that that Living Water was eternal life you receive when you trust Him as your personal Saviour. She got a drink of that Living Water that day and was so excited about it, that instead of moaning and groaning about it all the way back to town, she went running back to town and so convincing was her testimony that all the townspeople came out to see this Jesus that she told them about; the One who knew all about her and had obviously changed her life. Better never born? Not when you meet the Master.

Judas Iscariot

But wait! Jesus said, concerning Judas Iscariot, that it would have been better if he had never been born. Now, I didn't say that, Jesus did! Do you realize that Judas had opportunities that few people in history have ever had? Judas Iscariot heard the greatest messages ever preached for never man spake like Christ. He saw all the evidences of His deity. He saw Him unstop deaf ears, give sight to blind eyes, give speech to dumb tongues, give strength to lame legs. He saw Him as He stood and said, "Peace be still," to a stormy sea and the sea became as peaceful as a sleeping baby. He saw Him take a little boy's lunch of fish sandwiches, loaves and fishes, divide them and feed a multitude. He saw all that. He heard Him that day as He stepped to the tomb of Lazarus and say, "Lazarus, come forth!" and the one who had been dead four days walked out of the tomb. Judas Iscariot saw all the evidences of His deity; he saw an absolutely perfect life; the only One Who could say, "Which of you convinceth me of sin?" The One of whom Peter said He was the Lamb without spot and without blemish. You can find no flaw in His life, in His thought processes, in anything about Him! And Judas observed all that. Yet, with all these evidences, and all these great blessings, all these great sermons, and all of Christ's love that was so manifested in His ministry here in this world; Judas Iscariot sold Jesus Christ for thirty pieces of silver - the price of a slave - then came to the Garden of Gethsamane, placed the traitor's kiss upon His holy cheek as a signal that this was the One, then, later in remorse, not in repentance, he returned to the leaders and said, "I have betrayed the innocent blood. Take the money back!" When they refused to take the money, he threw it down and went out and hanged himself and went to Hell! Jesus said it would have been better if he had never been born.

Others

But what you say about Judas, you'd have to say about the rich young ruler we read about in Matthew nineteen. He had youth, he had morality, he had position, he had so many admirable traits and yet, when Christ showed him his need, he went away sorrowful because he had great possessions. He rejected Christ and it would have been better if he had never been born. There's Herod and Pilate. Both of them had wealth and position, but both of them were confronted by Jesus Christ and both rejected Him and it would have been better if neither had ever been born.

Now, I don't want to be misunderstood. It's pretty easy for us to say that the world would have been better if Hitler, Mussolini, and Joseph Stalin, and all that crowd, had never been born. It's pretty easy for me to make the statement that it would have been better if Adolf Eichmann, the one who murdered millions of Jews, had never been born. When we think of some of the Communist murderers around the world today, most good Americans would say it would have been better if they had never been born!

But what about the unsaved neighbor? The unsaved friend? Church member? Choir member? Sunday school teacher? Church leader? Preacher in the pulpit that has never been saved? I say to you, that if they die without Christ, it would have been better if they had never been born in the first place. That's speaking from a Scriptural standpoint.

Let me use an illustration. Most of us who have studied the history of the days preceding World War II, that awful war, remember with admiration Sir Winston Churchill. There were some things we did not admire about him, but he was a statesman. And it was his courage and his leadership that helped hold Great Britain together in those days before we, as a nation, entered the war.

Yet, I say, with all the good that he did for his country and for the world, from the Bible standpoint, it would have been better if Sir Winston Churchill had never been born. Why do I say that? And I do not mean to be unkind, but I understand shortly before he died someone asked him, "Sir Winston, are you ready to meet your Maker?" And he answered, "The question is not whether I'm ready to meet my Maker, but is my Maker ready to meet me?" Evidently, with that kind of irreverent attitude, as far as anybody knows, he went out into eternity unprepared. And, I say, having done so, it would have been better if he had never been born.

What about you? You may be a fine neighbor, you may be a very religious person, but have you been born again? That's the center of the issue. Jesus said in John, chapter three, "Except a man be born again, he cannot see the kingdom of God." How is a person born again? John 1:12 says, "As many as received him (Jesus Christ) to them gave he the power to become the sons of God, even to them that believe on his name." You are not born again by joining a church, or getting baptized, or trying to live a good life, or reforming your life, or getting a feeling; you're born again by putting your faith and trust in the Lord Jesus and receiving Him into your heart.

Let me show you something and I think this will help you see it clearly. If you are born only once, then you will die twice, and it would have been better, yea a million times better, if you had never been born once. However, if you've been born twice, you're only going to die once, if that many times. And then you can thank God you were born the first time, because it gave you opportunity to be born the second time and live with the Lord forever! This birth is from above, it's a spiritual birth. It's obvious that everyone of us here tonight has had one birth. I don't know if you've been born again. But, it's obvious we've all had one birth, which is a fleshly birth, an earthly birth. That made us a member of Adam's race, a fallen race, "for all have sinned and come short of the glory of God," and, "the wages of sin is death, but the gift of God is eternal life through Jesus Christ our Lord." When you come through Jesus Christ to receive eternal life, you are born again, born from above, born of the Spirit of God. It's not some kind of spooky thing, it's a wonderful, wonderful fact that when we trust Jesus Christ, the spirit of God makes us a new creature in Christ Jesus.

Having been born twice, I'm only going to die once, if that many times. You say, "What are you talking about?" Well, I may not even have to die once, because Jesus may come tonight, or tomorrow, or before I die. And if He comes before I die, the Bible teaches that everybody who's been born again and alive when the Lord comes back again will be caught up to meet Him in the air along with those Christians who have already died. They'll be raised first, according to First Thessalonians, chapter four, and then we'll be caught up together with them to meet the Lord in the air. Honestly, that appeals to me - being caught up without dying! I never did care much for dying. Six fellas carrying me around in a box never did appeal to me. Seems kinda confining doesn't it?

We stayed in the home of a funeral director one time. I told people we were staying at the house of the dead! He had the weirdest sense of humor. He'd come in wringing his hands. I'd say, "What's wrong?" He said, rather sadly, "All my friends are healthy." How could he pray for good business when he's in that kind of business? No, the blessed hope of the Christian is not death; the blessed hope of the Christian is Christ coming. He may come without our having to face physical death. However, if the Lord tarries, then, Christians, we will die. "It's appointed unto man once to die," and we will die. But that death will be just like an old, creaky garden gate that leads to a beautiful garden! "Yea, though I walk through the valley of the shadow of death, I will fear no evil for thou art with me."

We know the One Who said, "I am the resurrection and the life, he that liveth and believeth in me, though he were dead, yet shall he live. And he that liveth and believeth in me shall never die!" Christian, we're going to live until angels sing funeral dirges over the grave of God! That means we're going to live forever.

But, on the other hand, if you've only been born once, then you will die twice. You'll die physically, and then Revelation, chapter twenty, says at the Great White Throne judgment, "Whosoever's name is not found written in the book of life will be cast into the Lake of Fire. This is the second death." That's the death that never dies. Death is not a cessation of existence. Eternal death is conscious existence in a place called the Lake of Fire forever and forever! And that's the reason Jesus said it would have been better if Judas had never been born. And that's the reason it would be better if you never had been born, than for you to go on through life, rejecting Christ, and finally die without Him and go out into eternity lost.

I'm begging you, I'm pleading with you, make your calling and elections sure. You must not gamble with your eternal soul. Come to Christ now. Would you bow your heads please.

BUD LYLES

12

Good But Lost . . . Bad, But Saved

BIOGRAPHICAL SKETCH

Bud Lyles
(1927 -)

Bud Lyles was born on August 16, 1927. In 1944, at the age of seventeen, he trusted Christ as his Saviour and sensed the call of God to the ministry. Three years later he enrolled in Bob Jones University graduating in 1951.

He entered the ministry of evangelism in 1959 and has had the joy of preaching the Gospel in most of the states here in America as well as a number of foreign countries. He has conducted several hundred revival and evangelistic campaigns for individual churches in addition to several area-wide meetings sponsored by several fundamental churches. Dr. Lyles is an experienced soloist and song leader. His practical, Bible-centered sermons have been used by God to turn many to Christ. In 1970 he received an honorary Doctor of Divinity (D.D.) degree from Bob Jones University.

His wife, Dottie, also a BJU graduate, travels with her husband. Together they have reared five children. Two of their sons are ordained preachers, and one daughter and son-in-law are serving as missionaries to Australia. Dr. and Mrs. Lyles make their home in Greenville, South Carolina.

Evangelist Bud Lyles
P.O. Box 27121
Greenville, SC 29616

GOOD, BUT LOST...BAD, BUT SAVED
Bud Lyles

"And he spake this parable unto certain which trusted in themselves that they were righteous, and despised others: Two men went up into the temple to pray; the one a Pharisee, and the other a publican. The Pharisee stood and prayed thus with himself, God, I thank thee, that I am not as other men are, extortioners, unjust, adulterers, or even as this publican. I fast twice in the week, I give tithes of all that I possess. And the publican, standing afar off, would not lift up so much as his eyes unto heaven, but smote upon his breast, saying, God be merciful to me a sinner. I tell you, this man went down to his house justified rather than the other: for everyone that exalteth himself shall be abased; and he that humbleth himself shall be exalted." (Luke 18:9-14)

Jesus told this story to illustrate what it takes to get to Heaven. Obviously in His day, just as in our day, there was a great deal of confusion about that matter. The truth is that there are a great many people who are clean, decent, moral, law-abiding, even church members, who are going to be terribly shocked and surprised when it comes time to die, to find out that they are going in the wrong direction.

Several years ago in Michigan I went with a pastor to visit a man in the hospital. For some time this man had lived neighbor to the church where I was holding meetings. Although he lived side-by-side with that church, he never one time had been inside the building. Oh, he had his own church. He never went there either, but felt justified in never visiting the church beside his home. Now he was ill. We found his hospital room, walked in and introduced ourselves. As long as we talked about sports, or the weather, or newspaper headlines, the man was just as kind and congenial as he could be. But it was not long until we got around to the real purpose of our visit. We asked the man whether he was a Christian.

It was almost as though you could hear a needle drop into a groove and a record began to play. He had been over these things so many, many times that he had it all memorized. He ticked off one thing after another telling us what a fine man he was. He said that he was nice to his neighbors. He always paid his debts. He did not kick the dog. He never chased the cat and he never beat his wife, unless she needed it... one thing after another. Well, you know how a record does when the needle comes to the middle? It goes ptsh...ptsh...ptsh! Then the arm picks up and goes back and drops in place. You could almost hear it do that. He had finished his little speech and he was done.

We waited through all of that and when he was quiet, we turned to him and said, "But sir, if those are the things that get us to Heaven, why did Jesus go to the Cross and die?" As soon as we mentioned the death of Jesus on the Cross, this man turned livid with rage. His face became beet-red. I thought he was going to have a case of apoplexy right there in the hospital bed. He cursed! He swore! He used God's Name in vain and ordered us preachers to get out of his room and never come back again! Boy, was he angry!

We got him calmed down enough to where we could witness to him and leave him a Gospel tract and have prayer with him. Here was a man who wanted to be identified as a Christian. He wanted everyone to think that surely he would go to Heaven when it came time to die; a man who, when it came down to the one thing that makes the difference between Heaven and Hell for all men...and that is the death of Jesus Christ on the Cross...got so angry and so upset that he blew his cool, cursed and swore and ordered us out of the room. I am saying that there is a great deal of confusion about how to get to Heaven even in our day and time. So this story has its application to us.

The Pharisee

Will you notice that there are two main characters in the parable. One is identified as a Pharisee, a very religious person. The other is identified as a publican, a very irreligious person. I want us to examine these two men. The Pharisee was a good man by worldly standards. Notice several good things about him.

A Church Going Man

First, he was a church-going man. Jesus said, "Two men went up into the temple..." Now it is a good thing to go to church and people should go to church, but there are churches and there are churches. Do you know what I mean? There are some churches where it would do you as much good to spend two hours at the local country club on Sunday morning as it would to go to one of those churches. The fact is that you might better go to the country club, because the country club will not try to confuse you about how to get to Heaven, and some churches will. There are churches in your town where you could go for a lifetime and never see one person carry a Bible into that church...including the preacher. There are churches where you could be counted as a member and occupy eighteen inches of a church pew all your life and never hear a clear explanation of how to be saved. Now, what kind of a church is that? That is little more than a social club. Those churches might just as well be burned to the ground, and the preachers tarred and feathered and run out of town. I am not advocating that, you understand. I am just saying that some churches are not a help. They are a hindrance. Go to church, but go to the right kind of a church. Go to a church that believes and preaches that the Bible is the inspired Word of God word for word. Go to a church that believes and preaches that Jesus Christ is the virgin born Son of God. Go to a church that believes and preaches that Jesus died for our sins on the Cross and is the only hope of salvation for mankind. Go to a church that makes the way of salvation so plain and so clear in every single service that no visitor could come to a service in that church and go home not knowing how to be saved. That is the only kind of church worth going to for any of us. Yet going to church will not get you to Heaven.

A Praying Man

Notice also that this Pharisee was a praying man. Jesus said, "Two men went up into the temple to pray." It is a good thing to pray and people should pray. I know some unsaved people who pray more than some Christian people I know. It is a sad thing that Christians do not pray. Prayer is God's means for God's children to have what they need and want from God. Again and again God has promised to hear and answer the prayers of His children (Jeremiah 33:3; Matthew 7:7,8; John 15:7).

We have had some marvelous answers to prayer. For a long time we have had two cars. I use one to drive to meetings here and there around the country. My wife needs wheels while I am gone. So we have had two cars. We had two while our children were in college. I had used both of them on the road and they were well over 100,000 miles. They were getting to the place where I was fearful that they would break down somewhere and be expensive to repair. So I began flying to some meetings and that can be expensive, too.

Late one year I had a cancellation in my schedule on short notice...just two weeks. A young preacher trying to get a work started in Ohio had told me, "Brother Bud, if you have a cancellation, even on short notice, let me know and we will try to have you come." I called him and told him I could give him a Sunday through Friday and then would have to fly to North Carolina to start a meeting in Union Grove on Sunday. He said, "Let me pray about it. I'll call you back." A few days later he called and said I should come and we would try to have the meeting. I flew in. A man loaned me his car to drive back and forth to the motel. I did not pay much attention to it because it was his and I would be giving it back to him at the end of the meeting. It was a station wagon.

Earlier that year I had picked up a magazine and had seen an advertisement for the 1973 Ford Torino station wagon and it struck me that it was just what I needed. I began praying that God would give me a 1973 Ford Torino station wagon. I had prayed it would have a radio that would help me stay awake when I drove all night. Power steering and power brakes would be safety features and an automatic transmission would be good. I had said to the Lord that air-conditioning would be frosting on the cake. I had been praying that way and had my family praying as well.

We went through the week in Ohio and God blessed. We closed on Friday night. I was at the front of the building packing up some books I had brought so that I could mail them home. The man who had loaned me his car came and stood by watching me pack the books. He finally cleared his throat and said, "Brother Bud, do you think you could drive to North Carolina and get there in time for your meeting on Sunday?" Without looking up I told him I thought I could. I had all day Saturday to do it. He hemmed and hawed a little and then asked if I could drive the car I had been driving all week. I said, "Yes. I could drive anything that had wheels." It took me several minutes to realize he was trying to tell me he was going to give me that car. I want you to know what it was. It was a 1973 Ford Torino station wagon. It had a radio, power steering, power brakes, automatic transmission and yes, it was air-conditioned. The man threw in two snow tires to boot. Isn't that just like the Lord? That wagon had 8,100 miles on it when he gave it to me and when I finally traded it, it had 187,500 miles on it. I am just saying if you and I would pray and get answers to our prayers, we could convince this lost world that God has not died. It is little wonder they get that impression. We give them that impression by the way we live. We go through life acting like orphans. It is good to pray, but prayer alone will not get you to Heaven. You need more than that. This was a praying man.

An Honest Man

What else about this good man? Look at verse 11. The Pharisee said, "I thank thee, that I am not as other men are, extortioners..." What did he mean by that? He meant that he did not get his income from some illegitimate means. He put in an honest day's work for an honest day's pay. Well, God bless him! You know, people should be honest with employers. I know what it is to work in factories. I have worked for I.B.M., for Link Aviation, for Agfa Ansco. One time I was between things for the Lord and needed some income. I went to Agfa Ansco and filled out an application. The manager of the Personnel Office sat me down beside his desk and went over the application. Finally he said, "Well, Mr. Lyles, we are not hiring. We are just listening." Do you know that it is the wrong thing to say you're a Baptist preacher? He listened! I poured the Gospel into his ear for 15 minutes. He sat there and took it...a Roman Catholic man. Then he told me there was nothing open and if anything came up, he would call. About two days later the phone rang. This same man told me about an opening in the advertising shipping department. It sounded like a job any idiot could do and I figured I could handle it. He said, "If you are interested, come over and we will talk about it." I went and sat in the same chair, beside the same desk, in the same little office, and the same man told me about the job and how much it paid. He asked, "Are you interested?" I told him I was. He said, "I want you to understand one thing." I said, "What's that?" He answered, "We are not hiring you to preach." He had already heard me preach. "We don't expect you to bring a soap-box and spend all day preaching." I assured him they would get eight good hours out of me every day and I hired in.

That department hired both men and women and sometimes that is a worse situation than men alone or women alone. The stories were rotten and the language was filthy. I worked just a couple of hours when one of the men siddled over to my bench and started into a story. I thought I could tell what direction it was going and without being unkind to the man I said, "If the rest of that story goes the way I think it may, I don't care about hearing any more of it." His eyebrows shot right up under his hairline. I know he thought, "What kind of a nut do we have here?" It did not take long for that to get around the department and so those dirty stories did not come my way. I worked about three weeks and one day the superintendent came and threw his arm around my shoulder and said, "I don't understand this, Mr. Lyles, but the language around here sure has changed since you came."

Every morning and every afternoon there was a ten minute break for the cigarette suck...uh...the smokers, well, that's right you know. If you use cigarettes, you don't smoke. The cigarette smokes; you simply suck. You are a sucker if you smoke...anyway you look at it, friend. I don't use tobacco, so every morning and every afternoon I had a New Testament break. I am not a "Goody-goody." I do love the Bible and I carried my Testament to work and sat at my bench and read while they went out and smoked.

At noon time all the men disappeared. I wondered where they went. Then one day I found out. They were all down in the men's room playing poker. I don't gamble. So I sat at my bench and ate my lunch while on another New Testament break. One day I was sitting there eating and reading, when the man with the dirtiest mind and the filthiest mouth came back from the card game early. I guess he lost all his money and so was out of the game. He walked over to my bench and looked over my shoulder. "Hey, Bud, what are you readi...a...Bible." I witnessed to that man and showed him in the Bible how to be saved. Tears welled up in his eyes and rolled down his cheeks. He did not get saved that day, but he thanked me and from that day on he was my friend. If I ever needed someone to stand up for me, he was there. I worked there about a year and on my own time had opportunity to witness to everyone in the department including the boss. Then, going back into the Lord's work, I had to go back through the personnel office and be re-interviewed by the man who hired me. I sat in the same chair, beside the same desk in the same little office. That man looked up and down and said, "Mr. Lyles, I have worked for this corporation for more than twenty-five years and this is the first time anything like this has happened. A man called from your department and thanked me for hiring you. If you ever need employment again, you come right back here. There will be an opening somewhere."

Do you know why some Christians have no testimony in the place where they work? It is because they are lazy loafers. When there is work to be done, the boss has to come and hunt them up. This Pharisee said, "I am not like that. I give my employer an honest day's work for an honest day's pay." Now you should be honest with your employer, but that will not get you to Heaven. You need more than that.

A Law Abiding Man

What else about this man? He said, "I am not unjust." What did he mean by that? He meant, "I am a law-abiding citizen of my country." Christian people should be law-abiding citizens. Please turn in your Bibles to Romans 13. Let's read several verses beginning at verse one. "Let every soul be subject unto the higher powers. For there is no power but of God: the powers that be are ordained of God." That means, whatever you may think of him, God put the President in the White House, the Governor in the Governor's office, the Mayor in the Mayor's chair. Anyone who represents authority is there by the ordination of God. Verse two. "Whosoever therefore resisteth the power, resisteth the ordinance of God: and they that resist shall receive to themselves damnation." People who take part in civil disobedience riots and break the laws of the land simply because they do not agree with those laws, are not just defying the law. They are defying God Almighty. He is the One who established authority. They will bring down upon themselves and upon the land the condemnation of God. Verse three. "For rulers are not a terror to good works, but to the evil. Wilt thou then not be afraid of the power? Do that which is good, and thou shalt have praise of the same: For he is the minister of God to thee for good." Anyone who represents authority is God's minister.

That highway patrolman with the gumball machine on top of his car is God's minister. When he pulls you over, don't fuss with him. You are the one who broke the law. He is trying to help you do right. You should get out and run back there and thank him. That would flip him over, don't you think? He doesn't get that kind of reaction once in a lifetime. But he should. Verse four. "But if thou do that which is evil, be afraid; for he beareth not the sword in vain: for he is the minister of God, a revenger to execute wrath upon him that doeth evil." There is more, but we will not go into it. Is God in favor of capital punishment? You had better believe that He is! "He beareth not the sword in vain." Or the billy club, or the .38 revolver, or shotgun, or whatever he has. It is not in vain. It is for a purpose. Christian people should be law-abiding citizens. But obeying the law will not get you to Heaven. You need something other than that.

A Moral Man

What else about this good man? He said, "I am not an adulterer." Now I do not want to labor this point, but we all know what a serious problem this is in America today. We have so-called preachers who stand in their pulpits and advocate what they call "situation ethics." "If it feels good, do it." That has never been a Bible principle. The 7th commandment is still in this Book! "Thou shalt not commit adultery" (Exodus 20:14). And I remind you that Jesus, in the Sermon on the Mount (Matthew 5:27,28) said, "Ye have heard that it was said by them of old time, Thou shalt not commit adultery: But I say unto you, that whosoever looketh on a woman to lust after her hath committed adultery with her already in his heart." Not guilty of the outward act, but counted just as guilty as though he had gone into the sin, simply by entertaining the thought in his mind. Now this man is a Pharisee. He knows the Law. He knows the teachings of Jesus and what he is saying here is, "I am not guilty of the act of adultery. I am not even guilty of having the thought in my mind." Well, God bless him! Here is a man who is morally pure. You know, we need some moral purity in America today. City Number One for venereal disease in America is Washington, D.C., the Capital of our country. God help us! City Number Two is San Francisco, California, because of the queers, the homosexuals. I tell you, I have been shocked as I travel about the country. Every week that I am out on the road I hear another story of some good, fundamental preacher who has fallen in this area. Yes, I know the Devil is out to get preachers. I know sometimes preachers are counted fair game. And sometimes preachers have more opportunity in this area than do other men because women trust their preachers and come to them with their problems. But counseling sessions have turned into comforting sessions and before a man knows it he is trapped. Preachers above all people should be morally pure. However, moral purity will not get you to Heaven. You should be moral, but morality will not save you.

A Patriotic Man

There is more. The Pharisee said, "I am not even as this publican." Now a publican was a Jew who had sold himself out to the Roman government to serve as a tax-gatherer. Knowing something of his own people; their means, their livelihood, he was permitted to levy taxes against them and rake a percentage right off the top and put it in his own pocket. In that public office, then, as there often is in public office today, there was a great opportunity for graft, greed, and personal wickedness. Publicans were known to take advantage of their office. They were hated. They were counted as traitors to their country. The Pharisee was saying, "I am not like that publican, a traitor. I am a loyal, patriotic citizen." I believe Christians should be patriotic. We should be willing to salute our flag; willing to stand and face the music when we hear the National Anthem; willing to serve our country when our country needs our services. Thank God for many fine young people who are willing to wear the uniform of our armed forces; willing to fight our country's battles here or on foreign soil; to fight, to bleed, even to die in the cause of our country. Thank God for them. But even if a man gives his life in devotion to his country, that will not get him into Heaven. You will need something more than that. Patriotism doesn't save anyone.

A Fasting Man

What else? Look at verse twelve. He said, "I fast twice in the week." Now there is something largely gone out of practice in the Christian church. You don't hear much about fasting today, and some of us could stand to do some, just as a practical thing. A church in Pennsylvania invited me to come for a meeting and we set the dates. As soon as I walked into that church house, I could tell there was a difference. I could just feel it in the atmosphere. The song leader stepped to the pulpit and announced the first song. Now that is all he did. He did not have to pull at the people to get them to sing. Those folks sang! I had not heard singing like that since the days when I was a student in Bob Jones University. Bible college students sing and those people sang. Hey, do you know what? Congregational singing is not a spectator sport. That is your part in the service. I have seen people walk into a church building. They never pick up a song book or lift a voice to sing. Then they walk out muttering, "I didn't get any blessing out of the service." You didn't put anything into the service. You want to get something out of it? Then put something into it. "Well, I don't sing pretty." God didn't say you had to sing pretty. God said, "Make a joyful noise unto the Lord..." (Psalm 100:1). You may croak like a bullfrog, but do it for Jesus. Those people sang. The music director turned to lead the choir. I looked out over that congregation and women were getting into their purses. Men were reaching into their pockets and coming up with hankies and dabbing at their eyes. God was working in the music program.

It came time for the message. I was introduced. I read my text and began the message. Preacher, have you ever been in a church where, when you get up to preach, you feel as though you are batting your head against a brick wall? Man, I have. I have been in some real refrigerators. Yes, I have been in some churches that were so cold you could ice skate down the middle aisle. But not there. It was easy to preach and the people just pulled it out of me. When it came time for the invitation, we just announced the song and immediately the aisles were crowded. Here were people coming for salvation, for baptism, for membership, for rededication. It was wonderful and it was like that for every single service. Well, you know how it is. You get to know some of the people and you would like to get to know some of them a little better. There was a man in the church that I took a liking to and I said to him, "How about you and me having lunch together tomorrow?" He said, "I am sorry, Brother Bud. I can't." I said, "How come?" He answered, "Tuesday is one of our fast days." I didn't know that Tuesday was any faster than Monday. I said, "What do you mean?" "Well, in this church," he said, "we practice fasting twice in the week." Nothing is said in the pulpit. Nothing is printed in a bulletin. Nothing is posted on the boards, but as a group of believers, they have agreed that two days out of every week they will go without food in order to get that time to get alone and pray for God's blessing and God's power in their services and I want you to know, they have it! We had a wonderful meeting with people saved in every service. The last I heard from them, they were having to tear down the old building and build a bigger auditorium that will seat 2,500 people. But fasting, as good and right as that may be as a religious exercise to put down the desires and appetites of the flesh in order to give ascendency to the Spirit Who dwells within, won't get you to Heaven. Lost people can fast. Fasting doesn't save anyone. This man fasted.

A Tithing Man

What else? He said, "I give tithes of all that I possess." Here is a lost man who is tithing. I know some Christian people who do not tithe. I know some Christians who pay the rent. They pay the light bill. They pay the gas bill. They pay the grocery bill. They pay this and that. Then they come to church on Sunday morning and, if they have anything left, drop a quarter into the offering and feel as though they have sawed off a big one. You skinflint! You tightwad! It's no wonder you don't have anything. You are stealing from God. My Bible says, "The tithe is the Lord's" (Leviticus 27:30). Well, the whole thing is His isn't it? He gave you the strength to make it. All He asks is ten cents on the dollar. Look, if Uncle Sam can get his piece out of your paycheck before you ever see it, why don't you give God the benefit of the doubt and tithe on the gross and not the net? This man was tithing on ALL he possessed. A lost man and yet he is tithing. Why? Because he had found there is a blessing in giving to God. I wish Christian people would learn that. But tithing will not take you to Heaven. Now you should tithe, but that will not save you. You will need something else.

Here is a man who is good by nearly every standard men can think of, but he is lost. Why? Because goodness does not save anyone. People who trust in their own goodness are going to wind up in Hell. "All of our righteousnesses are as filthy rags..." (Isaiah 64:6). All of the good deeds a man can muster, built up over a lifetime, will not amount to a hill of beans so far as getting that man into Heaven is concerned. You cannot get to Heaven by doing good or being good. To get to Heaven you must admit that you are a sinner and repent of your sins and trust Jesus Christ as your Saviour.

A church in Omaha invited me for meetings and the dates were set. One of the Sunday School classes decided to have a nice dinner on Saturday night before the revival was to begin on Sunday. They called long-distance and asked if I could arrange to be there in time to speak to the group that night. I was glad to do so. It was a lovely meal in a hotel downtown. They had invited some prominent people in Omaha to that dinner. Elected officials and business people were there. They had a nice musical program and some entertainment, then introduced me. I gave a simple Gospel message, A,B,C, right down the line. One man was there who was an auto dealer. He had worked hard and built up his own business. He was a millionaire several times over. His showroom would cover half a city block. He just drank in the message and came to me afterward and said, "I have been a member of the _____" (almost told you what church he was a member of and I wouldn't want to embarrass anyone by telling you that he was a Presbyterian). "I have been a church member all of my life and have never heard anything like that. Could you and the pastor come and see me at my place of business?" I said we would be delighted to do so and we set an appointment for Tuesday at 10:00 A.M. We walked through the double doors of his showroom that morning. He showed us all around. He dealt in recreational vehicles, the kind you drive and the kind you tow as well as cars. We oohed and aahed. You know you can get anything you want in those RV's. You can get hot and cold water, air, gas, electric and carpet in them better than the carpet in my house. They will cost you a bundle too. Around the walls of his showroom were the trophies of his hunts. He had been a big game hunter. He had gone to Africa, India, Alaska, Northern Canada and here were the trophies, beautiful things, mounted around the walls. We spent nearly an hour in the showroom. Then he led us back to his own private office and sat down behind his desk. I sat in front of him and reached into my pocket and got out two copies of a 24 page tract. I opened one to page one and put it on the desk in front of him. I opened the other to the first page and held it in my own hand. We went through that little booklet word-for-word. There are forty-five Bible verses printed out and explained showing people how to get to Heaven. On page 23 there is a little paragraph that says, "Realizing that I am a sinner and believing that Christ died for my sins, I here and now trust Him to be my personal Saviour, depending on Him to forgive all my sins, change my heart, and give me everlasting life as He promised to do." Right below that paragraph there is a dotted line with the word "Signed." Now if anybody knew about dotted lines, this guy did. I called him by name and said, "Would you put your name on that dotted line? Would you do it?" That man dropped his head and sat there for a full minute with his head bowed. He was a good man. He had recently donated to the city of Omaha a building worth $400,000. He gave it to the city to be used as a youth center to try to help kids on drugs and kids in trouble with the law. He was getting up in years and was doing all he could think of to earn points with God. Now he sat with head bowed counting the cost. I know what he was thinking. "What will my wife say if I sign that? What will my business friends say? What will my preacher say?" I know that is what he was thinking. I know it. After a full minute, he looked up and shook his shaggy head. He said, "Preacher, I can't do it." I prayed for him then. I prayed for him afterward and sent him other literature. No doubt he is gone now. But I pray that before he died that man realized the one thing he must do to get to Heaven is to open his life to Jesus Christ and receive Him as personal Saviour. People who trust in their own goodness will go to Hell. Only those who put their trust in Christ will go to Heaven.

The Publican

Now look at the contrast. The publican probably was guilty of every sin the Pharisee had mentioned and many, many others the Pharisee never named. He so felt the guilt of his sin that he would not come close to the altar. He stood afar off. He would not so much as lift up his eyes toward Heaven, but smote upon his breast and cried out, "God be merciful to me a sinner!" Jesus said, "I tell you this man went down to his house justified rather than the other: for everyone that exalteth himself shall be abased; and he that humbleth himself shall be exalted." The good man went away lost. The bad man went away saved.

Justified is an interesting word. It means that judicial act of God whereby He declares righteous those who simply put their trust in Jesus. God knows and I know that Bud Lyles is not righteous. If I got what I deserve from God, I would be in Hell now and I know that. But because as a teenager I was willing to admit that I was a sinner and was willing to receive Jesus Christ as my Saviour, my sins are laid on Him and His righteousness is imputed unto me. I am justified...just-as-if-I'd never sinned. Nothing held against my record. My sins, past, present and future are gone. They are under the blood of Christ.

A church in North Carolina invited me for meetings. They were assembling in the basement of a home. By putting out folding chairs they could accommodate about 125 people. I started on a Sunday morning. That night I preached on soul-winning and hearts were stirred. A fine young Christian man took a burden for his uncle who was known as the town drunk. That man had had his first serious brush with the law at age fourteen and was sent away to a reformatory. He learned more about serious crime inside than he could have learned outside in those three years. So when he left there at age seventeen, he was ready for a life of lawlessness. He got into one scrape after another and finally got into the illegal booze business. He got caught at it and was sent away to prison. Out again, in again was the story of his life. Now finally he had become his own best customer and everyone knew him. His nephew went to him and said, "Uncle _____, I want you to go to the revival with me." "Naw," the man said, "I don't go to church." "That's OK," said the nephew. "There'll be lots of visitors. You won't be the only one." The uncle said, "Naw, I don't have clothes to go to church." "You don't need fancy clothes to come to our church." "Naw," said the uncle. "I don't want to go." "Please, Uncle _____, I want you to go as my special guest." Finally he talked him into it. The man came Monday night dressed in bib overalls, a blue denim shirt cut off at the sleeves, a day's growth of beard, scraggly hair and scruffy shoes. He didn't feel quite right in that situation so he sat on the very last row. He liked what he heard so he was back on Tuesday. He had found a clean shirt and a pair of slacks and had shaved. He moved a little closer to the front. He liked what he heard Tuesday so he was back on Wednesday. Now he had gotten a haircut, found a tie and shined his shoes. He moved still closer. He liked what he heard Wednesday so he was back on Thursday with a sport coat and looking like the other folks. He moved a little closer. He enjoyed what he heard Thursday so he was back on Friday sitting in the third row with a couple of empty chairs in front of him. I preached and gave the invitation. "Heads bowed. Eyes closed. How many here would like to be saved? Lift your hand so we can pray for you." Among others Uncle _____ raised his hand. We prayed and sang inviting those who raised a hand to come forward. Several did so, but Uncle _____ did not. I asked the crowd to sing another verse with heads bowed and eyes closed. As they sang, I slipped off the little platform and stepped in the row in front of Uncle _____. He was holding the back of the chair and I laid one hand on his. He looked up. I said, "You raised your hand for prayer that you wanted to be saved." "Yes, I did, Preacher, but I believe I can be saved right here as well as down there at the front." "I do, too." "You do?" "Yes, do you really want to be saved?" "Yes, sir." I asked him to bow his head and I prayed for him while people continued to sing. Then I said, "Now you pray." He used the word "reprobate." Something like this: "Lord, if you can save an old reprobate like me, I want you to do it." I said, "Did you really mean that?" He said, "Preacher, I never meant anything more in all my life." I said, "Would you shake my hand on it?" He nearly wrung the fingers off my hand shaking it. So I suggested that he come to the front and let me tell the people he had just been saved. "Naw, Preacher, I ain't ready for that." We dismissed the service and folks went home.

The next night, Saturday, we had announced a special youth emphasis and had reserved the first three rows on each side of the aisle for teenagers. There was a good crowd and Uncle _____ was sitting in the last row where he had been on Monday night. But tonight he was smiling and taking in the service. I preached a message to challenge young people to live all out for the Lord. At the invitation a dozen or more lined up across the front of the room for a special prayer of dedication. We were singing the invitation song and there was movement in the last row. Here came Uncle _____. He was lifting them up and putting them down and he marched down the aisle. I got him by the hand and said, "What is it, Mr. _____?" He replied, "Preacher, I'm ready for you to tell these people I got saved last night." We had him turn and face the crowd. I said, "You people know this man. He comes tonight to let you know that last night standing right there in the third row, he opened his heart to the Lord and received Jesus Christ as his Saviour. Is that right, Mr. _____?" He said, "Yes, sir." And a big "AMEN" went up from that crowd. People in that part of the country know how to say "Amen." I don't know what is wrong with people in some other areas. I have been back in that region for meetings in other churches and each time that pastor came to hear me preach. I would spot him in the crowd and could hardly wait to get to him after the service. I asked him how he was doing and how the church was doing. Then I said, "How's Uncle _____?" He would answer, "Brother Bud, he's going on with the Lord. You know we are building a church house and anytime I announce a work night, I can count on Uncle _____. He is there with his bib overalls and claw hammer, ready to pound nails for the Lord."

Friends, there is just one way to get to Heaven. It is the same for the up and out sinner as it is for the down and out sinner. You come to Jesus, helpless and guilty in your sins. You repent and say, "Lord, save me." And He does it. He does the saving. He does the cleansing. He does the forgiving. He does the keeping. Start to finish, Jesus does it all. Put your trust in Him. Do it now!

KEN LYNCH

13

The Forgiveness Of Sin
BIOGRAPHICAL SKETCH

Ken Lynch
(1946 -)

Born on October 28, 1946 in Wilmington, Delaware, Ken is the second of three children born to Evelyn and Grevirson Lynch. He has an older brother and a younger sister. In 1950, his family moved to Chester, Pennsylvania, where his mother still lives.

One of the first things his parents did upon moving to Chester was to find an independent, Bible-believing, Bible-preaching Baptist Church. His parents did not just send their children to Sunday School and church; they all went together as a family and were there for every service, including the midweek prayer meeting.

Raised in a Christian home, Ken asked "Jesus to come into his heart" when only five years old, but, not understanding the reality of sin, was not truly saved until ten years later at the age of fifteen in March of 1962. By that time he was an active, baptized member of an independent Baptist church. He had memorized more than 350 Bible verses in Sunday School and had taken a counselor training course in a youth program.

Just days before his conversion he had sung in a youth choir on the last night of a revival meeting in a church not far from his home. In fact, the church was so full that night that the choir was unable to leave the choir loft. He recalls only one statement that was made by a shouting, pulpit-pounding evangelist, "You can believe the whole Bible and still go to Hell!" That was the phrase God used like an arrow to strike conviction deep into his heart. Several days later, his mother had the joy of leading him to Christ in the front seat of their old 1948 Dodge not far from his home.

Two and a half years later he entered Bob Jones University as a music major, but, sensing God's call to preach, he changed his major to prepare for the ministry. He graduated from the Institute of Christian Service in 1969. After graduation, and his marriage to the former Barbara Nichols, he served the Lord for eight years as Minister of Music and Visitation as well as serving as Sunday School Superintendent and Youth Sponsor working under Pastor Bob Walter, now with the Lord.

In September, 1977 the Lord led him into the ministry of full time Missionary-Evangelism. While ministering in churches of any size, his special burden is to minister to and encourage small churches. As of this writing, he has conducted more than 700 meetings in nearly every state in the U.S.A., as well as numerous foreign countries. One country that has become very dear to him is the land of India where he has preached a number of times and has a continuing ministry.

Ken is an accomplished musician and, while his proficiency is on the violin, he also plays a variety of other instruments including the vibra-harp, clavinova, glass armonica, and theremin, an electronic instrument dating from the 1920's. He has also produced a number of albums of conservative sacred music in addition to a nationally recognized video seminar on the evils of "Christian rock" music. He has authored two books, Gospel Music: Blessing or Blight? and The Evangelist: His Life & Ministry To The Church & The World.

His wife, Barbara, conducts special children's meetings during their crusades together. On January 22, 1975, Ken and Barb were blessed with twin daughters. Jennifer and Joanna were raised "on the road" and participated in the musical ministry with vocal and piano solos and duets. They are currently entering their fourth year at Bob Jones University. KWL

Evangelist Ken Lynch
1810 Edgmont Ave.
Chester, PA 19013

THE FORGIVENESS OF SIN
Ken Lynch

Take your Bibles, please, and turn with me to Psalm 32. In Psalm 32 we have one of the great passages in Scripture that deals with the great subject of the forgiveness of sin. I want to read for you the first five verses of this great chapter.

"Blessed is he whose transgression is forgiven, whose sin is covered. Blessed is the man unto whom the LORD imputeth not iniquity, and in whose spirit there is no guile. When I kept silence, my bones waxed old through my roaring all the day long. For day and night thy hand was heavy upon me: my moisture is turned into the drought of summer. I acknowledged my sin unto thee, and mine iniquity have I not hid. I said, I will confess my transgressions unto the LORD; and thou forgavest the iniquity of my sin." (Psalm 32:1-5)

Notice first, in verses one and two, the Condition of Sin; then in verse three, the Condemnation of Sin; in verse four, the Conviction of Sin; in the first part of verse five, the Confession of Sin; and in the latter part of verse five, the Cancellation of Sin.

Shall we bow together in prayer as we ask for God's blessing to attend the preaching of His Word this morning.

"Our Father, we thank Thee, first of all, for the person of the Lord Jesus Christ. Then, Father, we thank Thee for the great work of redemption that He did in our behalf, as our substitute on the Cross of Calvary, dying in our place that we might live. And, Father, we are grateful for this great passage of Scripture. We pray that You will minister to each of our hearts and meet the needs that may be there. Do that work of grace that needs to be done, whether the work of salvation, the work of surrender, or the work of service. And may the Lord Jesus alone be glorified, and we'll give Thee all of the praise because we ask it in Jesus' name. Amen."

The Condition of Sin

Please note with me as we consider the Condition of Sin in verses one and two that there are three different words used to describe that condition. Notice in verse one the words "transgression" and "sin" and in verse two the word "iniquity." Now each of these words comes from a different Hebrew word and conveys a slightly different aspect regarding the condition of sin.

"TRANSGRESSION": The word "transgression," in verse one, literally means "rebellion against the rightful authority of God." And, dear friends, one thing we must all come to grips with is the simple fact that God, by virtue of Who He is, as the Eternal, Sovereign Creator, IS the rightful Authority over ALL of us! It doesn't matter whether or not you like it, or believe it, or reject it! God IS the rightful Authority over all of us. Man, however, in his sin, in his "transgression," has rebelled against that rightful authority of God.

In Psalm 14:1, the Bible says, "The fool hath said in his heart, There is no God." Now in the King James translation, the two words "there is" are italicized meaning that they were not in the original manuscripts, but were added by the translators of 1611. If you read Psalm 14:1 and reverently delete those two words, it reads simply, "The fool hath said in his heart, No God." In other words, it is not that the self-acclaimed atheist does not believe that God is, but rather that he refuses to acknowledge that God is!

Dr. Matthew Henry, writing three and a half centuries ago, said this, "No man will say that there is no God until he becomes so hardened in sin that it becomes his best interest that there should be no one to call him to account." That's a good evaluation. You see, recognizing and acknowledging that God is also acknowledges that there is ultimate accountability to Him. Every one of us will one day stand before that God and be held accountable to Him. "Transgression," then, is rebellion against the rightful authority of God.

"SIN": Notice, also in verse one, the word "sin," which denotes the idea of "missing the mark." A similar word is used in Romans chapter three and verse twenty-three where the Bible says, "For all have SINNED and come short of the glory of God."

I must confess to you that, in spite of the fact that I come from an area of great sports' teams in all of the professional sports, I grew up with a great dislike for athletic sports. To me, "sports" is fishing, swimming, boating, etc. Even worse to me than Latin and Algebra, was gym class. But I was forced to take all such courses! And I thought that, when I graduated from high school and went to a fundamental, Bible-believing, Christian college like Bob Jones University, I would, at last, be free from the scourge of Phys Ed! Alas, to my utter dismay, even there I was subjected to four semesters of my "favorite" course!

Now the big sport on campus at that time was soccer. To me, soccer was too much like football, and one sport I did not like was football! A bunch of grown up men dressed up in those silly looking costumes, running around in sub-zero temperatures kicking a bag of zipped-up air, waiting to get their wind knocked out! So I said "No" to soccer.

Then there was basketball. Basketball is certainly an exciting game, and me, growing up in the shadow of the world's greatest basketball team, the 76ers! I could run in those days and I could dribble but, somehow, I never seemed to be able to co-ordinate doing both at the same time. So

I thought to myself, "No way am I going to make a fool of myself trying to play basketball!"

So, I signed up for two semesters of Beginning Archery. Have any of you ever used a bow and arrow? A number of you. Then you'll appreciate this! Understand, the only bow I had ever held in my hands was a violin bow! The only thing I knew about archery is what I had seen on Robin Hood. My, did Errol Flynn make it look so easy! I knew that you took a crooked stick with a string tied to both ends with which you shot another stick at a target so big and colorful only a blind man could possibly miss it. Brother, was I naive!

My ignorance of archery was so bad that, when the instructor suggested I begin using a 35 lb. bow, I looked at the bow, then looked at him and said, "You mean that thing weighs thirty-five pounds?" Thus began my career as a fumbling, embarrassed archery student. I couldn't hit that target if my life depended upon it, no matter how hard I tried! In fact, my archery was so bad that, at the change of semester, all of the archery students received new coverings for their targets - except me! Years later, a friend finally discovered what I was doing wrong; I was looking down the shaft of the arrow with the wrong eye! Now, your eyes may only be a couple of inches apart, but those couple of inches are magnified many times over at fifty yards!

As I look back on those days as a fumbling, embarrassed archery student, I cannot help but think how much like that is the average person here in America today. The target set before us is the standard of God's infinite, divine perfection. It is His holiness, His righteousness, His purity, His sinlessness, His perfectness that is His glory! There is nothing and there is no one more perfect than God! God is the essence of perfection. Because God is holy, He requires that every thing in His presence be holy.

We TRY to aim the arrow of our life in the right direction. We TRY hard to do our very best. But, as we release the arrow of our life, and we have but one life - one arrow, somewhere down the line we sin and, because of our sin, the arrow of our life misses the mark; the target of God's perfection. My friend, Perfection and imperfection cannot dwell side by side! If God were to simply overlook man's sin and all his imperfections, He would cease to be holy and perfect and would, therefore, cease to be God.

"INIQUITY": Notice in verse two, the word "iniquity." The word translated "iniquity" means crookedness, distortion, that which is perverted. The prophet Jeremiah said it well in Jeremiah 17:9, "The heart is deceitful above all things and desperately wicked. Who can know it?" That is what we call a rhetorical question; that is, that it needs no answer. The human mind is not capable of understanding the wicked, foul, perverted depths to which it is capable of stooping and wallowing in its total degeneracy and depravity! Your heart, my heart, all hearts, are desperately wicked beyond comprehension in their natural state.

This terrible condition of sin, my dear friend, is a condition that effects ALL of us for the Bible says in Ecclesiastes 7:20 that "there is not a just man on the earth that doeth good and sinneth not." "There is NONE righteous, no not one" (Romans 3:10). "We are ALL as an unclean thing, and ALL of our righteousnesses are as filthy rags" (Isaiah 64:6). And Romans 3:23 says that "ALL have sinned."

The Condemnation of Sin

Going on to verse three, notice there the Condemnation of Sin. "When I kept silence, my bones waxed old through my roaring all the day long." David talks here about something we don't like to talk about or even think about - a thing called old age.

Now I realize that, to a degree, old age can be a relative thing; you are only as old as you feel. However, that does have its limitations. Why, I can remember when I thought an "old" person was a high-school senior. That's because I was only in the third grade! But when I became a senior, I didn't feel "old." I then reached a point when I thought a person was "old" at fifty; an "antique" at sixty; an "artifact" at seventy; and just "well pickled" at eighty and beyond. And now, my own dear Mother is nearly ninety!

Did you know that, according to medical science, your body replaces all of its cells (with the exception of brain cells) every seven years? Now that's great when you're a little baby because the cells are replaced by bigger and better cells during every seven-year cycle. But, once you pass five cycles of seven, that's thirty-five years, (which is half of the Biblical "threescore and ten"), each cycle is not quite as good as the previous one. So, the body begins to break down and deteriorate.

Some of you men find that your nice dark hair has begun to fade. Now you can use Grecian Formula if you like, but I wouldn't recommend it as a good investment for some of you. Some of you used to have the waves and now you've got the beach! And for you ladies, there is a "miracle" product on the market that is international in scope. The promoters want you to believe that if you begin to use this product when you're sixteen, when you're seventy-six you'll look like you're forty-six. Do you know what it's called? No, not Oil of Olay but Oil of "Delay!" In spite of what they claim, it cannot hold back the frost-heaves of life known as wrinkles!

Seriously, though, with all kidding aside, we can chuckle about it now, but it is a very serious matter. You can use Grecian Formula, Oil of "Delay," or any of a number of other products. You can lose some weight and have your "chin tucks" and maybe make yourself look twenty years younger. But, friend, there's one thing you cannot do: you cannot roll back the clock of time and take those years off! And, if God tarries His coming, and all things take their natural course, old age will eventually lead you to the most inescapable event in human history - physical death! The Bible clearly teaches us that physical death is God's condemnation or sin.

God told Adam and Eve, way back in the Garden of Eden, that the day they ate of the forbidden fruit, they would die. Remember, please, that death is separation. Physical death is separation of the soul from the body and spiritual death is separation of the soul from God. The day Adam and Eve ate of the forbidden fruit, they, in fact, died; first, spiritually in that they were at once separated from God. That is why God cried out to man, "Adam! Adam! Where art thou?" God knew where man was, but His question demanded that he be held accountable. Then, secondly, they began the process of dying physically for up until that time, their bodies were not deteriorating nor showing signs of increased age. It was only after the Fall that those things became apparent.

The Bible says, "The soul that sinneth, it shall DIE" (Ezekiel 18:4). The question is not IF you die; that has already been settled. The question is, rather, WHEN, and HOW you die; but die you will! "As by one man sin entered into the world, and DEATH by sin; so then DEATH passed upon all men, for that all have sinned" (Romans 5:12). "The wages of sin is DEATH" (Romans 6:23b). Wages are that which you earn. There will come a day when you have to leave this life. And, as you do, you'll have to go by the paymaster's office and pick up your paycheck. And the paycheck for a life of sin, my friend, is death; both physical and spiritual!

The Conviction Of Sin

Going on to verse four, notice with me the Conviction of Sin. Notice the emphasis on the hand of God. David said, "Day and night THY hand was heavy upon me: my moisture is turned into the drought of summer." Turn in your Bibles, please, just a couple of pages, to Psalm 38. As I read the first few verses, notice the clear working of God. "O LORD, rebuke me not in THY wrath: neither chasten me in THY hot displeasure. For THINE arrows stick fast in me, and THY hand presseth me sore. There is no soundness in my flesh because of THINE anger; neither is there any rest in my bones because of MY sin. For MINE iniquities are gone over my head: as an heavy burden they are too heavy for me." Jump down to verse 17. "I am ready to halt, and my sorrow is continually before me. For I will declare my iniquity; I will be sorry for my sin" (Psalm 38:1-4,17,18). Wait a minute! "Sorry for my sin" is NOT a sorrow that

I got caught in my sin; NOR a sorrow that I now have to face the consequences of my sin; but, a sorrow that I ever committed sin in the first
place and offended a holy God! Go back to Psalm 32.

When we come to the conviction of sin, we come to that part of
salvation that is the work of God alone. For too long there has been taught
in some circles that we are out to get souls saved when we go soul-winning.
Friend, understand clearly, that no man, no preacher, no one, has any
ability or any authority to save anyone, or even convict, anyone of their
sin. We can tell you what the Bible says about your sin and the remedy
for your sin, but we have no power to convict or save anyone! Our job
is not to "get people saved." Our job is to faithfully "sow the seed" of the
Word of God, and reap the harvest as God, Himself, provides the increase
(I Cor. 3).

There are some people ("super-Gospel-salesmen" I call them) who go
into a person's home on visitation to witness to the individual. Instead of
just sharing the Gospel and being sensitive to the Lord's leading, they
over-stay their visit and really put the pressure on until, around midnight,
they finally get a "decision." The person to whom they have been "wit-
nessing" becomes so exasperated that he or she finally prays a "prayer";
not because they recognize their need of Christ; not because they truly
desire to be saved from their sin and not because they want to go to
Heaven and miss Hell! The only reason they pray such a prayer is to get
this over-bearing, high-pressured religious "nut" out of their house! And
yet, they're just as lost as if they were already in Hell! And the personal
worker leaves the house in glee saying, "Boy, I got another one saved!"
Oh, how God Almighty must be grieved.

My friend, I want you to understand something, tonight. God says in
His Word, the Bible, that His Word will not return unto Him void (meaning
empty or fruitless) but would accomplish that which He pleases and would
prosper in the thing where unto He sent it. Friend, you and I are not
responsible for the fruit and the results of our labors. That is God's business.
The Apostle Paul says in First Corinthians 3, "So then, neither is he that
planteth any thing, neither he that watereth, but God that giveth the
increase." God the Holy Spirit must do His work or there can never
be salvation. Without conviction there can be no conversion. Without
repentance, there can be no regeneration.

Now any preacher can use what is called crowd psychology and manipu-
lation and get people to respond the way he wants them to. You see it
all the time on so-called religious TV. But if God Almighty hasn't worked
in your heart and life, my friend, it doesn't make any difference how many
times you raise your hand in a meeting like this. It doesn't matter how
many times you walk an aisle, or pray a prayer (remember that prayer is
an outward expression of an inward heart attitude. One can physically

and verbally say a prayer, but if one's heart attitude is not right with God, there is no salvation). It doesn't make any difference how many times you sign a decision card, or get dunked in somebody's baptismal pool, or join a church! If God the Holy Spirit has not done His work of conviction in your heart, there is no salvation! You don't get yourself saved; God does the saving - and the keeping, too! When we give the invitation, I am so thankful that I am not responsible for the decisions that are made or not made in our meetings. The invitation is not my time to "prey" on souls but to pray for souls to get right with God! What you do with the invitation is your responsibility before God. If you only respond because you think it will please me, it means absolutely nothing.

The Confession Of Sin

In verse five, we have the Confession of Sin. David continues, "I acknowledged my sin unto thee, and mine iniquity have I not hid. I said, I will confess my transgressions unto the LORD." There are three words that David uses to describe the confession of sin.

"ACKNOWLEDGED": "I **acknowledged** my sin unto thee." The word "acknowledged" means to admit personal responsibility. We need to stop blaming Aunt Tizzie and Uncle Harry. We need to stop blaming Mom and Pop. We need to stop blaming the school system and the government. We need to stop blaming everybody and everything else for our sin, and come to the place where we are willing to admit that we, and we alone, are responsible for our own sin.

Back in the early 1950's, when I was just a boy, I had an experience that will help to illustrate the point I'm trying to make. A neighbor across the street had bought a brand new shiny black Ford pick-up truck. You know that's how you spell truck - "F-O-R-D!" Right? Well, anyway, my family had never been able to afford a new car. To us, a new car was someone else's ten-year old trade-in! So I really admired that truck. I cannot recall ever seeing that truck dirty. It was always clean and it sparkled like a diamond in the sun! I remember gently rubbing my hands over the smooth paint on the fender of that truck. Oh, it felt so good to touch.

One day, as I was admiring that truck, I did something terrible. I don't know why I did it, but I did it. I found a rusty nail in the gutter which I picked up and, holding it tightly with both hands, proceeded to, not scratch but, carve my initials, "K-W-L," in the fender of that truck. Talk about stupid! Imagine! Carving my initials, of all things!

Later that afternoon, when my father came home from work, I saw that man walk across the street and start talking to my dad. I remember thinking, "What does he want?" After all, we lived in the city where neighbors (other than those directly next to you) don't even know each other, much less talk to each other. Let me tell you, I found out what he wanted. My father came to me and asked me point blank, not, "Son, did you do it?" but, "Son, WHY did you do it?" I mean there was no benefit of the doubt. Now, my father had been on the United States Naval Academy championship boxing and wrestling team back in the class of 1924. Dad used to say those were the days when the Navy had "wooden ships and iron men!" So you didn't mess with my dad. Boy, was he mad that day! I honestly don't remember what I told him. What could I say, anyway?

In a way, my dad lied to me that day. He told me he was going to give me the "whipping of a lifetime." Now to me, that means you get one whipping and it lasts you the rest of your life. Man, I got those things two and three times a week! That's why I say he lied to me. Dad was mad at me and I was mad at him.

Have you ever been so mad that you talk to yourself? Well, a couple of hours later, while my mother was getting supper ready, I was up in the bathroom getting washed up. As I looked into the mirror, there was the meanest looking kid glaring back at me. Do you know what that kid said to me? He said, "The next time I'll carve my brother's initials in it!" What I didn't know was that my brother was standing right outside the door waiting his turn to wash up. When he heard what I said, he slid down the banister (how many times I wished there had been a big splinter in that railing pointing north!) and told on me.

Have you ever seen a softball pitcher winding up for the pitch? Well, that's what my dad looked like, only he was winding up his belt in his hands before he even hit the staircase. Man, I want to tell you, I got two whippings of a lifetime in less than two hours! Now, here's the point I want to drive home. I had to acknowledge to my father that day that I, and I alone, was soley responsible for that act of vandalism. There was nobody standing over me with a .38 pointed to my head saying, "Carve, kid!" I did it because I wanted to do it and I had to admit it to my father.

My friend, that is exactly what this word, "acknowledge," means in relationship to you and your Heavenly Father. You cannot blame your sin on anyone else. You must come to the place where you are willing to admit that you, and you alone, are responsible before God for your own sin. And you will never be saved until and unless you do!

"NOT HID": Notice the next statement, "mine iniquity have I **not hid**." That means "to cover or conceal." The question is not, "Are you a sinner?" The answer to that is obvious: of course you are. If you're honest, you know that. We are all sinners, myself included. So the real question is, "What are you going to do about your sin?" That's the issue here.

Now here's what most people do. Oh yes, they recognize that they are a sinner. After all, nobody's perfect! But they try to cover, or conceal, their sin by putting on the garment of religion, or the cloak of baptism, church membership, sacramentalism, and a host of other things; thinking that all of their religious "coverings" will conceal their sin from God. Friend, that will never do. What you need to do is stop trying to cover and conceal your sin. You need, rather, to strip off the garments of religion, baptism, sacramentalism, church membership, or whatever else you've been trusting in, and literally bear your souls naked before a holy God crying out to Him, "Oh God! Here I am, in all the filth and the magnitude of my sin!" And until you do that, dear friend, you'll never know the saving grace of a loving God!

"CONFESS": Then there's the last word dealing with the confession of sin and it is the word "confess." "I said, I will **confess** my transgressions unto the LORD." The word confess literally means to "agree with," or to "say the same thing as," God. And in this case, it deals particularly with the matter of agreeing with God about our sin. Too many people say, "Of course, I'm a sinner, but I'm not that bad." But God says you are that bad. True confession means that when God says I'm a sinner, I say, "That's right. I agree with You!" When God says that I'm going to go to Hell, I say, "That's right. I agree with You!" When God says that I deserve to go to Hell, I say, "That's right. I agree with You!"

Please take careful notice to whom such confession of sin is to be made. It is NOT to be made to the preacher or the priest, but only to the Lord Himself! "I will confess my transgressions to the LORD." Why? Because only the Lord has the power and the ability to forgive us our sin. No man, no matter who he is, what he is, or where he is, can do that. The Bible says that there is but one mediator between man and God, and that is the Lord Jesus Christ (I Timothy 2:5).

The Cancellation Of Sin

Finally, will you notice, also in verse five, the phrase, "...and thou forgavest the iniquity of my sin." Here we have the Cancellation of Sin. There are three different words that the Psalmist uses to describe for us the cancellation of our sin. You will find them back in verses one and two. Please be patient with me. I'm almost through.

I was preaching from this passage of Scripture a number of years ago during a meeting in the Pittsburgh, Pennsylvania area. A young boy, maybe seven years old, came to church for the first time to hear the musical glasses. During the service he sat right on the aisle on the second row so he could see well. Since he was by himself, the pastor sat next to him to make sure he behaved himself.

All during the message he talked right out loud. As I was trying to preach, I could hear every word he said. Even those sitting in the back of the church could hear everything he said! He was most disconcerting, let me tell you. And what he said was even worse! He kept saying things like, "Man, he's long!" or "When's he gonna be done?" or "Ain't he done yet?" The pastor quietly pointed him to the end of verse five and whispered, "Do you see that word, 'Selah'?" And the kid bellowed out, "Yeah! I see it!" Pastor quietly continued, "Well, when he gets down to that, he's going to quit." "Oh. OK!"

So I got down to the end of verse five and I said, "All right folks, go back with me to verses one and two." Well, did I have that boy's attention! I mean to tell you, he sat right up in his seat and cried out so that the whole church burst into laughter, "Man alive! He's startin' all over agin'!"

No, I'm almost finished. Do notice with me, though, in verses one and two, the three words or expressions used to describe the cancellation of sin.

First, the word FORGIVEN. "Blessed is he whose transgression is **forgiven.**" Dr. Alexander Maclaren (one of my favorite Bible expositors) says that the word "forgiven" means "to lift off, as a heavy burden from aching shoulders." And isn't that exactly how David described the burden of sin in Psalm 38? "As an heavy burden, they are too heavy for me." (Psalm 38:4b) My friend, you'll never, in your life, ever carry a heavier burden than the burden of unconfessed sin. But, if you will confess your sin to Him, acknowledge your own responsibility and stop trying to cover and hide your sin, God, in His wonderful grace and mercy, will reach over the battlements of Heaven and lift that heavy burden of sin from your aching shoulders! As a teenager, we used to sing a great gospel song: "Leave your heavy burdens at the Cross and, sinner, GO FREE!" My dear friend, you don't have to carry that load of sin a moment longer, if you will come to Jesus.

The next word in verse one is the word, "COVERED." ["Blessed is he] whose sin is **covered.**" Again, Dr. Maclaren describes the word "covered" as "God shrouding the foul thing from His pure eyes so that His action is no longer determined by its presence." In Old Testament times, the saints of God offered the blood of the animal sacrifices which served as a covering for their sin. Hebrews 10 makes it emphatically clear that the blood of bulls and goats could not take away sin, but it did cover sin temporarily, pending the ultimate sacrifice of Jesus Christ (Hebrews 10:1-5). But, the Bible also makes it crystal-clear that the "blood of Jesus Christ, His Son CLEANSETH us from all sin" (I John 1:7). John the Baptist said of the Lord Jesus, "Behold the Lamb of God which taketh AWAY the sin of the world!" (John 1:29). Thank God, dear friend, that there is "power, power, wonder-working power! in the precious blood of the Lamb!"

The final expression is the phrase "IMPUTETH NOT." "Blessed is the man unto whom the LORD **imputeth not** iniquity." That phrase literally means that one's sin is no longer laid to his own account but has been transferred to another's. When we trust in Christ, our sin is transferred to Him and paid for by His substitutionary sacrifice on the Cross. "He bore our sins in His own body on the Tree." (I Peter 2:24)

When the Lord Jesus was hanging on the Cross, He made several utterances that have come to be known as the "Seven Sayings from the Cross." One of those sayings is a three-word English translation of one Greek word. The English translation is the phrase, "It is finished," which comes from the one Greek word, "Tetelestai," a commercial term used in the marketplace of our Lord's day. The term meant basically the same thing as the phrase we use today which is, "Paid In Full."

Ah, dear friend, thank God, Jesus didn't pay only part of my sin debt. He didn't just make an installment or two. He didn't even pay most of my sin debt. But, Jesus paid it ALL! Every last bit of it is paid for! As the hymn-writer penned the words so many years ago:

> "Jesus paid it all; all to Him I owe.
> [While] sin had left its crimson stain
> [Thank God] He washed it white as snow!"

Oh, my dear friend, have you personally known that wonderful forgiveness of sin? If not, you need to, and you can, right now. The Bible says, "These things are written, that ye may KNOW that ye have eternal life" (I John 5:13). Will you trust Him right now?

BOB SHELTON

Bob Shelton

14

The Serpent Crawls Through Bible Prophecy

BIOGRAPHICAL SKETCH

Bob Shelton
(1929 -)

Born on June 1, 1929 and reared in a godly home, Bob Shelton grew up under the ministry of Dr. H.H. Savage at First Baptist Church of Pontiac, Michigan. Following his graduation from Bob Jones University in 1951, he, along with several other young evangelists and seasoned missionaries, went to Taiwan to preach God's Word in Chinese army camps. This ministry was sponsored by the late leader of Free China, Generalissimo Chaing Kai-Shek. Thousands of his soldiers professed to receive Christ as Saviour.

In early 1952, Bob began to evangelize the people of the Pescadores, a chain of islands between Taiwan and Mainland China. Twelve of the islands had never heard the Gospel of Jesus Christ; eight of those had never been visited by a white man.

Bob returned to the states and married the former Nancy Harrison. A few weeks later they went to Okinawa where they served their first term as missionaries. Those were blessed years with much fruit among the nationals as well as a rewarding ministry among American servicemen.

After furlough they went to Viet-Nam where they intended to spend the rest of their earthly ministry. They learned the language and entered into a work of evangelism and Bible conferences that took them from one end of the country to the other.

They returned to the States for furlough with their three children. (Their daughters, Becky and Shari, were born on Okinawa and their son, Dan, in Saigon.) It was during furlough that the war broke out in Viet-Nam and they were not able to return to that field to do the work that was so close to their hearts. But God had other plans. Following Dr. Savage's 38 year ministry at Michigan's First Baptist Church, the congregation extended the call to Bob to become their next pastor.

There were several highlights to the work in Pontiac. The greatest being the many who received Christ as Saviour. The radio ministry under Pastor Shelton's ministry covered the globe with responses coming from 36 countries. Perhaps one of the greatest outreaches was the television program, "There Is An Answer," which weekly saturated the greater Detroit area resulting in the conversion of many people and the edification of countless Christians.

Since 1974, the Sheltons have been in a full-time ministry of evangelism and Bible conferences. Nancy travels with Bob and enjoys a fruitful ministry among children.

In addition to their evangelistic and Bible Conference labors, Bob now has a weekly radio broadcast that reaches into many states as well as overseas. He also spends from four to six weeks every year ministering in foreign countries.

The Sheltons make their home in Greenville, South Carolina.

Evangelist Bob Shelton
10 Wallingsford Rd.
Greenville, SC 29616

THE SERPENT CRAWLS THROUGH BIBLE PROPHECY
Bob Shelton

From the dawn of creation until this present hour, Satan's influence among men has been profound. But, according to Bible prophecy, his power will be felt in an even greater way in the days ahead. The subject at hand deals primarily with things to come, but before considering God's prophetic blueprint as it relates to Satan, it would be well to take a brief look into history, as well as a glimpse of the present.

Satan In History

First, we will look at Satan's past. "How art thou fallen from heaven, O Lucifer, son of the morning! how art thou cut down to the ground, which didst weaken the nations! For thou hast said in thine heart, I will ascend into heaven, I will exalt my throne above the stars of God, I will sit also upon the mount of the congregation, in the sides of the north: I will ascend above the heights of the clouds; I will be like the most High. Yet thou shalt be brought down to hell, to the sides of the pit. They that see thee shall narrowly look upon thee, and consider thee, saying, Is this the man that made the earth to tremble, and did shake kingdoms; That made the world as a wilderness, and destroyed the cities thereof: that opened not the house of his prisoners?" (Isaiah 14:12-17). This passage records the account of Lucifer's fall and the prophecy concerning his eternal destiny. Much has happened, and will yet take place, before the prophecy is fulfilled. But where is Satan in this present age?

Satan Today

Note first that Satan has access into the presence of God. Job 2:1 declares: "Again there was a day when the sons of God came to present themselves before the Lord, and Satan came also among them to present himself before the Lord." The question arises, "Why is Satan allowed to appear before Almighty God?" The answer is recorded in Revelation 12:10 where Satan is pictured standing before God as the "accuser of the brethren." Every Christian should be careful to maintain a consistent testimony because God is not the only One who is viewing our lives. Satan is also aware of our deportment and is quick to make accusations before the throne of God.

Next, we understand that Satan has access to the earth. Job 2:2 goes on to state: "And the Lord said unto Satan, From whence comest thou? And Satan answered the Lord, and said, From going to and fro in the earth, and from walking up and down in it." Sometime ago, I heard of a liberal pastor who wrote, "There is no such thing as a devil." A certain Christian read that statement and responded by saying, "I feel like the prizefighter who was receiving a terrible beating at the hands of his opponent. As the weary boxer leaned on the ropes about to fall, his manager said, 'Come on, he is not even hitting you.' The fighter replied, 'He isn't? Then watch that referee because somebody is!'" The inference is clear. If there is no devil, who is responsible for the things that only Satan can do? Alfred Hough had this in mind when he penned this satire:

"Men don't believe in the Devil now, as their
    fathers used to do.
They've forced the door of the broadest creed to
    let his majesty through.
There isn't a print of his cloven foot or fiery dart
    from his bow
To be found on earth or air today, for the world
    has voted it so.
Who dogs the steps of a toiling saint and digs
    the pits for his feet?
Who sows the tares in the fields of time
    Whenever God sows the wheat?
The Devil is voted not to be, and, of course, the
    thing is true;
But who is doing the kind of work that the Devil
    alone can do?
We are told that he doesn't go about as a roar-
    ing lion now,
But whom shall we hold responsible for the
    everlasting row
To be heard in home, in church and state, to the
    earth's remotest bound,
If the Devil by unanimous vote is nowhere to be
    found?
Won't someone step to the front forthwith and
    make their bow and show
How the frauds and crimes of a single day spring
    up? We want to know.
The Devil was fairly voted out, and of course,
    The Devil's gone;
But simple people would like to know who carries
    the business on?

God's Word is clear on this subject. "Be sober, be vigilant; because your adversary the devil, as a roaring lion, walketh about, seeking whom he may devour" (I Peter 5:8).

Satan not only has access into the presence of God where he accuses the brethren night and day, and access upon the earth where he roams as a roaring lion, but he is also showing his presence in outer space. The Apostle Paul declares: "Put on the whole armour of God, that ye may be able to stand against the wiles of the devil. For we wrestle not against flesh and blood, but against principalities, against powers, against the rulers of the darkness of this world, against spiritual wickedness in high places" (Ephesians 6:11,12). Earlier in this epistle Paul refers to Satan as the "prince of the power of the air" (Ephesians 2:2).

It is interesting to note the enchantment that people seem to have with life in outer space. From many modern-day psychics and astrologers, statements like these have become commonplace: "Some day soon UFO's will be landing upon the earth." "Representatives from other planets are gathering for an interplanetary meeting." "Contact with earth by a civilization in outer space . . ." "Space probes to Mars will reveal new evidence of ancient alien civilizations and of recent landings there by UFO's." One author has written a book in which he tells us that kids are singing a rock song which says, "The star machines are coming down and we are going to have a party." He goes on to say, "The odds seem very good that something is penetrating our air space" The BAPTIST BULLETIN carried an interesting review of the book UFO's: What On Earth Is Happening? In part, that review stated: "Over 15,000,000 people claim to have seen UFO's (Unidentified Flying Objects). Skilled scientists, astronauts, and pilots from various countries are numbered with this group. Among the many suggestions as to the identity of UFO's, the top three are weapons of some government, interplanetary humanoids, and demon activity. After radar screening, 3,000 aircraft chases and thousands of photographs, UFO's elude a sure explanation. The conclusion of this data-packed book is that UFO's represent demon activity, especially in preparation for the Antichrist."

It seems clear that Satan is not only getting the world ready for the coming of Antichrist, but is, no doubt, preparing men for the Rapture of the Church. Though Scripture does not record what will appear in newspapers following the catching away of the Bride of Christ, it may be reported that UFO's have finally arrived and have successfully snatched away millions of people who called themselves Christians.

Robert Emenger in his book, UFO's, Past, Present, and Future, relates the opinions of a panel of leading psychologists supervised by Dr. Leon Testinger of New York's School for Social Research. They concluded that "aliens from outer space could land on the White House lawn tomorrow and science fiction, would hardly bat an eye . . . the majority of Americans would simply go on with their everyday business and probably lose interest in them soon." It should not startle believers to hear of all of the strange events associated with outer space, for remember that this is Satan's domain.

Satan In Prophecy

The day is coming, however, when Satan will be cast out of the atmospheric and celestial heavens above us. This truth is presented clearly in Revelation 12:7-12: "And there was war in heaven: Michael and his angels fought against the dragon: and the dragon fought and his angels, And prevailed not: neither was their place found any more in heaven. And the great dragon was cast out, that old serpent, called the Devil, and Satan, which deceiveth the whole world: he was cast out into the earth, and his angels were cast out with him. And I heard a loud voice saying in heaven, Now is come salvation, and strength, and the kingdom of our God, and the power of his Christ: for the accuser of our brethren is cast down, which accused them before our God day and night. And they overcame him by the blood of the Lamb, and by the word of their testimony, and they loved not their lives unto the death. Therefore rejoice, ye heavens, and ye that dwell in them. Woe to the inhabiters of the earth and of the sea! for the devil is come down unto you, having great wrath, because he knoweth that he hath but a short time."

Lucifer lost his first estate, as was noted earlier in Isaiah 14. Now in Revelation 12, a fearful battle is waged between the forces of Heaven and the forces of Satan (Lucifer). Michael and the angels of Heaven will win the war, so those in Heaven can rejoice over God's great victory. But ". . . Woe to the inhabiters of the earth and of the sea! for the devil is come down unto you, having great wrath, because he knoweth that he hath but a short time" (Revelation 12:12). This battle will take place in the middle of the Seventieth Week of Daniel.

At that point, Satan will be cast to the earth, no longer permitted to appear in the presence of God or to roam in the celestial heavens above. He will be confined to the earth. It is interesting to note that Revelation 12:7-12 records the casting out of Satan to the earth, and in the following verses, the Great Tribulation is introduced. During the three and one-half years that follow, Satan will do all within his power to kill as many people on earth as possible. His special hatred will be aimed at those who trust Christ as Saviour, but he will also feel a fiendish glee over the millions of unbelievers who die without Christ and without hope. Jesus declared in Matthew 24: "And except those days should be shortened, there should be no flesh saved. . . ." (verse 22). It would appear that if Satan had but a few more months, his goal of ridding the earth of its total population would be accomplished. It should be understood that many of the judgments that will take place in those days will be from the hand of God against a wicked and perverse generation, but it will be Satan who will put into the hearts of nations the desire for battle. He will also bring untold misery through hunger and ravenous animals. It will certainly be the most chaotic time in human history. It has been properly called, "the Great Tribulation."

The Bottomless Pit

As the serpent continues to crawl through the prophetic scene, the next major development will be his confinement in the bottomless pit. "And I saw an angel come down from heaven, having the key of the bottomless pit and a great chain in his hand. And he laid hold on the dragon, that old serpent, which is the Devil, and Satan, and bound him a thousand years, and cast him into the bottomless pit, and shut him up, and set a seal upon him, that he should deceive the nations no more, till the thousand years should be fulfilled: and after that he must be loosed a little season" (Revelation 20:1-3). This confinement will follow the Battle of Armageddon. The thousand years that Satan will be chained will be the same thousand years in which Christ will be ruling in His Kingdom. The prayer that has been offered for nearly two thousand years will at last be answered. "Our Father which art in heaven, Hallowed by thy name. Thy Kingdom come. Thy will be done in earth, as it is in heaven" (Matthew 6:9-10). The will of God may be done today in the hearts of those who have trusted Christ as Saviour, but God's will will never be done on earth as His will is done in Heaven until Satan is chained in the bottomless pit and Christ is sitting upon the throne of His father, David.

Satan Loosed

One would think that after a thousand-year prison term Satan would learn something; but the sacred record tells us that after a millenium in the bottomless pit, Satan will be loosed out of his prison and will go out to deceive the nations. He will gather all of those who have been born in the Millenium and have failed to trust Christ as Saviour into one last rebellious army. They will follow Satan's leadership in defying the exalted position of Jesus Christ, but they will meet the wrath of God. Revelation 20:10 becomes a fitting conclusion for our present consideration: "And the devil that deceived them was cast into the lake of fire and brimstone, where the beast and the false prophet are, and shall be tormented day and night for ever and ever." It should be understood that Satan will be cast into the Lake of Fire where the Beast and the False Prophet are. The word is "are," not "were." That is, at this point, the Antichrist and the False Prophet will have been in the Lake of Fire for a thousand years. It should be remembered that they will be cast into the Lake of Fire following the Battle of Armageddon (Revelation 19:20). Satan will finally be cast into the same place a thousand years later only to discover the Antichrist and the False Prophet are still there. Those who argue that the Lake of Fire is a place of annihilation certainly have a difficult time explaining Revelation 20:10. We can rejoice that Satan will be in the Lake of Fire for all eternity. After all, that place was prepared for the Devil and his angels (Matthew 25:41). It was never God's intention that any human being should go to Hell, but those who reject His Son as Saviour will be cast into that eternal place (Revelation 20:15). As sure as God's Word is true, they will spend the countless ages to come with Satan.

Earlier I presented a passage from Isaiah 14. I would like to close with that same portion of God's revelation. "Yet thou shalt be brought down to hell, to the sides of the pit. They that see thee shall narrowly look upon thee, and consider thee, saying, Is this the man that made the earth to tremble, that did shake kingdoms; That made the world as a wilderness . . ." (Isaiah 14:15-17a). What a tragedy to think that some who hear these words may actually repeat this passage in Satan's ears as they suffer the torments of Hell throughout all eternity!

PHIL SHULER

15

Two Beggars

BIOGRAPHICAL SKETCH

Phil Shuler
(1924 -)

Phil R. Shuler, the youngest of seven born to the family of R.P. (fighting Bob) Shuler & his wife Nelle, arrived on the scene December 29, 1924, in the beginning of his Father's campaign to "clean up Los Angeles." Dr. Bob Shuler was (and remained for 37 years.) Pastor of Trinity Methodist Church downtown, Los Angeles.

At the age of 14, Phil listening to his Father preach on Rom. 3:23 & Rom. 10:9-13, and under deep conviction walked the aisle to accept Christ as his personal Savior. The next year, in a summer tent revival, sponsored by Trinity Church, and under his brother Jack's preaching, Phil answered the call to preach.

Before his 18th birthday, (and under the signature of his Father,) Phil joined the Navy & became a radio man. He was attached to landing parties for the purpose of setting up ship-to-shore communication for the 1st Marine Division, and was in three invasions, making nine landings. Upon his return from WWII, Phil entered Bob Jones University, then in Cleveland, Tennessee, where he graduated in 1950. Upon completing his formal education, Phil joined his brother Jack's Evangelistic team and became his field director and advance man. (You spell that; "FLUNKIE.") During these two years, Phil was most impressed that Evangelism was God's will for the remainder of his life.

When Phil was six years of age, he sat in his Sunday School class next to a shy little girl named Marie Lemmon; in 1948, he married her! She was not only the girl that filled his thoughts, she was the only girl that would put up with him! Marie studied to be a concert pianist, & brought to Jack's team that expertise.

In November, 1951, Phil and Marie left the Jack Shuler team for a ministry of their own. The first two years was a mixture of city-wide & single church revivals, starting with Tabernacle Baptist Church, Roswell, N.M. (Howard Ingram, Pastor). Phil's heart, however, was for the small, struggling churches of 50 members or less, and is to this day.

Phill & Marie have two daughters, both married to Pastors. Debbie (born during that Roswell Meeting) married Dan Mauldin, Ass't Pastor, Beth Eden Baptist Church, Denver. Julie, born 2½ years younger than her sister, married Ross Davis, Pastor of Falls Road Baptist Church, Rocky Mount, N.C. These unions have given Phil & Marie five Grandchildren, all perfect! The eldest is in college in California, the second oldest is at Bob Jones, the third oldest will enter Clearwater in 1996, and the other two are trying to catch them!

1996 was a special year to Phil & Marie. In Phil's first year at Bob Jones College, he began holding revival meetings on weekends, preaching pool halls on Saturdays when he had no meeting, and Sunday jail services. The three summers of his college days were booked in Revivals. So, on January 15, 1996, Phil & Marie completed 50 years in the Field of Evangelism. His reputation has been his recommendation to Churches all over the 50 states, and many foreign mission fields. If one were to sum up the ministry of Phil Shuler, it could be done in three little words he uses to close each letter. "Yours For Souls".

Evangelist Phil Shuler
8800 Eton Ave, # 60
Canoga Park, CA 91304

TWO BEGGARS
Phil Shuler

If you have your Bibles, open them please to Luke the sixteenth chapter, beginning at the nineteenth verse. Here is a very interesting story, one that is not preached on very much today, but one that should be preached. Luke sixteen and verse nineteen:

"There was a certain rich man, which was clothed in purple and fine linen, and fared sumptuously every day: And there was a certain beggar named Lazarus, which was laid at his gate, full of sores, And desiring to be fed with the crumbs which fell from the rich man's table: moreover the dogs came and licked his sores. And it came to pass, that the beggar died, and was carried by the angels into Abraham's bosom: the rich man also died, and was buried; And in hell he lift up his eyes, being in torments, and seeth Abraham afar off, and Lazarus in his bosom. And he cried and said, Father Abraham, have mercy on me, and send Lazarus, that he may dip the tip of his finger in water, and cool my tongue; for I am tormented in this flame. But Abraham said, Son, remember that thou in thy lifetime receivedst thy good things, and likewise Lazarus evil things: but now he is comforted and thou art tormented. And beside all this, between us and you there is a great gulf fixed: so that they which would pass from hence to you cannot; neither can they pass to us, that would come from thence. Then he said, I pray thee therefore, father, that thou wouldest send him to my father's house: For I have five brethren; that he may testify unto them, lest they also come into this place of torment. Abraham saith unto him, They have Moses and the prophets; let them hear them. And he said, Nay, father Abraham: but if one went unto them from the dead, they will repent. And he said unto him, if they hear not Moses and the prophets, neither will they be persuaded, though one should rise from the dead." (Luke 16: 19-31)

"Holy God and Heavenly Father, we ask now Thy blessing upon the preaching of Thy Word, that it shall not return to Thee void, but accomplish its purpose, we pray, in Jesus' holy and precious Name. Amen."

I'm speaking tonight on "Two Beggars"; one who begged for time, and one who begged for eternity. Now I'm going to ask you to be the judge of a monologue tonight. We're going to take you back in the figment of the imagination to the seat of this story. And by the way, let me say, this is not one of the parables that Jesus taught. Jesus is giving you a first-hand description of the testimony of a man that went to Hell; the only one that we have in the entire Bible. You say, "How do you know it's not a parable?" Because the rule of a parable is they do not give proper names or nouns. And here people are named, Lazarus and Abraham, therefore we know the characters in the plot. It is the story of a man who went to Hell. And Ladies and Gentlemen, it is better to get it from the "horse's mouth" than to get it through speculation. Let's find out exactly what Hell is like. Let's find out if it's a myth. Let's find out by taking the story that Jesus gave of a man who went there and his explanation of it, and let's lay it before us in a kind of monologue.

The Rich Man

Taking you back several thousand years now to the seat of the story. And I'm going to, in the figment of the imagination, bring you to the rich man's house and start with him first. I do this because the Bible says that he "fared sumptuously," and the key phrase is "every day." Now preacher, you and I've had good days, but we've had bad days. Every now and then I've had a bad day. But this man had a good day every day! He fared sumptuously every day, so we're going to slip up to his house.

We come about, oh, seven-fifteen, seven-thirty in the morning up on the veranda of that beautiful house on the hill; lovely, lovely home. And we hear the tinkling of a little silver bell as the butler stands at the bottom of a staircase. He rings his little bell and says, "Breakfast will be served in the drawing room in ten minutes." And upstairs the father steps out in the hall and looks at his gold pocket watch while waiting for his wife. The children come, the boy dressed up in the very finest of clothes, knickerbockers on; the girl in a pinafore. The wife comes in the very latest fashion, puts her hand on the arm of her husband, and that lovely family comes down the winding, golden stairs, as it were, to the drawing room, where there's a great big King James table, (and I believe this is where most rich people lose their kids). They sit at those big long tables; they can't tell what's going on at those big tables. I sat at some when I was on trips with my dad and they tried to impress us. These rich people would have a table thirty-five feet long. Mom and Dad sat at one end, the kids sat on the other, and they hardly knew they were growing up. They'd see 'em every now and then and say, "My, you've grown a foot since the last time I saw you." (I like to get close together when we eat.) But there they sit at the table and the butler and maid serve them. After they've had a lovely meal, Father looks at his watch and says, "Well, I've got to get down to the office. I've got to foreclose on a widow woman before the bank does. Got to make money, you know, to keep this thing going." He said, "Now Wife, look after your children. They're the rich man's children. Kids, I want you to act like the rich man's children. Young girl, I don't want you to walk around with just anybody. Remember who you are. You belong to the rich man's family. And Son, one of these days all that I have is going to be yours. Everything is going to be yours. Don't you deal with common people! You deal with the 'hoy-toy' [elite]. You deal with our social register."

Pastor, did you hear about the Idaho potato that fell in love with the Irish potato? You didn't? Well, they fell in love and got married, and in due time they had a Sweet potato. And the Sweet potato fell madly in love with Paul Harvey. But Momma Tator and Poppa Tator were agin' it, because he was just a Common Tator, you see. Stay away from the Common Tators. You get some of these rich people, they don't want you to deal with the common people on the wrong side of the tracks.

So he said, "Now you two children, go to school and keep your heads high! Now," he said to his wife, "here's a hundred bucks. Go buy yourself a hat. I'm going to the office." And he goes down and gets into his beautiful, beautiful carriage, drawn by two beautiful Morgan horses, and he says, "To the office, James." And the horses go clickety-click, clickety-click, down the cobblestones, while he looks at his holdings and says, "Oh, yes, there they are." He looks out yonder and there are wheat fields as far as you can see, hybrid corn coming up; he comes by the stable and looks in there at the finest thoroughbred Quarter horses you ever saw. Right along side is the hog pen. There's Berkshire, Yorkshire hogs the boys are raising for 4H. They always win a blue ribbon with those.

Everything he has is the very finest. Until he gets to the gate. And suddenly, in horror he looks, and there, outside of his gate is a poor, old fella. He's got scabs and running sores all over his hands and his face, and a dog is licking him for comfort. And this man reaches out with his hand and he says, "Please, sir, please just a crumb from your table. I'm starving to death. Won't you please give me a crumb?" And the rich man picks up his speaking tube and says, "Whip those horses! Get me to my office! And when you let me off, you go to the Chief of Police and you tell him to get that bum outta here! I've got my rights!"

Lazarus

Well, let's look at this "bum" for a minute. He had a mother and dad, too, at one time. He grew up in a home, too, at one time. He fell in love at one time with a lovely girl. He was married. Children graced their home, too. But the children began to grow up and they began to have their friends over to the house. And dad came home from the office one day and he had a skin condition. It was itching, and his finger nails became loose, and his eyebrows began to fall, and his hair began to recede. And pretty soon these little itches became sores and then scabs but, of course, he didn't know what a leprous condition was. Then it began to "snow" decaying flesh around the house. And the boys and girls, who were beginning to date then, went to Mom and said,"Mom, we love Dad. We don't have anything against Dad. But, please, we can't bring our friends in here. This isn't a place to date. This isn't a place to show our future loved ones off. Listen. Mom, put Dad in the back room. Get him away from us. We love him but it smells bad when he's in here."

And so they finally made a little office back there for Dad and put his bed in there. But that's not good enough. Pretty soon they say, "We've got to get rid of him. We hate to do it. Dad, we love ya, but it's either the poor farm or...hey, wait a minute! Wait a minute! You know, I was coming home from school the other day, and I came by the rich man's house. Do you know they throw away garbage better than we eat? They've got the very finest food there. Mom? Listen. If we can get him down by the rich man's house, I'm sure the man is benevolent. I'm sure he's a philanthropist. Certainly he would give him food. Certainly that would be our answer!"

And so they take old scabby Dad, they put him in a wheelbarrow, and they carry him down to the rich man's house and they dump him off. The poor old fella. He lies there with a dog for a friend. And the evening comes. And the sun goes down. And his teeth begin to chatter and he says, "Man, it's cold. Oh, it's cold!" And he gathers his outer garment about him and snuggles next to the dog for warmth. And he prays, "Oh, that I might feel the rays of the sun upon me again!" And in the morning the sun comes up again, and, for a moment, it seems to be peaceful until the sun begins to scorch upon his body and the sweat begins to trickle down into the open sores and it burns like fire and smarts him! And he prays, as he opens his outer garments to the wind, "Oh, that I might feel the cool rays of the night to comfort me!" And this goes on; the cold and the heat, and the cold and the heat, and the Bible says that the only friend he had was a dog!

Well, I told you that you were going to be the judges tonight. Right now, in this story, which of these two men would you most like to be? You say, "That's easy. I don't even have to think about that. Why, you give me the position of the rich man any day! I'd rather have that than the other." Well, let's go on.

The Death Of Lazarus

This poor old fella one night, as he's freezing to death, and the wind is chilling his bones, lies there praying for the heat of the day when suddenly, a warm zephyr seems to hit him. He says, "Oh. Boy, that's nice. Must be a Santa Ana coming my way. I'm...I'm comforted by this."

Then suddenly, he realized it was no wind. It was nothing from this earth. The Bible says that the poor man died and was taken by the angels into Abraham's bosom. He felt the warm wings of an angel about him, as the angel carried him up and away into the throne where Abraham sat. It doesn't say a thing about his body. Doesn't talk about a funeral. I think I know why it doesn't talk about a funeral. I think the same dog that cuddled up against him was the dog that ate him! They did that in those days. These weren't domestic dogs. These were wild dogs. The dogs knew from the man's condition he wouldn't last long; just like a vulture always appears before death. It could smell death. It knows it's there.

But don't worry about the body, Ladies and Gentlemen. If you're a born again Christian and you die, your body means nothing anyway. God'll get it all back together again. Don't worry about the body; the soul is Home with Jesus Christ! Now if you're unsaved and you die, then people have a concern over your body. But, Ladies and Gentlemen, to a Christian, to be absent from the body is to be present with the Lord! Don't worry about the body.

Now, I'm saddened, very saddened to see so many Christians over this country more interested in propagating a body that is decaying than they are to try to get that soul saved before it decayed. They're interested in the body. Friend, let me tell you something. Nothing is in that body worth keeping. It used to be worth a $1.72; now it's worth $6.18. That's what inflation has done. But the body's worth $6.18 in chemicals. The soul is worth more than the world to Almighty God; He sent His Son to die for it!

He dies! He was carried by the angels into Abraham's bosom! Say, listen! You can't beat that! Why, now, he's in Abraham's bosom and old Abraham takes his hands and wipes away the wrinkles in his face and he's young again! And he looks at the beauty of that place and the Tree of Life, and the River of Life, and he's happy there! Everybody that goes there is.

The Death Of The Rich Man

The next day the rich man comes by. You see, he's had a fight with City Hall but he hasn't won yet. He's putting on lobby pressure. But they won't take that bum away because that domain is not his. See, that's public domain. He can sit there if he wants too. He's outside his gate. And he's mad at the City Hall, he's mad at the Mayor, he's mad at the Governor, he's mad at everybody! And he's going to get even with them at election time.

When he comes by the next day, he looks out there, and, behold, somebody's gotten him! Isn't that great? Somebody's gotten him. He's gone! He says, "Good riddance to bad rubbish!" I hear that man say,"Get me down to the office as quick as you can!" And he goes down to the office and he has a good day because nobody's out there to bug him when he drives by.

All week goes by, maybe a month goes by, maybe a year, maybe five, maybe ten years, it doesn't tell. But it doesn't matter. One day, he's giving dictation to his secretary. He says, "Now take a letter...(cough, cough)...take a letter...(cough, cough)...I've got something in my throat here. You know, that's been coming on me (cough). I've got a little lump in there that kinda (cough) grips me every now and then. I wonder...get me a glass of water, secretary." Two or three days later, he's coughing and he looks in his hands and sees a little fleck of blood there. He said, "Hey, I don't like that." He goes to a doctor. The doctor looks down there and says, "I don't understand this at all. You know, your throat looks perfectly normal except the right side of it's beginning to bulge out a little bit. It's kind of closing in on the left side. It's going to squeeze your windpipe in a little while. I don't know what that is."

And the man comes back from the office a couple of days later and says, gasping, "I can hardly breathe! Call the doctor! Call the doctor!" So they call the doctor and the doctor looks in and his throat is almost closing. They didn't know how to diagnose cancer in those days. And as he gets worse, the greatest doctors are brought in, all the specialists are brought in. Everyone that money can buy is brought in! But he gets worse, and worse, and worse. Finally, the death rattle is heard in his throat. His wife, the loving wife, the faithful wife, sits by that bedside and says, "Please. Help my husband. Keep him alive. Keep him alive!"

William Randolph Hearst, died with two hundred million dollars cash in the bank, which is a little more than the pastor has I guarantee you. He died with six Cadillac limosines, three mansions, all alike, all of them furnished alike, so that no matter where he was, the socks were in the right drawer, the tee shirt was in the right drawer, everything. William Randolph Hearst, who owned the largest diamond stick pin collection in the world at that time, and the third largest art collection in the world, when he was dying turned and said to his doctor, "Keep me alive! Keep me alive, I'm not ready to die!" He said, "You'll receive five thousand dollars cash every day you keep me alive. I'm not ready to die." And he died saying that! That was the condition here. Keep him alive. Oh, the wife was worried; she loved him. And the children were in the next room. They were going through a terrible, a terrible, traumatic experience. They were arguing over who was going to get the biggest cut in the will.

It breaks my heart, as I go around the country, and see these kids that have been given hundreds of thousands of dollars in their teens to help skid the way to Hell a little more easily, to grease the path so they can get there quicker! I told both of my girls, when they got married, "You marry well," and they did - they married preachers. You can't marry better than that because God takes care of preachers. I said, "You marry well, cause you're not going to get much money when I die." Everything that I have in the way of funds when I die goes to perpetuate the Word of God. One tenth of my will goes to the church. By the way, I think every Christian ought to do that. I don't think there's a Christian sitting before me that ought not to go back and rework your will and tithe it when you're dead, so that when you're dead, you still speak with your money. The government doesn't eat it up. The church can use it. If you don't believe in your church, get in a church where you can believe in it. Get with a pastor you do believe in. When I die, I'm going to die with a grin on my face, if I do die. I believe I'll be here when the Lord comes, but if I do die, I'm going to die with a grin on my face because I know that ten percent of it goes into the church to continue to preach the Gospel in my locale, and the other ninety percent is going to go to Bob Jones University or some other school that is propagating the Word of God. I'm not going to waste it. And listen, if we would all do that we wouldn't have a problem today; God would take care of us in our lifetime and we would die with peace in our heart because we would know that we are perpetuating the Gospel with our death. Don't worry about your kids. You got along without your parents' money. They can get along without it. It makes better character to dig for it a little bit. I really believe in that.

Now here they are, and the rich man dies, the Bible says, "and was buried." Now it tells you where his body went. He had a funeral. Oh boy, howdy, did he have a funeral! It was one to stop all funerals. Why, this was the rich man. And they took him down to the First Church of the Deep Freeze and they put him in a coffin there. And I'm telling you Doctor Pussyfoot stood up there and preached that old boy into the first row of the choir in Heaven, and said, "He was such a gooooood man. Why, we could always depend on him for a big contribution for the building fund." And the Lodge was there. And the band was there. And they said, "Oh, we're going to miss him!" Sure. He always picked up the tab. He was a rich man.

But I've got news for you. When they threw roses down on that grave, he wasn't there. He wasn't there. You see, the Greek language does not have a colon in it here, it has a comma. It means "next thought follows," you're not to divorce it. So let's look at it that way. "And the rich man also died and was buried comma and in Hell." Now hold on a minute. To the Christian, absent from the body is present with the Lord. To the unsaved, absent from the body means present in Hell!

"And in Hell," notice, please, number one, he "lift up his eyes," in other words, he could see. He could see. He saw Abraham, he saw Lazarus, he saw the beauty of that place. That's going to be the worst aspect of Hell; the fact that you can see. Do you kids remember this morning I told you about when we went in to get Doolittle's boys and we brought them back from Sasebo, Japan, in World War II? We brought twenty-eight of these boys back, and practically all of them had no fingers or thumbs up to the first joint. They'd been burned off. The Japanese would put bamboo under the fingernails, sliver it under the skin next to the bone. Bamboo burns without oxygen, you know. They'd light it and let it burn. And each day they'd do this until they burned their flesh right off. They would torture these kids trying to find out information about the next invasion, where they were from, what was coming toward them, and so forth and so on. All kinds of punishment was given to the extent, as I recall, of the twenty-eight we took aboard there wasn't but two or three that were rational. The rest of them were vegetables. They were out of their heads. They just walked around with male nurses to keep them from falling over the side or committing suicide.

But there was one major. I'll never forget him. I pal'd around with him for a while. He had a sense of humor he said that got him through. And he did have a good sense of humor. He had no fingers, like the rest of them. But now the war was over. We had lights on the ship; we could go with lights, now. We were standing back toward the fantail of the ship in the evening. And he was smoking a cigarette with these stubs. I said to him, "Major, I don't want to bring up any bad memories to you, but," I said, "Of all the punishment that you went through, of all the punishment, what was the one that finally broke the men?" "Well," he said, "I think that's pretty easy to explain to you." He said, "It wasn't the bamboo up the fingernails, the water torture, or these others things they did to us, the beatings. After this was all done, they would put us in a cell of isolation. They would give us just enough water and fish heads to keep us alive; just barely keep us alive. And then, about the fifth day of this fast, we'd wake up from kind of a coma in dreamland. We would smell American food! We'd look out of our cell and there was a big banquet table with a table cloth on it, and American coffee steaming, and American T-bone steak, medium well, French fries, salad with Roquefurt cheese dressing; all these things. The things we loved at home - there they were! And there was a little Japanese boy with a bamboo fan behind it, fanning that aroma in the cell." He continued, "We'd crawl to the cell door. And there would be a Japanese officer with an American cigarette. He'd inhale it and then blow it in our faces. We'd smell that. We'd say, 'Please! Please! Give me something to eat!' And the officer would say, 'Tell us what we want to know, and you can have all you can eat.'"

"Then they would take an urn of ice water and they would put it down here with crinkling ice in it and they'd let the dogs drink it! And we were starving for water! And we'd reach and say, 'Please! Give us water!' And they would slap our hands with the flat of a sword and say, 'Tell us what we want to know, and you can drink all you want.'"

I'll never forget that major as he told that story in almost a monotone. He flipped that cigarette over the side of the ship. It hit the screw and churned up in the water. He turned around to me and looked right into my face and he said, "Mate, that was hell!" And I said, "That's exactly what it was." And I pulled out my New Testament and took my little flashlight off my life jacket and I shined it down there to Luke 16 and I showed him what Hell was!

Here was a man that was in Hell. He could see the Tree of Life! He could see the beauty of eternity with Christ! He could see all the goodness that Heaven had but he knew he'd never attain it! That's Hell. That's Hell. "He lifted up his eyes and SEETH Abraham and Lazarus in his bosom" And he cried (he had a voice) and said, "Father Abraham..." Now, stop just a minute. Who told him that was father Abraham? Had he ever met Abraham? No. Well, then who told him? Did Abraham have one of these little "Hello, I'm Abraham" get acquainted tags on his lapel? No. Well then, how did he know? I'll tell you how he knew, and you'd better get this doctrine; it's there. When we who are saved, when we die, when we see Christ, the Bible says "we shall be like Him;" we shall have the mind of Christ. If any of you have a brother or sister that died before you were born, like I have a brother that died before I was born, you'll never have to go to Jesus and say "Where's my brother or sister?" You'll go right to them and recognize them. Why? Because you'll have the mind of Christ, you'll know as He is known, the Bible says. But that same attribute is going to be the curse of Hell! God will see to it that every lost soul will have an unfailing memory. You say, "Listen, don't bug me on this business of getting saved! If I go to Hell, it's my business! I'm not hurting anybody!" Oh yes you are! Yes, you are! You reject Jesus Christ and say, "I'll not have Him to rule over me!" Listen! Listen! When you die, you say, "Well, I'm goin' to Hell, but it's only me." No, your sons; they respected you and honored you, and they're going to be like you. So they're going to go to Hell someday, and then they're going to have children that respect and honor them, and they're going to go to Hell someday. And they're going to have children that respect and honor them and they're going to go to Hell someday, and you're going to be down their crying, "Please! Warn the future generations!" You say, "Where do you get that?" Right here. "I have five brothers, that he might go and tell them of this terrible place of torment." Ladies and Gentlemen, you're going to be there in Hell, those of you who reject Christ, forever and ever, and forever and forever, and forever and forever, as long as God exists, you're going to be in Hell. And you're going to be watching those who come after you, who have followed your pattern and also rejected Jesus Christ, and you can't do a thing about it. You wouldn't give a nickel to missions now, but you'd give anything to be a missionary then.

"And he said, Father Abraham have Lazarus come down and dip the tip of his finger in water and cool my tongue for I am tormented in this flame." Man, that's the hardest thing in the world for me to grasp with my mind. I'm a farm boy, folks, and my dad would not allow us to go in and get a drink of water on our farm until our hoes were dull. I don't know whether you had a dad like this or not, but dad would say, "Don't ask to go get a drink of water till your hoes are dull." Man, you'd get out there, you know, and be hoeing for a couple of hours; you'd be dehydrated. We'd say, "Dad, can we go in and get a drink of water?" "Let me feel your hoe." He'd feel it, and say, "That isn't dull, yet. Keep hoeing."

Well, we knew how to solve that. You know, after a while, you'd find a rock; there's enough of them around. We'd start beating that rock. We'd say, "Dad ..." He'd say, "Let me feel your hoe. Yea, it's dull. All right, boys. Go on in and get your drink of water, and sharpen your hoes. Be sure to get all the water you can drink." Oh, we would. We had a big, deep well. We lived at El Monte, which is right over a clear lake. We could drill down not too far and get nice, cool, spring water. I mean, before they put all the junk in it, it was pure, beautiful water. And we would fill, (right above the well house), a fifty gallon drum that was encased in straw that was wet all the time. Kept it ice cold. And that gravity fed down to a pipe that had a brass spigot on it. That was our drinking fountain. And we would turn the spigot on, with that fifty gallons of fresh water up there; we'd turn that spigot on just fast enough to keep up with it. Then we'd sterilize it by wiping our hand across it once, 'cause my brothers had used it, you see. Then we'd let all the air out (of ourselves) so we could fill up on it. And we'd wrap our mouths around it and gulp, gulp, gulp, just bloat up like an old blood leech.

When I drank, I drank! I never in my life understood the use of a demitasse cup. Those things never appealed to me. Those little bitty cups they hand you, you know. A sip of tea! Thimble full. Man, listen, I... I was a milk drinker when I was a boy. I used to drink skim milk. If we didn't, the hogs would. And we didn't want the hogs to get it all. So we'd drink skim milk. I was raised on skim milk, and my wife used to drink a lot of coffee. And I told her, "Honey, you're going to have to quit that coffee." And she said, "Well, you're going to have to quit drinking skim milk. It's getting to you. You're drinking too much." And I was. Well, I was drinking a quart a meal! Every meal I'd drink a quart of skim milk. Marie was drinking, maybe, three cups of coffee each meal. So I said, "I'll tell you what I'll do. I'll limit myself to one glass of milk a meal if you'll limit yourself to one cup of coffee a meal." She said, "OK. You're on."

Then I went downtown and bought a quart glass! She never knew how much it was, until about three months later. I was still going with my quart a day, when somebody came along and said, "Boy, I'd like to get one of those quart glasses. Where did you buy it?" And Marie said, "That'll do it!" Well now, Friends, when I drink, I like to drink a lot. I don't like to drink just a little bit, I like to drink. And here, can you imagine, what one drop of water means to a person in Hell? When one drop of water can comfort a person in Hell, what a terrible place that must be!

Now, I want you to get this next part. He said, "Son, remember that thou in thy lifetime receivedst good things, and likewise Lazarus evil things; now he is comforted and thou are tormented. Now the answer to this is, when he was young, he had faith in the Law and kept the Law. He was one that offered sacrifices. He was a good Jew. And by that it was counted to righteousness. But you wouldn't do that. Instead, you became a money man, instead you became a wealthy man, but you would not have faith in what the Bible then said to be salvation." And then he says something that staggers the mind, "And beside all this, ..." Now, stop here just a minute, because in Connecticut, 1953, I held a revival meeting in a church where a Catholic woman came to me and said, "Preacher, I've never heard a Gospel like this before." She said, "Would it be offensive to you if I asked you to speak to our priest?" And I said, "Not at all. I'd be glad to speak to him." So she took me to the Catholic priest having made an appointment. She said she was bringing a friend. That's all she said. And I got there and talked to an elderly priest who later became a Cardinal in that area. So I'm not talking to a novice, I'm talking to an educated man. And I asked him where he got his New Testament doctrine of Purgatory, the in-between position of purification that the Church believes in. They believe that Pope John Paul the First, who died today, is there now. He's being purified. He will go through a period of purification where he will be burned so that the dross burns up and his soul will come through unscathed. It (the soul) gets out, presumably, by the number of prayers and the number of Masses that are said for him, which are purchased Masses. The Kennedys have already purchased over two million dollars worth of Masses for their two sons. I have been told. Now this is what he [the priest] explained to me. I said, "Where do you find this?" And he said, "The main reference we have is in Luke 16." He said, "This, that He refers to, the opposite of Paradise, is Purgatory." So I said, "Who is out of Purgatory?" He said, "Several of the popes, not all of them, but most of them, are out and those who have been beautified, or made saints, are out." Now, they've thrown Christopher back in again! But the rest of them, when they are beautified, or made saints, come out. Now this man is a Cardinal, and he said, "Other than that, we are not sure of any Catholic that is not in Purgatory." Now, here is his reference for it.

Please, will you read it with me very carefully? Now, I want you to have an open mind on this. Catholics here, please, have an open mind to the Scripture that they lean on, if you will please. This is verse twenty-six. "And besides all this, between us and you" (that's the Paradise part or the Heaven part at that time, and this, what he [the priest] calls the Purgatory part) "there is a great gulf" (now get the word, underline it) "FIXED." Now the word "fixed" is the same word in the Greek that is used when Paul said that His word is "<u>established</u> forever and forever." Established, it means "foundationed." For instance, if I were to drive down the street and I were to see a pile of leaves, I would say, "Those are not permanent. Those are transient." I can drive through them or I can scatter them with my foot. But if I were to go to the Empire State building in New York, I would say, "That's established. That's there. I can't move it. It can't be moved. It has to be destroyed before it can be moved." Now, that's what this word means. "There is a great gulf fixed," now watch it, "so that they which would pass from hence to you," what? "CANNOT, neither can pass to us which would come from thence." Now, wait a minute! Jesus is giving the story. And He says that Abraham said that there is no way - impossible - no way, for a person, once they're there, to get out!

Now, I'm warning you, folks. You might say, "I don't like his preaching. It's not what I've been taught. I've been taught differently." Please, don't read books about the Book; read the Book. Don't trust people who tell you about the Book; trust Jesus Who wrote the Book. Please, don't lean upon the teacher; lean upon the Author! Jesus Christ said there is no way you can get out of that place. No way. It's a permanent thing. As long as God lives, you'll be there, until you're resurrected at the Great White Throne, and then you answer the one question, "What have you done with Jesus that is called the Christ?" And having rejected Him, the Bible says in Revelation you'll be sentenced to the Lake of Fire where the worm dieth not, and the fire is not quenched. You and Satan will be there forever and ever, and forever and ever, and forever and ever, and then, you'll be having breakfast. You'll never get out.

Now, the last question. At this stage of the game, which of these two men would you like to be? You say, "Well, that's a gray horse of a different color. Now when you put it that way, Shuler, I guess the answer would be I'd rather be a beggar for time than to be in Hell for eternity! Yes, yes. And yet, isn't it a thrill, Christians, that we're not even beggars for time? For, when we accept Jesus Christ as our personal Lord and Saviour, "my God shall supply all your needs according to His riches in glory in Christ Jesus." There's not a need in your life that God Almighty will not supply. And to boot, eternal life.

You see, Paradise is no longer in Paradise. The Bible says that Jesus Christ died on the Cross of Calvary two thousand years ago, and they put Him in the tomb of Joseph of Arimathaea. But the Bible says when they rolled the stone and sealed it with the Roman Seal, Jesus entered Sheol, the very place I'm telling you about. He entered Hell. And the Bible says that He wrestled Satan for the keys of sin and death and He defeated Satan! And He rose conquering and to conquer. And the Bible says when He rose many graves were opened. You say, "Where do you find that?" In Ephesians four, verses four to eight. You'll find that Jesus Christ went down into the lower part first and led captivity captive. All the Old Testament saints arose with Him. All those, at the time of Jesus and before, rose with Him. They are present with Him, where ever He is. Now, since the resurrection of Jesus Christ, every sinner that dies goes into this same Hell that I've described to you from Luke 16; only there is no Paradise left: only the beauty of the place. Nobody's there. There are no persons there. There might be the trees and the land, even the chair that Abraham sat in, all these things; but nobody's there! Just the joy of the place, just the peace of the place! Nobody's there. All of those people, plus everyone who has died in Christ since Jesus Christ, have gone home to be with Christ, Who'll come some day in the air to gather us, the Bible says.

Now folks, I'm going to just ask that you realize that this is not the figment of the imagination of this Evangelist tonight. This happens to be the one and only story Jesus Himself told, when He was on this earth, of a man who actually went to Hell. And I pray God that nobody in this building, knowing better, shall say, "I resolve that I shall not accept Christ, but I'll take my chances on that place I can never escape; I'll take my chances on Hell." I hope you won't do that. I hope you'll use good, common sense.

Bow your heads and close your eyes, please.

JERRY SIVNKSTY

16

What Changed My Life As A Teenager

BIOGRAPHICAL SKETCH

Jerry Sivnksty
(1942 -)

Evangelist Jerry Sivnksty was born on September 10, 1942 and raised in the small coal mining camp of Areford, West Virginia, near Fairmont, where his father spent more than forty years working in the coal mines.

As a young man he was quite the outdoorsman and sportsman playing both football and baseball as well as enjoying hunting, fishing, trapping and hiking.

He was saved at the age of seventeen out of a Roman Catholic background through the faithful ministry of a Pastor Douglas Rutherford. After his conversion, he enrolled in Bob Jones University to prepare for the ministry, graduated in 1965. He also attended graduate school for a year and a half.

While a senior Bible major at BJU, the Lord enabled him to start the Fellowship Baptist Church (Independent) in Anderson, South Carolina, which he pastored for five years.

In 1970, Jerry, his wife, Sharon, and his family entered the field of fulltime evangelism and has been greatly used of God in the years since in more than 1,000 meetings all across America. He is especially popular as a youth evangelist. Recognizing the importance of memorizing Scripture, he wrote his own Bible memorization program entitled, The Two Edged Sword Memory Plan, a soul-winning diary, and a gospel tract entitled, The Most Important Thing In Life Is ...

In 1980, Maranatha Baptist Bible College in Wisconsin honored him with a Doctor of Divinity degree. In 1987, he was given an honorary Doctor of Humanities degree by his alma mater, Bob Jones University.

He and his wife have three sons and a daughter, and make their home in Starr, South Carolina. KWL

Evangelist Jerry Sivnksty
P.O. Box 141
Starr, SC 29684

WHAT CHANGED MY LIFE AS A TEENAGER
Jerry Sivnksty

Tonight, my message basically deals with what changed my life as a teenager. You know, teenagers, there has to be one truth that grips your heart, that will change the way you live as a Christian. What I'm going to tell you right now is what changed my life after Christ saved me. And I pray to God that some young man, or some young lady, or many of you, may get a grip on what God used in my life, and what I am, really, is because of this one great truth.

Second Timothy, Chapter three and verse sixteen is our text. Let's all stand right now, please, if you will. And would you please listen very carefully to verse sixteen. "All scripture is given by inspiration of God, and is profitable for doctrine, for reproof, for correction, for instruction in righteousness." I would pray, in Christ's Name, that I might have your undivided attention as I give out God's Word at this time. Let's pray. FATHER, IN JESUS' NAME, WE PRAY YOU MIGHT BLESS AS WE GIVE OUT THE WORD OF GOD, WE ASK IN THY NAME. AMEN. You may be seated.

Our text begins by stating, "All scripture is given by inspiration of God." Look up! You all know what the word inspiration means? The word inspiration means "God-breathed." And that means the Bible actually came from God Almighty's mouth.

Jeremiah 1:9 - "Then the Lord put forth his hand and touched my mouth, and the Lord said unto me, Behold, I put my words in thy mouth."

II Samuel 23:2 says, "The Spirit of God spake by me and his word was in my tongue."

Exodus 32:16 says, "And the tables were the work of God and the writing was the writing of God." That means the Bible came from the very mouth and divine finger of God, Himself.

Since that's true, young people, that means the Bible is completely trustworthy!

John 17:17 says, "Sanctify them through thy truth; thy word is truth."

John 15:3 says, "Now are ye clean through the words which I have spoken unto you."

I Kings 8:56 says, "There hath not failed one word of all his good promises."

In John 10:35 - Christ says, "The Scripture cannot be broken."

Isaiah 40:8 - "The grass withereth, the flower fadeth, but the word of our God shall stand forever."

Matthew 5:18 - "Till heaven and earth pass, one jot or one tittle, shall in no wise pass from the law until all be fulfilled."

Psalm 119:89 - "Forever, O LORD, thy word is settled in heaven."

I Peter 1:25 - "But the word of the Lord endureth forever."

In Psalm 138:2 the Word of God says, "Thou hast magnified thy word above all thy name."

Young people, there is a great truth we stand on tonight. That great truth is this: "All scripture is given by inspiration of God."

God Gave The Bible To Grow

But why did God give you the Bible? The answer is in our text. First of all, He gave the Bible so you may GROW. Look back at our text. "All scripture is given by inspiration of God," now, get this, "and is profitable for doctrine." That small statement there, "profitable for doctrine," shows you that God gave the Bible so we may grow.

II Timothy 2:15 says, "Study to show thyself approved unto God."

Psalm 119:18 says, "Open thou mine eyes that I may behold wondrous things out of thy law."

Look here. Every time you open your Bible, you ought to bow your head and say, "Dear God, give me understanding as I read Thy Word." Why is that so? Because the way you grow, the way you mature is by the in-take of the Bible within your life.

When I first got saved. I didn't even own a Bible. Hey, guys, my whole life was a sports realm. I played football for three years. I was outside linebacker offensive end for three years in a public high school of twelve hundred students in West Virginia. I played baseball in the outfield for three years. My entire life was that of an outdoorsman. I hunted, I fished, I trapped, I ran the hills of West Virginia.

One day though, when I got saved, my Sunday School teacher made a challenge to twenty teenagers. He said, "The first teenager who memorizes John 14:1-15; I will give him whatever he wants." I said, "Man, these Baptists must be millionaires! I'm going to memorize that and get me a new bat!" I needed a new bat real bad, so I said, "I'm going to memorize that." So I went home, borrowed my mother's Bible, and memorized John 14:1-15.

The next Sunday I went to class and the teacher said, "Did anybody memorize John 14:1-15?" And no one raised their hand, and finally I said, "I did, sir." He said, "You did?" I said, "Yes, sir." He said, "Well then, stand up in front of the class and quote it." Man, I went into shock! I never did that in my life. And when I got scared, I stuttered a great deal. And man, I started stuttering; I got so scared I said, "J-, J-, J-, John fourteen, one through fifteen." Listen, I'm part Russian, and I rushed right through the whole passage! Well, when I got through, he said, "Jerry, that's good. What do you want?" I said, "Sir, I want a new ball bat." He said, "Are you serious?" I memorized that for one reason: I wanted a new ball bat!

The next Sunday I went to Sunday School and I saw my teacher standing outside with his hands behind his back. I knew he had my ball bat. I went running up to him as fast as I could. When I got there, he said, "Here, Jerry!" and he gave me-- a Bible! Can you imagine that? A Bible! An Old Scofield Reference Bible. My heart sunk to my feet and I wasn't a bit thankful. Honest. I was disgusted. And I said, "Thank you." I didn't want the Bible; I wanted the ball bat. That was my entire life.

Well, I took my Bible home, went downstairs in the basement one night, sat down in my dad's coal-mining chair, opened my new Bible up to the Gospel of John, began to read - listen guys - began to read the Word of God; and when I did, I could not put the Bible down! And every evening I'd go home; I'd do my chores; I'd go downstairs and begin to memorize, and memorize, and study the Word of God. And here's the one great truth that changed my life: I started memorizing something that was going to last forever. And I'll tell you that one great truth has changed my life. I am memorizing, I am reading, something that's going to last for all eternity. "Heaven and earth shall pass away, but thy word shall never pass away."

And I want to tell you as a testimony, young person, we need a revival among you young people; a revival where you make this Bible greater than soccer. You make this Bible greater than volleyball. You make this Bible greater than basketball. You make this Bible greater than football. You make the great love of your life the Word of God! The Bible says in Colossians 3:16, "Let the word of Christ dwell in you richly in all wisdom."

Joshua 1:8 - "This book of the law shall not depart out of thy mouth, but thou shalt meditate therein day and night."

Revelation 1:3 - "Blessed is he that readeth and they that hear the words of this prophecy."

I Peter 2:2 - "As newborn babes in Christ, desire the sincere milk of the word that ye might grow thereby."

And young people, the way you grow is to recognize that God Almighty gave you the Bible that you might grow!

God Gave The Bible To Groom

But, second of all, look back at verse sixteen, please, because the Word of God goes on to say that He gave the Bible that He may groom our lives. "All scripture is given by inspiration of God and is profitable for doctrine," now get this, "For reproof, for correction." Second of all, God says, "As you grow, I want to groom your life."

Would you all take your Bible and go to Titus two and verse twelve? I want to show you a great passage. If there's one verse I would to God was in the life of every Christian on the wall of your home, it would be Titus two and verse twelve. Here, the Word of God shows how He wants your life to be lived after He saves you. Look at Titus 2:12. It says, "Teaching us, that denying ungodliness and worldly lusts, we should live soberly, righteously, and godly in this present world." Look here! You say, "Jerry, how should I live my life?" You should live sober, which means "sound in your reasoning;" righteous means "righteous in your living;" godly means "godly in your example." Now, how does God take any one of you and make you a "sober, righteous, and godly" individual? One word: "teaching us that DENYING." And there's the key: DENIAL. Denial has always been God's way of shaping the life of an individual. The Bible says in Matthew 16:24, Christ Himself said, "If any man will come after me, let him deny himself and take up his cross and follow me."

Galatians 5:24 - "And they that are Christ's have crucified the flesh with the affection and lusts."

Romans 13:14 - "Put ye on the Lord Jesus Christ and make not provision for the flesh to fulfill the lust thereof."

I Peter 2:11 - "Dearly beloved, I beseech you as strangers and pilgrims, abstain from fleshly lusts which war against the soul."

Over and over God says, "Denial. Denial." Denial is the key. That means this, young man, young lady: you must come to the place where you put your life under the authority of the teaching of God's Word. Did you hear me? I said you need to put your life under the authority of the Bible where you are tender and you obey what God's Word commands you!

Many years ago, I was preaching in Minnesota. Now, this is not a problem today like it was back then; but this was many years ago when guys wore long hair, OK? I was preaching in Minnesota and the church was packed; I did not know who was there, just like I don't know who is here tonight. It's a Bible principle. And I said this, "The Word of God says whenever God sees a man, God wants a man to look like a man!" Amen? And, girls, God wants a girl to look like a girl, not a Notre Dame fullback! All right? And so I said, "The Bible says in First Corinthians 11:14, 'Doth not even nature itself teach you that if a man have long hair, it is a shame unto him?'" I said to the congregation, "What would you kids think if I had long hair, down to here? a golden earring in one ear? a purse on this shoulder? if I had high heel shoes on?" And I said, "Now, you guys, would you like that?" I said, "If you would, I'd take my purse and slap you up the side of your head!" When God sees a man, God wants a man to be a man! I got through preaching; I'm standing in the back of the church;

a man with long black hair on his shoulders comes walking up to me--
I'm five nine when I stand up straight; this guy was six five or six nine-
black hair, this long on his shoulders, walks right up to me, grabs my
shoulder, squeezes my shoulder; points his finger right in my face and
said, "You preached on long hair tonight, didn't you?" And I looked at
him and said, "Yes,sir." He is squeezing me tighter all the time on the
shoulder and he said, "You know what?!" Brother, I did not know what!
I said, "No. What?" He said, "God spoke to my heart!" I said, "He did?"
He said, "Yes, And tomorrow night when you see me, I'm going to have
my hair cut like a man!" I said, "Praise the Lord!" Now, why didn't that
guy get mad at me? Because his heart was tender to the Word of God.
He put his life under the authority of God's Word. Here's my observation.
If I could look you right in the eyes and say this to you one on one, I
would do that. Your problem is not your rock music. Your problem is not
the Contemporary Christian Music. Your problem is not the magazines.
Your problem is not the hair. The person's problem is always the heart.
Show me a person whose heart is tender to the Word of God; he automati-
cally puts his life under the authority of the Bible. So whatever God
condemns, he'll never condone. What God forbids, he'll not endorse.
What God denies, he'll never embrace. Why? His life is under the authority
of God's Word. God's commandments, God's law, God's statutes, God's
teachings: his heart is tender and God can shape his life.

Psalm 119:9-11 "Where withal shall a young man cleanse his way?
By taking heed thereto according to thy word. With my whole heart have
I sought thee. O let me not wander from thy commandments. Thy word
have I had in mine heart that I might not sin against thee."

God Gave His Word To Guide

Young people, God says, "I gave My Word so that you might GROW.
I gave My Word so that I might GROOM your life." But, last of all; look
back at verse sixteen; the Word of God says He gave the Bible, last of
all, that He may GUIDE you. The latter part of verse sixteen says "for
instruction in righteousness." That's very crucial. The Bible is God's instruction for righteousness! In other words, the only way a man can know he's
going to heaven is by what God has revealed in the Bible. No angel's
going to write your name across the sky; no one's going to come down
from heaven and tell you to get saved. No. When God saves a person,
He saves him through preaching, teaching about Jesus Christ.

There's a man in the Bible in Acts eight who was one day reading the
Word of God. As he read the Bible, a man of God said to him, "Understan-
dest thou what thou readest?" The man said (Acts 8:31), "How can I,

except some man should guide me?" Now I thank God for that man's heart. He was not like the average American, "Hey, man! I'm not a heathen! What do you think I am? a heathen? Why, sure I've got my religion. I'm OK!" Now this man was not proud; this man was humble. He said, "How can I, except some man should guide me?" Now, I would to God today, you had enough common sense in your heart, young man or young lady, you'd have enough character in your life that you'd admit no one has ever taken a Bible, no one's ever shown you from the Word of God how to be saved.

And, when that man said that, Philip opened his mouth and opened the Scriptures and preached unto him, Jesus. Here's my observation. Throughout the Bible, where ever you go, the Bible will never focus on religion. The Bible will never focus on a denomination. The Bible will always focus on Jesus Christ. If I had a big screen, and I could just throw verse after verse after verse before you, would you see this invisible screen, and listen to God's Word?

"Believe on the Lord Jesus Christ and thou shalt be saved." Acts 16:31.

"Neither is there salvation in any other." Acts 4:12.

"For God sent not his son into the world to condemn the world, but that the world through him might be saved." John 3:17.

"In whom we have redemption through his blood." Ephesians1:7.

"I am the door; by me if any man enter in he shall be saved." John 10:9.

"I am the light of the world." John 8:12.

And throughout the Word of God, time and time again, the Bible will just always draw you to Jesus Christ. Let me ask you a question, right now. Please look at me. If I took this preaching finger, and as you have observed, I'm left-handed, and I pointed you out right now where ever you are, in the back row, or over here in the middle, and I said, "Stand up right now and come down here. Has anyone ever taken the Bible and shown you how to be saved? Give your answer before God." What would you say, young man? What would you say, young lady?

I was in meetings last week in Minnesota. While I was there, in my office on Wednesday morning came a knock on my door. I said, "Come in." A lady came in, and she was weeping. I said, "What's the matter, Ma'am?" She said, "I've not slept all night." I said, "What do you mean?" She said, "I don't think I'm saved." She went on, "Do you know what I did when I was a little girl? I went down the church aisle. They said, 'Just weep and pray, and it'll be all right.'" She said, "No one took a Bible and showed me how to be saved. And I want to be saved!" And I took the Word of God and showed that lady from the Word of God how Christ could save her, and she got saved. After last night's service, when I got through preaching, a lady called for me and said, "There's a young teenage girl here who would like to talk to you." I won't embarrass you, but I thank

God you got saved, young lady. This young lady's a Roman Catholic, and she was searching; she wanted me to take the Bible; and I took the Word of God and sat down with her in this tent, opened the Word of God and showed her how Christ could save her; and she asked Jesus Christ to save her.

I want to tell you something. I've got a son whose name is Scott. I always wondered about my son, Scott--I've got three boys-- but Scott, I never saw tears in his eyes over anything spiritual. I've got a problem with you, guy, if nothing ever moves you to tears. Lady, I've got a problem with you if nothing ever draws you to tears over the things of God. And I looked at my wife, two weeks before this happened, and I said, "Sharon, something's bothering me about Scott." She said, "What's that, Honey?" I said, "I've never seen Scott ever shed tears over anything spiritual and that bothers me." Two weeks later I was at Northland Youth Camp. At the conclusion of one service, I felt this peck on my shoulder and I turned around and there was my son, Scott. He said, "Dad, can I talk to you?" I said, "What is it, Scott?" He said, "Dad, I've gotta get saved." You know what I could've said to that boy? I could've said, "Hey, Scott, you got saved under Dad's preaching, remember? When you were just a little boy, Dad led you to Christ." You think I did that nonsense? No. I said, "Scott, let me take the Word of God and show you," and I took my son to a side room. And I sat down, like I'd do with anyone in this room, and I showed Scott the whole way of salvation. I said, "Scott, would you like for Christ to save you?" And he said, "Dad, I want to get saved." And that young man, my son, wept. He asked Christ in his heart. We went home to South Carolina, he went down the aisle, he made public his faith in Christ, he gave a testimony and he wept publicly. Anyone who knows my son, Scott, knows he's not a sissy; he's on the Karate team at Bob Jones University. But Scott said, "You know, Dad, I do not remember what I did and no one ever took the Word of God and showed me how to be saved." He does not remember anything about it [his childhood "decision"].

You know what, young man, or young lady? That could be you! No one's ever taken the Word of God; no one's ever explained, and all you're trusting is a denomination of religion. You've never had anyone take the Bible, and the Bible has been given to guide you to Jesus Christ! Let us bow our heads and pray, please.

HAL WEBB

17

Three Crosses At Calvary
BIOGRAPHICAL SKETCH

Hal Webb
(1926 -)

The name of Hal Webb brings back many delightful memories to generations of folks who knew of him and sat under his preaching as teens in the 50's and 60's during his ministry as a popular youth evangelist with Youth For Christ. I am no exception. In fact, Hal Webb has had the greatest influence, outside of the Holy Spirit, of course, on my being in evangelism myself; so I am very grateful to the Lord for having had the privilege of knowing him personally for nearly forty years. I sat under his ministry as a boy of ten when he and Theron Babcock conducted one of their early crusades together as a team in my home church. I am delighted to present him here.

Hal was born in 1926 in Conklin, New York to George and Ada Mae Webb. He came to know the Lord Jesus Christ as his personal Saviour at the age of eleven during a revival meeting being conducted by Evangelist Charles Young at the Conklin Center Baptist Church. It was four years later that he surrendered to preach while attending a youth camp at the old Pine Brook Bible Conference in the Pocono Mountains of north eastern Pennsylvania.

During World War II Hal served his country in both the European theater as well as the Philippines. While in the Philippines he directed the GI Gospel Hour in addition to his work with Youth For Christ (YFC).

In 1949, he married the former Nell Sue Wachob a year before graduating from Bob Jones University in 1950. The Lord blessed them with three children, one of whom, Barry, is serving the Lord as an evangelist as well.

It was in 1956 that Theron Babcock joined him and the Hal Webb Evangelistic Team was formed. They have just recently completed forty years together as a team. In addition to strong Bible preaching, one of the unique ministries of the team is Theron writing a new gospel chorus each service based on a theme or title suggested by a member of the audience In addition to their regular meetings, Hal and Theron air some 350 radio broadcasts each year as well as speaking in hundreds of Christian school chapels.

Hal has written several books including the trilogy, Why Not?, Why So?, and How Come? He and his wife make their home in Conklin, New York. KWL

Evangelist Hal Webb
P.O. Box 195
Conklin, NY 13748

THREE CROSSES AT CALVARY
Hal Webb

Now, tonight, I want you to take your Bible and we will turn to the twenty-third chapter of the Gospel of Luke. And in the twenty-third chapter of the Gospel of Luke, we are going to see tonight a picture of the crucifixion of the Lord Jesus Christ. I believe with all of my heart, one of the tragedies of today is that so few are preaching on the Cross. It has come to the place where millions of people who profess to be born again into the family of God cannot even shed a tear, cannot even have a tremble in their soul, cannot seemingly express any real broken-heartedness over the tremendous cost that Jesus paid for us on that horrible giblet of shame! The twenty-third chapter of Luke; and I believe Christians ought to read it at least once a month, and even more. Beginning at verse thirty-three, we read,

"When they were come to the place, which is called Calvary, there they crucified him, and the malefactors, one on the right hand, and the other on the left. Then said Jesus, Father, forgive them; for they know not what they do. And they parted his garment, and cast lots. And the people stood beholding. And the rulers also with them derided him, saying, He saved others; let him save himself, if he be Christ, the chosen of God. And the soldiers also mocked him, coming to him, and offering him vinegar, and saying, If thou be the king of the Jews, save thyself. And a superscription also was written over him in letters of Greek, and Latin, and Hebrew, THIS IS THE KING OF THE JEWS. And one of the malefactors which were hanged railed on him, saying, If thou be Christ, save thyself and us. But the other answering rebuked him, saying, Dost thou not fear God, seeing thou art in the same condemnation? And we indeed justly; for we receive the due reward of our deeds: but this man hath done nothing amiss. And he said unto Jesus, Lord, remember me when thou comest into thy kingdom. And Jesus said unto him, Verily I say unto thee, Today shalt thou be with me in paradise. And it was about the sixth hour, and there was a darkness over all the earth until the ninth hour. And the sun was darkened, and the vail of the temple was rent in the midst. And when Jesus had cried with a loud voice, he said, Father, into thy hands I commend my spirit: and having said thus, he gave up the ghost. Now when the centurion saw what was done, he glorified God, saying, Certainly this was a righteous man. And all the people that came together to that sight, beholding the things that were done, smote their breasts, and returned. And all his acquaintance, and the women that followed him from Galilee, stood afar off, -- beholding -- these -- things." (Luke 23:33-49)

"Oh, Dear God, tonight, we would bow our heads and our hearts in this great area-wide crusade. And oh, Dear Lord, we would cry out to Thee, for human utterance of divine truths. We would ask, Holy Spirit, that Thou wilt captivate this mind, and this tongue, and from Thy book, the Word with great clarity. We pray Thou wilt speak to each and every heart wherever this message will be heard. And, oh God, may it, because it is thy message, empowered by Thy spirit, bring thousands to Thee across the nation, we pray. And we'll give Thee praise as we ask for those seated all over this auditorium, both Christians who've grown cold and indifferent, and those who need to kneel at the foot of the cross to be saved. May Thy spirit and Thy presence and Thy power break our hearts together and mold us, and wet our cheeks with tears, and with a new touch of desperate devotion and love to the one who gave his all for us, we pray, for we ask it in Jesus' name. Amen."

One of the great tragedies of men and women in the human race, is that it seems that if in these days, millions of people are incapable of saying, "Thank you." When it comes to the great citizens of our land who have done so much, they're quickly forgotten. When it comes to the great war heroes who have stood for freedom, and the millions of our boys in the wars that have died to provide the freedom we have; how quickly people forget! The great statesmen of the past, whose laws and whose writings went into the Constitution and the Declaration of Independence, and the Bill of Rights; how quickly these men are forgotten and set aside.

But I believe with all of my heart, there could be nothing worse done on the part of anyone of us than for us to forget the tremendous price, the awful penalty, the terrible thing that happened, when Jesus Christ, God's Son, went to the cross and gave His life in the most horrible death recorded in all eternity for a world lost in sin!

The Religious Sinner

Now, careful scrutiny of these verses we just read, reveal several groups of people that stood there when Jesus died. Why do I mention them? Because those same groups are very visible in every meeting wherever we travel throughout the world in evangelistic endeavor today. Why, we read there were the chief priests, and the elders. These were the religious crowd, the intellectuals of the day, those who were angered when Jesus taught that all men have sinned; those who scoffed when He pointed out that, outside of the new birth, there was no way to reach heaven; those who were depending on their works and their religious beliefs, and all of the things that they had followed for so very long, and who had added many man-made religious ideas, as well. This religious group; why, the

Lord in one place, called them "snakes in the grass," warned them that they were vipers, asked them who it was that had warned them to escape the judgment of hell. And yet, many of the accusers of Jesus Christ were simply great religious leaders of His day, who would not believe Him to be the virgin born Son of God who would shortly shed His blood for a world that was lost in sin.

But, before you condemn these religious leaders, remember our generation is even more packed full of these unbelieving rascals. For everywhere, the modernist and the ecumenical crowd are spreading like the great hideous cancer, like a great brooding bubonic plague of evil and sin; the great crowd of unbelieving people who still smack of something religious, but deny the Lord Jesus Christ, Saviour, Lord and Master, His place in this world and hence, lose their eternal hope of salvation. Oh, how tragic, that these are here in every meeting everywhere, wherever the Word of God is preached - some unbelieving; how tragic in the schools of America there are many unbelieving scholars; many ugly college professors, who have turned from the truth, who deny the great tenants of the gospel. My beloved friend, there's never been a time in the history of man when there were more religious, unbelieving rascals than there are in this age and day! Great denominational seminaries have become cemeteries, and deny the very truth they should be teaching their pupils. Great denominations have turned away from the truth to the cunningly devised fables of man and to the socialistic pink gospel of Russia and to every manner of evil manifestation of the fact. They are not willing to follow the truth. Long-tailed, striped-trousered rascals stand in the pulpits of our nation's churches and damn their congregations by crying out against the great, old gospel fundamental truths, which without belief in, no one can be saved.

And, oh, I warn you; if you've not been born again, you need Christ. If all you are is a religious person; that won't save your soul! If all you can muscle together is good works; that won't bring redemption! If you've been baptized once, twice, three times, or only dry cleaned; that won't do it either! If your life has followed the path of man made religious reform; that is not enough! The Bible pictures the whole human race as dead from the crown of your head to the soles of your feet and every inch of unsaved mankind filled with running, putrid sores in between!

The Common Everyday Sinner

There was a second group. We'll call them the common, everyday people - stirred up; a mob that had watched Him feed the multitude and perhaps enjoyed some of the food; a crowd that had wagged their ugly heads at much of His teachings; a group now stirred up much as you can stir up strikers, or agitators today; more easily stirred to become a mad mob who march past the Saviour wagging their head, scoffing, and spitting and howling as they went, ready to reject the Christ. It was this foolish, man-confused crowd that would accept Barabas and would cry, "Away with Him! Crucify Jesus Christ!"

There are millions of puzzled, religious people in the world; millions of them who are religious and yet religiously lost and confused. And, yet, many others, who have nothing to do with the Church or the things of God at all; a crowd of people, marching and turning and influenced and confused, and turned off to anything spiritual by the things of this world; influenced by the false leaders and forgetting that each man and woman on the face of this earth is responsible to God for your very own life.

The Lost Soldiers

Then, there were the soldiers. Now, to these soldiers, the crucifixion was just another crucifixion. Just another thief! Just another robber! Just another criminal! It was a job to be done; a messy chore to be finished. And they were so devoted to the cause of soldiering, and to their Roman government; this Jew was just another body to put away in a grave, to throw into the dung heap in the valley below! And so they wanted to get it over with. As they gambled and they split the clothing of Jesus, they pictured, oh, so many today involved in money, involved in the pursuit of fame, chasing after the god of business, or the exciting god of pleasure, devoted to things, but blank to God's appeal. Why, there are millions of people today who've heard something about Christ, something about a crucifixion; but to them, everything about the cross has no interest whatsoever. They are only interested in their own goals and their own life and their own future. They care little for the cause of Jesus Christ.

The Observing Sinner

Then, there were those standing by, observers only. Every pastor in this great crowd can easily identify these sitting in your congregation. They come when it's convenient, when the rain doesn't come down, or it's not too cold, when a sick headache does not threaten, or when a noisy evangelist is not within range! They come and sit. They sit in a sort of stupor, as if to say, "Well, here I am. Hurry up and get it over with." If you go past noon on Sunday morning, you're in terrible trouble, pastor! They come, they sit, they listen! There are teens that way - not a spark of interest for God, not an ounce of zeal for Jesus, not a bit of abandon-ment, putting self totally out of the way, and surrendering completely to

Jesus Christ. Everywhere you look, there are those who are religious, those who have a Bible, but those who seem to have no commitment.

They stood there, a great crowd at the crucifixion; they saw, they heard, they watched, and then, the Bible says, they smote their breasts! That's the equivalent in Jewish culture of, "Not for me. I've seen it. I've watched it. I've been here and it's over now. I'll make no commitment. It was an interesting afternoon. He probably deserved what He got." And off they walked: wishy-washy people who had stood and watched the Miracle of the Ages, the greatest fulfilled prophecy of eternity, when God sent His own Son to but a vile, dirty, crooked world of sinners! And, yet, they smugly walked away and said, "It is nothing to me!" and did nothing at all. They do that still today. Every service, every meeting, every crusade, you can watch somebody settle back in their seat and walk out of the door saying, "Not for me! Not for me! Some other time! Some other situation! Some other place! Not for me! I'll NOT make my decision for Christ!"

John, chapter twelve; in verse thirty-seven, it says, "They believed not on him." And in verse thirty-nine, it says, "They could not believe on him." And I would warn you, that, when you hear again and again, the gospel of Jesus Christ, and go out of the building, making no commitment, smiting your chest, or patting your back, or making your excuse, you put yourself in the most dangerous place of all; for once you have heard, and once you know that you need to be saved, and go out without Christ, then you have committed the most terrible sin you could possibly commit!

Far Off Christians

But, oh, there's a fifth group. And I cry every time I come to it and think about it. It says, "And those he loved stood afar off - beholding - these things." I thank God for every blessing of these days. I thank God for every faithful person who has come to this crusade, and for every pastor who has kept his promise to be here every night with his flock. But, I cry, and I tremble, and I wonder how quickly revival could spread across America, if every Christian, every follower, every believer, would begin to be faithful to his Church, and faithful to fundamental evangelistic meetings. Isn't it sad that, here in this town, many who should have been here have stood afar off. There are many that bear the name of a fundamentalist, but they've got the spine of a modernist; who bear the name of a fundamentalist, who want to be in a fundamental Church, but who are not willing to lay down their all and sacrifice and come together. Every Church today has people sitting in the pew who are God's people but who are involved in the world, they're involved in selfish things, they're involved in the pleasures of life, they're involved in so many things that are time wasters, that don't count. They're married to their television, they're involved in their pleasure, they're wound up in their sports, they're lazy in their homes, and they just do not stand close to Christ and the cross and the challenge that the Church must give in these last days.

And I ask every Christian in this great auditorium; I ask you, how near are you standing? How much of God's Word are you reading? How much time on your knees are you spending? No wonder the Bible says when He comes, "Will He find faith on this earth?" In a day when fundamentalism ought to be growing and surging like a floodtide of God's blessing, in many areas it's standing still, simply because millions of God's people are standing afar off!

Perhaps we all need to stop a few moments more and take a close look at what happened so many years ago when Jesus gave His life, for you and for me. And I said earlier, I was there in the land of the Bible, in the land and in the city of Jerusalem. And it was there, as I walked in tears and a broken heart from place to place, that God changed my preacher heart and life, and I'll never be the same.

I want us to sit in these closing moments as hushed as possible, with as little confusion in the auditorium as possible, and I want you just to turn your mind and your imagination for a moment; and I cry to you Lord, to help this tongue of clay, led of the Spirit, to picture how it must have been. We go back, back, back, hundreds of years in our imagination now, until we walk down, through the gate, through the arch and down the long, narrow streets, or paths, or little lanes, that still today look the same as they did in Jesus' day in the old city. Amazed, because we do not see the many people we expected to be packed and jammed into the area. Ah! There is a beggar. We'll ask him. Perhaps he can shed some light on the subject. "Oh beggar! Beggar, sir! Tell me, we expected to see ..." and he looks up at us with bloodshot eyes, holds out a bony hand, and cries, "Money, Master! Money, ere I die!" And so we reach in our pocket; we'll flip him a few coins, and we'll ask him, "Tell us, please, where are the people? Something very unusual must be taking place. Tell us, please." It is then the beggar would tell us the story, first of all, of what he had heard the night before. The man, Jesus, taking three of His disciples with Him that He most loved and worked with, went into the garden to pray. I've stood at the rock tradition says is where He prayed, and I thought, oh my, the tremendous, tremendous pressure that must have been there. Jesus left His disciples, as the beggar continues the story of what he had heard to our listening ears, near the gate of the garden, as He went further along to pray. Falling down by a great stone, He cried out to His Father in the heaven above, realizing He was in the very last few hours before He was to be taken and crucified. How heavy must the pressure have been upon the holy, perfect, Son of God! Perhaps desiring a little bit of manly, warmth of seeing and talking and fellowship, He went back to His disciples. Finding them asleep, He awakened them and said, "Watch and pray;" went back to the stone and there began to come to His great, holy self the tremendous, awful price He would have to pay in a few, short hours. And He agonized there in pain against that great boulder in the garden just across the valley from the city of Jerusalem. Back again, to find the disciples asleep, He awakened them again, and said, "What? Could ye not watch with me one hour? Watch and pray that ye enter not into temptation."

Back to the stone, and this time, with such agony and with such suffering as He began to vision and see in the great mind of the Saviour, the awful, terrible cup of all the vile, hideous sin that had ever been, or ever would be committed; and as He, the holy, spotless, perfect Son of God, saw all that was about to come upon Him very, very soon, He cried, "Oh my Father, if there be any other way ... nevertheless, if this cup must come upon me, nevertheless, not my will, but thine be done." And the Bible says He agonized in such a terrible way that, in place of the sweat drops, great drops of blood broke out through the pores of His face and trickled down as He agonized in the horror that would soon be His. And yet, somehow I feel, it was not just that, but it was the great, great love in His heart, as He yearned for a world lost in sin, that He was willing to go through the horror that would soon be upon Him.

Then the beggar would tell us that he heard that a man named Judas, one of the twelve, had run into that garden scene; and, rushing up, faked love and affection, and kissed repeatedly Jesus, so that the soldiers and the religious leaders would surround Him and be ready to take Him away. And step by step, the awful horror, terrible horror, developed as the hours went by. I've stood in the judgment hall, and as I stood there with our tour of people, it was my turn to pray. And I don't think I've ever had a more difficult time composing myself as I tried to vision what had happened in that horrible judgment hall.

Early in the morning, the sound was outside of the gate; the multitude grew with screams and jeers, and pounded on the gate as the soldiers sought to hold it closed, and, finally, pushing their way more and more. Pilate was notified; his wife asked him as he left the chamber, "What did that man say? They've got Jesus? Oh, I dreamed about Him tonight, terrible things. Be careful what you do. You better have nothing to do with Him." And Pilate came out on the judgment throne and porch; ordered the gates to be opened, and a floodtide of evil humanity pushed forward, shoving before them Jesus Christ, the Son of God. His hands were bound, tied tightly. Can you imagine? the hands of the Saviour - no criminal, no prisoner - but His hands were tied. Hands that had stretched

forth to heal the sick now were bound. Hands that had raised the dead;
now the cords of man's hatred cut deep into the flesh. Hands that had
fed the hungry multitudes now were bound while thousands of angels
above strained, ready to sweep the multitude into hell, if He would just
make one beckoning call!

Someone in the crowd had brought some of the oriental, spiked thorns.
Perhaps you've never seen them. Three to five inches long, every single
thorn. And having twisted it into a circle, someone put it upon His head
and pushed it down. And the points of the thorns pierced His brow, and
the blood began to trickle in little rivulets down the sides of His face, and
in and out of His loving eyes, as He stood there, in patience, waiting for
all to be fulfilled. And some vile, wretched one of humanity, for which
He had come to die, stepped forward and grasped a great handful of His
beard, and with a tearing rip, pulled it from His face. And the blood,
trickling down, now found companionship with other beads of blood and
sweat that oozed from the pores of the wounded Saviour's face. He was
beaten about the head. The Bible said back in the book of Isaiah that
Jesus would be taken, and prior to being hung on the cross, His face
would be so beaten that it would not even resemble the face of a man.
The Greek indicates that many, many in the throng smote Him and beat
Him about the face again and again, until it was bruised and swelled, until
some particularly evil one, using the Jewish sign of hatred, cleared his
throat, dragged up all of the scum from deep, down in his throat, and
spat in Jesus face! And the grayish, slimy, spittle of the infamous man
who hated God's Son, joined the blood oozing through the beard, and
the wounds of the Son of God! And He stood there, taking it all. It was
then that Pilate felt that giving Him a flogging would appease those who
cried for His blood.

They stripped Him of His clothing. Can you imagine the awfulness of
the holy Son of God, standing stripped, hands tied high to a pillar, according to Roman history; two great, strong soldiers with, what we would
remember as a "cat-of-nine-tails," with great whips with sharp pieces of
stone and thorns, and whittled sharp things on the ends, stood, one on
each side and smote the back and beat the shoulders and, with each pull
of the whip, the objects embedded themselves in the flesh, and then, with
a coarse jerk, strips of flesh are pulled loose from the back which hung
in horror as He suffered, and as His body was shaken with each new beat
of the lash.

They took Him down, and someone said, "He's got a crown! He needs
a robe!" And they put a robe of royal purple about Him, and adjusted the
crown on His brow with another thunk of hatred. And, as He stood there,
they hailed Him, "King of the Jews!" And man mocked the Son of God.

Pilate, realizing something had to be done quickly, for the mob was so angry, they would tear Him to bits, reminded them it was the time that he could release a prisoner, and quickly sent the soldiers down in the dungeon to get the man called Barabas; the most vile, thieving, insurrectionist man he had in the dungeon. And they brought him up and stood him next to Jesus, and Pilate said, "Which of these will you that I release unto you?" And they cried, like one man, "Release unto us Barabas, but crucify Jesus!" And so they chose; they chose the crook; they chose the thief; they chose the worst murderer of the day, and set him loose, but screamed all the harder, "Crucify Jesus Christ!"

Oh, they took Him, and they brought the cross out of its storage place, as Pilate washed his hands in picture and token of the fact that there would be no guilt upon himself. And yet, I want to remind you, that Pilate, and anyone hearing this warning, who has not yet received Christ as Saviour, will never, never, never, never, ever be able to wash from your hands the guilt of the rejection of Jesus Christ, the Son of God.

Oh, they put the cross on His shoulder. They took Him out of the judgment hall, and He started up that trail where the archways meet one beyond the other, where there's ten or fifteen feet, then you have to step up; ten or fifteen more feet, step up. There is nothing level in Jerusalem anywhere. And so up the trail they went, up the trail they led Him; further and further and further He carried the cross. And the crowd nearly carried Him along with their hatred. And He fell; and they got another to help Him as the cross was borne along the way.

And we say to the beggar man, "Go on, tell us! Speak! Speak! Speak! Please, tell us what happened." And the beggar said, "As you can see, I cannot know, for I could not move from this spot." And so we'll say, "Well, which way did they go?" And he says, "That way. If you hurry, you may yet observe what happened to this man called Jesus." And so we'll throw down another coin or so and say, "Thank you." And we'll push along the way, stumbling up the trail on and on. I've walked that way and I thought, as I climbed with weary feet, what a terrible way it must have been carrying that tremendously heavy cross, with all of the agony and the pain that, already, Jesus had been forced to bear. Let's go. Let's move along. Hurry, folks! Come with me! The message is nearly finished, and we want to see what climax came to the Son of God.

Push our way along, back through a little garden that is still there today; up a little narrow trail that winds around until we'll come to that place, the place--oh, look!--it DOES resemble a skull! You can still see it today: the eye sockets, and the place where the nose would have been - but in a skull, of course, it falls away and only the hollow is left.

The Cross of Rejection

Excuse me! Out of the way! Let me see! And so we'll push our way through. Look out, please! We're visitors! We want to see this scene! And we'll stand underneath -- a cross. On it is a thief. A vile man. A murderous man, one who is being killed upon a cross for the sin and the evil that he has committed. And we'll look at this man and we'll say, "There, you're getting your just reward for the things that you have done!" We'll look at that cross a minute-- and, let's see, we must name it before we close. Oh, we'll name it ... wait! He speaks. And the man looks at the Man, oh ... how horrible! That's a man? He doesn't even resemble a man! Wait! He speaks to that broken, mass of flesh, nailed to the center cross, and he says to Him, "Lord, Lord, why don't you get off that cross? Why don't you get off that cross and get us too, and save us and get us outta here?"

And we look at that man on that cross and we'll come up with a name of the cross of Rejection, because on that cross, that thief rejected Jesus Christ! It was not words of belief. It was not words of willingness to follow. It was a mere echo of the jeer of the crowd, "If you're the Christ, get off of the cross and save us too!" And we call that cross the cross of REJECTION.

But, I warn you, all that thief had to do to miss heaven was to reject, refuse, the Man called Christ. And, ladies and gentlemen, this whole world is full of people who are like the thief on the cross of Rejection, who refuse again and again and again and again to believe on the Lord Jesus and accept Him as their Saviour. All you've got to do to die and go to hell is what he did. To die and go to hell, reject Jesus Christ!

The Cross Of Reception

Oh, the crowd pushes and we're shoved to the other side where there's another cross--oh, look--another thief! This thief, however, does not have the coarse, hard look on his face. Oh, look, he's turning also to the Man, oh, so horribly beaten, on the center cross. And this man is saying, "My Lord, remember me when Thou comest into Thy Kingdom." And, from the center cross, comes a broken voice, "Today, thou shalt be with me in Paradise!" And we marvel and we rejoice and we give it the name of the cross of RECEPTION, because, on this cross, this thief repents and believes on Jesus Christ and receives Him as Saviour; and that is all you have to do to be saved. Ladies and gentlemen, teenagers, boys and girls, repent of your sin and believe on the Lord Jesus Christ and you, too, can be saved!

The Cross Of Redemption

Now, we're shoved, but I'll not be denied the opportunity to stand here in a closing moment, and, as we look at a man barely resembling a man, bloodied, purpled, beaten, beard plucked from his face, spat upon, we marvel, for there's something about Him that says, "I'm not a victim! I'm not a criminal! This is no accident! I AM not before My time! I AM fulfilling the word of My Father and the will of God!"

Why, Roman history tells us, always, when they arrive at the crucifixion scene, the soldiers leap and tie the criminal down on the cross, because they have super human strength in their struggle to fight what they know comes next. Roman history records none of this for Christ! When the cross had been placed, He lay upon it, stretched out a hand, and they nailed it! Stretched out the other, and they nailed it! Crossed His feet, and nailed them! He opened not His mouth! Like a lamb is led to the shearers, dumb, and without complaint, Jesus Christ did not complain, for He knew this was fulfilling God's plan of redemption for a world lost in sin.

They lifted the cross. It had fallen into the sockets that are there, always ready for a new crucifixion, and it struck the bottom with a flesh-tearing thud! The blood continued to trickle, oozing from wounds on His back, wounds on His face, wounds in His forehead, and every move drove the thorns deeper into His brow. The way they're crucified makes a person slump down, unable to breathe, and, he has to push up on the foot with the nail in it to get a breath, and fall again for a few more minutes of agony and pain.

And we'll stand and look just a minute. It's an awful scene. The blood trickles down, finds its way down the cross making little rivulets and pools on the rocks below. The heat is unbearable. The tongue is protruding through the lips, having swollen so. The face is so swollen and beaten, it doesn't even resemble the face of a man. And we watch. And we watch. And all of a sudden, blackness!

The people fall and scream in terror, the soldiers grab their weapons and move the people back in case it is some kind of a trick. And everyone stands and trembles in horror. There is a blackness through which no eye can see!

Then, from the middle--I'm so glad God drew the curtain of darkness-- no eye ever made could have stood what happened next--and the Son of God, Who did not even whimper at all of the horrible things that man did to crucify Him, suddenly, from the blackness, that voice did cry, for the first time: "ELI! ELI! LAMA SABACHTHANI?" MY God! My God!

WHY have you let me down?" He could stand the beard being plucked; He could stand the foulness of spit in His face; He could stand the crown of thorns piercing His brow; He could stand the horrible pull of the nails on His hands and feet; but in the blackness of that darkness, when God lifted God's own sword of judgment and smote his own Son, Christ cried, "Oh God!"

We can't stand it any more. We've been stirred, and broken, and frightened, and tearful, and almost nauseated by the horror, and we've seen the darkness, after three hours, begin to fade itself away. We peer up, and He's still there. But His head's tipped down; the blood seems to have stopped running. Everything seems to be finished. I guess it's over. I guess we'll leave. And so, we turn, and we start to move off the top. And something causes us to turn back. There's a movement--yes, there's a movement. And that head--it's moving. It lifts again, and the body seems to strain against the horrible, agonizing restraints, and it summons one last cry, "IT IS FINISHED!"

And the plan of God, from the beginning of the world, is completed! And the Son of God has died. And the veil of the temple is rent. And there's a way to heaven for the vilest, lost sinner who will believe in the cross of REDEMPTION in the Christ Who died for you and for me.

And as we walk away, we're brushed aside by a marching group, the clean-up squad of Roman soldiers. Roman history and law requires that every crucified victim must have his legs broken as the last sign of hatred, to crush out the last spark of life. And they break the legs of one thief; and they break the legs of another. And they come to Jesus, and, for the first time in Roman history it is recorded; they didn't break the legs of the crucified prisoner. Why? Ah, bless God, hundreds of years before, an Old Testament prophet had pictured the horror of the crucifixion scene and told just what it would be like, and said, though He would be bruised, and beaten, and bloodied, and his form barely resembling the form of a man, not a bone of his body would be broken! And, instead, they thrust in a spear under the rib, and out flowed, what a doctor told me, could have been absolutely nothing but a literal broken heart.

They took Him down. And a rich man, who had a tomb in the garden just below, never yet used, perhaps prepared for himself, begged them to let him have the body. And, because it was getting late, and they wouldn't even have the time to properly prepare the body for burial. They carried it down a little trail. There the slot was hollowed in the side of the cliff, the great rock was there, the great cavity dug back in, and, outside of the main, just to the right, was one place prepared. And there they lay the Son of God. And coming out, many shoulders rolled the stone rumbling down the slot and sealed Him in. And the Devil rejoiced, and the fiends and the foulness of hell screamed in glee, "The Son of God, Jesus, is dead!"

The Christian disciples fled everywhere to hide, lest there be a great mop-up campaign and wipe them out as well. Christianity is dead. This man, Jesus, has joined the ranks of every other religious leader. At last, death claims every one!

But, on the morning of the third day, down came the angels to roll back the stone, not to let the Saviour out, but to let the world look in. He was gone! And I've stood in that tomb. I went back one day, alone, and knelt in that tomb. He isn't there. Everything about it fits the picture of the Bible. He isn't there. Why, His clothing was neatly folded, like a very neat, perfect person who would get up, not need it now. Jesus is ALIVE! Jesus has risen! How do I know? He's in my heart! He's in my life! He saved my soul! And I've seen Him do it to tens of thousands of others, and He'll do it to you right now, if you'll but bow your head, and confess that you, too, are a member of the lost, hell-bound, sinful race, and cry out to Him, "Lord, be merciful to me a sinner, and save me for Jesus sake."